In this groundbreaking work, Liston tackles admirably the thus far unexplored use of Third Article Theology as a lens for exploring the relationship between the church of Christ and the kingdom of God. Most impressively, Liston not only accomplishes this task with scholarly depth, clarity, and maturity, but also in a pastoral way that winsomely invites the church on a Spirit-led journey to imagine, experience, and practice even now her own transformation into the image of God's coming kingdom. A *tour de force*!

— Leopoldo A. Sánchez, Professor of Systematic Theology,
Concordia Seminary, USA

Karl Barth famously referred in his final years to the possibility of a theology of the Holy Spirit. Greg Liston has answered the call here with an ecclesiology taking its rise from the third article of the creed, that of the Spirit. His book is both stimulating and provocative, and it will no doubt spur the church onwards as it reflects on the work of the Spirit and its own identity and task in the third millennium.

— Kimlyn J. Bender, Professor of Christian Theology,
Baylor University, USA

Using the Holy Spirit as his lens, Liston grants us a challenging view of the church as the anticipation of the Kingdom of God to come. Anyone who reads this will never view the nature and mission of the church the same way again.

— Frank D. Macchia, Professor of Systematic Theology,
Vanguard University, USA

Third Article Theology has been making inroads into contemporary theology for some time and with this work it speaks into areas previously overlooked. *Kingdom Come* offers readers something unique: a perspective on the church, the Spirit, and the eschaton in equipoise and one that manages to speak into the present ecclesiological chaos with an ordered word of the Spirit. Liston starts at the end and works backwards in order for the rest of us to start where we are and move forward. *Kingdom Come* offers insight and hope to the Body of Christ as we see how the Spirit is guiding the church to its intended *telos* and is transforming it in the process. Bringing Christ and church, Spirit and Kingdom together, and starting with eschatology, is a masterstroke the rest of us can benefit from.

— Myk Habets, Head of Theology, Laidlaw College, New Zealand

The proof of the pudding is in the eating. This saying applies to Gregory Liston's book, where he not only offers a systematic-theological reconstruction of an eschatological ecclesiology through the lens of a comprehensive pneumatology, but also shows how the apostle Paul addressed the followers of Jesus in Corinth from a similarly constructed point of view. And it tastes good! This is how systematic theology should be done, not in isolation from biblical scholarship, but in direct conversation with the bible! In doing so, Liston presents a great example of what David Tracy called analogical imagination.

— Cornelis van der Kooi, Professor Emeritus of Systematic Theology,
Vrije Universiteit, Amsterdam

The Christian church is a work in progress, a community being formed to participate in the coming kingdom of God. In this penetrating analysis of how that transformation takes place Greg Liston draws our attention to the vital role of the Spirit who makes Christ present and draws into the church's present life anticipations of the kingdom that will one day be realised in full. More than just a theory, this book offers practical guidance on how the Spirit is at work among us.

— Murray Rae, Professor of Theology and Ethics,
University of Otago, New Zealand

Recent years have seen a greater emphasis on understanding the significance of the third article of the creed not only for accounts of the Holy Spirit but as a dogmatic *res* from which to build other theological loci. This book shows the fascinating and generative results that come about when the intersections of pneumatology, eschatology and ecclesiology are explored in a richly theological and biblical way.

— Tom Greggs, Marischal Chair (1616) and Head of Divinity,
University of Aberdeen, UK

KINGDOM COME

An Eschatological Third Article Ecclesiology

Gregory J. Liston

LONDON • NEW YORK • OXFORD • NEW DELHI • SYDNEY

T&T CLARK
Bloomsbury Publishing Plc
50 Bedford Square, London, WC1B 3DP, UK
1385 Broadway, New York, NY 10018, USA
29 Earlsfort Terrace, Dublin 2, Ireland

BLOOMSBURY, T&T CLARK and the T&T Clark logo are trademarks of Bloomsbury Publishing Plc

First published in Great Britain 2022
Paperback edition published 2024

Copyright © Gregory J. Liston, 2022

Gregory J. Liston has asserted his right under the Copyright, Designs and Patents Act, 1988, to be identified as Author of this work.

For legal purposes the Acknowledgements on p. x constitute an extension of this copyright page.

Cover image: SunFlowerStudio / Alamy Stock Photo

All rights reserved. No part of this publication may be reproduced or transmitted in any form or by any means, electronic or mechanical, including photocopying, recording, or any information storage or retrieval system, without prior permission in writing from the publishers.

Bloomsbury Publishing Plc does not have any control over, or responsibility for, any third-party websites referred to or in this book. All internet addresses given in this book were correct at the time of going to press. The author and publisher regret any inconvenience caused if addresses have changed or sites have ceased to exist, but can accept no responsibility for any such changes.

A catalogue record for this book is available from the British Library.

Library of Congress Cataloging-in-Publication Data
Names: Liston, Gregory J., author.
Title: Kingdom come: an eschatological Third Article Ecclesiology / Gregory J. Liston.
Description: New York: Bloomsbury Academic, 2022. | Includes bibliographical references and index. |
Identifiers: LCCN 2022004216 (print) | LCCN 2022004217 (ebook) | ISBN 9780567707413 (hardcover) | ISBN 9780567707451 (paperback) | ISBN 9780567707420 (pdf) | ISBN 9780567707444 (epub)
Subjects: LCSH: Eschatology. | Holy Spirit. | Church.
Classification: LCC BT821.3.L57 2022 (print) | LCC BT821.3 (ebook) | DDC 202/.3–dc23/eng/20220513
LC record available at https://lccn.loc.gov/2022004216
LC ebook record available at https://lccn.loc.gov/2022004217

ISBN: HB: 978-0-5677-0741-3
PB: 978-0-5677-0745-1
ePDF: 978-0-5677-0742-0
ePUB: 978-0-5677-0744-4

Typeset by Deanta Global Publishing Services, Chennai, India

To find out more about our authors and books visit www.bloomsbury.com and sign up for our newsletters.

*For my parents,
John and Frances Liston,
who have always been loving and supportive*

CONTENTS

Acknowledgements x

Chapter 1
TOWARDS A THIRD ARTICLE ECCLESIOLOGY 1
1.1 Third Article Theology 2
1.2 Third Article Ecclesiology 8
    1.2.1 A Christological Third Article Ecclesiology 9
    1.2.2 A Trinitarian Third Article Ecclesiology 11
1.3 The grammar of eschatology 15
1.4 Constructing an eschatological Third Article Ecclesiology 20

Chapter 2
TWO CONTRASTING ESCHATOLOGICAL ECCLESIOLOGIES 25
2.1 Eschatological and teleological tensions 25
2.2 Barth and the eschatological tension 28
2.3 Hütter and the teleological tension 36

Chapter 3
THE CHURCH'S JOURNEY THROUGH TIME 43
3.1 Constructing a Spirit eschatology 44
3.2 The pneumatological journey of the church through time 50
3.3 Conclusion 57

Chapter 4
AN ESCHATOLOGICAL *MUNUS TRIPLEX* 59
4.1 A timebound view of the *munus triplex* 60
4.2 An eschatological view of the *munus triplex* 63
4.3 Christ and the church's prophetic eschatological office 64
4.4 Christ and the church's priestly eschatological office 67
4.5 Christ and the church's kingly eschatological office 71
4.6 Conclusion 75

Chapter 5
EUCHARISTIC TRANSFORMATION 77
  5.1 The church as the proleptic anticipation of the kingdom 77
  5.2 The eucharist in ecclesial transformation 80
    5.2.1 Imagination 82
    5.2.2 Presence 84
    5.2.3 Practice 85
  5.3 A concrete account of eucharistic transformation 89
    5.3.1 Love and unity 89
    5.3.2 Abundant life and joy 92
    5.3.3 Truth and holiness 94
    5.3.4 Justice and equality 96
  5.4 Hütter and Barth on the eucharist 98

Chapter 6
AN ESCHATOLOGICAL THIRD ARTICLE ECCLESIOLOGY 107
  6.1 Ecclesial transformation through prayer and praise 111
  6.2 Ecclesial transformation through gospel proclamation 118
  6.3 Constituent features of an eschatological Third Article Ecclesiology 125

Chapter 7
READING 1 CORINTHIANS AS AN ESCHATOLOGICAL
THIRD ARTICLE ECCLESIOLOGY 129
  7.1 1 Corinthians 15: Pneumatologically enabled transformation 132
  7.2 1 Corinthians 1–2: Pneumatologically enabled imagination 136
  7.3 1 Corinthians 3–4: Pneumatologically enabled unity 142
  7.4 1 Corinthians 5–10: Pneumatologically enabled community 146
  7.5 1 Corinthians 11–14: Pneumatologically enabled worship 150
  7.6 Conclusion 154

Chapter 8
TOWARDS A THIRD ARTICLE THEOLOGY OF ECCLESIAL MISSION 157
  8.1 The relationship between ecclesiology and missiology 157
  8.2 A pneumatological and dialogical relationship 163
  8.3 Towards an ecclesiologically informed missiology 166
    8.3.1 The Christological connection 167
    8.3.2 The Trinitarian connection 168
    8.3.3 The eschatological connection 170
  8.4 Conclusion 172

Chapter 9
CONCLUSION 173
   9.1 A coherent Third Article Ecclesiology 174
   9.2 Applying an eschatological Third Article Ecclesiology 176
   9.3 Future research directions 184

References 187
Author Index 197
Subject Index 200

ACKNOWLEDGEMENTS

The themes of Spirit, church and God's coming kingdom interweave through the pages of this book like recurring melodies through a symphony. And these same themes have also infused the process of its writing.

First and foremost, this research was undertaken with many prayers that God's Spirit would inform and guide what was written. Further, it is offered with ongoing prayer that the Spirit will enable those reading to see through the halting prose to the profound pneumatological truths about who the Spirit is and what the Spirit does in the world – truths that words cannot convey completely, accurately or convincingly but truths that are rich and beautiful, nonetheless. I have enjoyed writing about the transforming and perfecting work of God's Spirit. But to see and know that this Spirit is truly at work in this world is an even greater joy.

Second, this research has been influenced by many of my brothers and sisters in Christ. People from my current local church family, Mt Albert Baptist Church, who inspire me with their integrity, creativity and drive. Like Rebecca McLeay, whose graphic design expertise proved to be hugely helpful in choosing the book's cover. People from previous church families, like my brothers Nick Drake and Rob Winthrop, and like Craig Allen, who knows the best and worst of me and still chooses to travel alongside. And people from my wider church family, like my colleagues at Laidlaw College, whom I sincerely thank for their loving acceptance.

I am particularly grateful for Myk Habets, who provides leadership, support and guidance beyond what is expected or deserved. I look forward to many more years of mutual collaboration. Thanks also to the Laidlaw College leadership for granting me study leave in the last half of 2019 that enabled this work to be completed. My recent thesis students continue to inspire. I sometimes wonder if my own work adequately measures up to the quality of thought and expression regularly demanded from them. Taryn Dryfhout, Soon Young Kwon, Jackson Kurian, Jacqueline Kotula and Sam Song: I have appreciated and learned a lot from each of you.

It is perhaps to my nuclear family, though, that I owe the greatest human debt. Diane, Emily and James continue to be my primary support and greatest joy. And now my parents, John and Frances, have moved closer so that we are getting to spend more time together again. This book is dedicated to Mum and Dad, in grateful thanks for many years of (often unacknowledged) thoughtfulness, prayer and ongoing support. Your love for us is greatly appreciated.

Finally, this research has inspired a much more concrete, nuanced and substantial eschatological hope. Indeed, perhaps the most enduring takeaway has been the recognition that for all the great and important things the Spirit is doing now in leading and transforming us as a church, we can and should look forward to so much more. This world matters, but from an eschatological perspective, right now is primarily about practising our scales, about gathering in the green room, about tuning our instruments. Imagine what it will be like when the conductor strides onto the stage and the orchestra starts to play. Come Lord Jesus.

Soli Deo Gloria.

Chapter 1

TOWARDS A THIRD ARTICLE ECCLESIOLOGY

As followers of Jesus, our ultimate destination is breath-taking. The captivating description of God's coming kingdom in Revelation 21–22 paints a picture of the church as Christ's radiant bride, fully and completely united with him, living in a world where every remnant of evil and darkness has been swept away by God's all-encompassing goodness and light. We are growing towards this future together while also looking forward to a coming radical transformation that will finally make it a full and present reality. Given our ongoing journey and ultimate destination, the important question raised is how the church presently grows into a more complete knowledge of and unity with God. How does God go about transforming the church so that this breath-taking picture of our future reality increasingly becomes a part of our lived experience now? If the church is on 'the Way',[1] how is this journey occurring?

Some overemphasize the journey's discontinuity, radically separating the church from the coming kingdom and thereby eclipsing the Spirit's present transformational mission. From this perspective, the church is merely a holding pen for believers until the kingdom truly comes. Others emphasize the journey's continuity, closely identifying the Spirit's work with the church or its practices and thereby failing to adequately account for how the Spirit works outside of and, at times, even against the church. The purpose of this volume is to utilize the methodology of Third Article Theology to examine the intrinsically pneumatological relationship between the church and kingdom. The broad and overarching thesis being developed is that exploring the relationship between church and kingdom through the lens of the Spirit enables the construction of a nuanced account of the church's ongoing transformation, an *eschatological* Third Article Ecclesiology. The church, as pictured in this volume, is the proleptic anticipation of the coming kingdom. Through enabling Christ's kingly presence, the Spirit draws back to the present church characteristics of the coming kingdom. This enriches, influences and transforms the present church towards its intended *telos*.

---

1. One of the prominent descriptions of the members of the Christian community in Acts is that they belong to 'the Way'. See, for example, Acts 9.2; 19.9, 23; 22.4; 24.14, 22. Inherent in this characterization is the idea that the church is on a journey.

This initial chapter lays the foundation for the development of this thesis. It introduces the fundamental concepts of Third Article Theology, explaining how a dialogical 'Wolterstorffian' methodology fits naturally with this approach. It then briefly revises the pneumatological understanding of the church developed from the vantage points of Christology and the Trinity, as explored in a previous volume on Third Article Ecclesiology: *The Anointed Church*.[2] Given that the central task of this volume is to examine the church through the lens of the Spirit from the vantage point of the coming kingdom, the next topic considered in this initial chapter is the pivotal doctrine of eschatology. Recognizing the ground and grammar of eschatological thought, and the importance of simultaneously attending to both its continuity and discontinuity with our present reality, is a necessary precursor to the constructive work that follows. The final section outlines the structure of the rest of the book, explaining how the argument and thesis unfolds.

1.1 Third Article Theology

'Third Article Theology is a new, exciting, and ambitious project.'[3] While it intentionally prioritizes pneumatology, the third article in the Apostles' Creed, Third Article Theology, goes well beyond traditional pneumatology. Indeed, the aim of Third Article Theology is nothing less than to re-envisage the whole of theology through intentionally 'starting with the Spirit'.[4] As Habets comments, 'Pneumatological considerations are not left to a postscript or conclusion but are, rather, incorporated into theological discourse right from the beginning.'[5] Perhaps the most common image used to illustrate Third Article Theology, then, is to view the Holy Spirit as a lens. A lens is transparent and difficult to focus on in and of itself, but when it is looked through, the object being examined comes into perspective. Similarly, Third Article Theology looks through the lens of the Spirit in order to see other theological realities more clearly. Indeed, it views pneumatology not just as the starting point but as the connecting link that binds all the different theological doctrines together. 'Pneumatology is not so much one specific chapter of Christian theology as an essential dimension of every theological view of the

---

2. Gregory J. Liston, *The Anointed Church: Toward a Third Article Ecclesiology* (Minneapolis: Fortress, 2015).

3. Kirsteen Kim, 'Foreword', in *Third Article Theology: A Pneumatological Dynamics*, ed. Myk Habets (Minneapolis: Fortress Press, 2016), xiii–xiv.

4. D. Lyle Dabney, 'Starting with the Spirit: Why the Last Should Now be First', in *Starting with the Spirit*, ed. Stephen Pickard and Gordon Preece (Hindmarsh: Australian Theological Forum, 2001), 3–27.

5. Myk Habets, 'Prolegomenon: On Starting with the Spirit', in *Third Article Theology: A Pneumatological Dogmatics*, ed. Myk Habets (Minneapolis: Fortress Press, 2016), 14.

church and of its spirituality and liturgical and sacramental life.'⁶ Third Article Theology thus aims to utilize the Spirit as a God-given lens through which we can conduct theological enquiry, explicitly allowing the Spirit to guide us into all truth (Jn 16.13).

Detailed explanations of and justifications for Third Article Theology are becoming more common, as increasing numbers of theologians become familiar with and adopt for themselves this fruitful theological approach.⁷ The explanations often begin by noting that the term *Third Article Theology* refers to both the methodology of intentionally starting with the Spirit and the theological understanding that emerges when this approach is utilized. They often contrast Third Article Theology with First or Second Article Theology, which respectively prioritizes the Father or the Son.³ Explanations also regularly note that while First and Second Article Theologies tend to focus on universals – our universal tendency towards God (as created image bearers of the Father) or our universal rejection of God (as fallen humans in need of Christ's redemption) – Third Article Theology is intrinsically particular. 'Third Article Theology begins with the localised claim that in *this* people, at *this* time, the Spirit is present and drawing us as a community towards redemption.'⁹ It is precisely this specific and localized aspect that makes Third Article Theology an appealing methodological approach through which to explore the relationship between the church now and the coming kingdom, and how the church is transformed through time towards its ultimate destination.

Justifications for Third Article Theology often note the many compelling biblical, theological, philosophical and contextual reasons for utilizing this methodology. The biblical recognition that God often initiates his work through the Spirit suggests that we can also learn of God this way. Theologically, the realization that our relationship with God implicitly starts with the Spirit who draws us to the Father in Christ justifies the idea of making our explicit theological method match this implicit prioritization. Philosophically, the twin premises that reality is fundamentally relational and that relationality is intrinsically the province of the Spirit lead to the conclusion that pneumatology should be primary in our theological explorations. As McDonnell says, 'Pneumatology is to theology what epistemology is to philosophy. Pneumatology determines the "rules" for speaking

---

6. Boris Bobrinskoy, 'Holy Spirit', in *Dictionary of the Ecumenical Movement*, ed. Nicholas Lossky, et al. (Grand Rapids: Eerdmans, 1991), 470.

7. See, for example, Liston, *The Anointed Church*, 7–33. Also Habets, 'Prolegomenon: On Starting with the Spirit', 1–20 Note also the helpful introductory explanation in Ben Pugh, *SCM Studyguide to Theology in the Contemporary World* (London: SCM Press, 2017), 46–52.

8. See particularly Dabney's early explanations of this characterization: Dabney, 'Starting with the Spirit', 3–27.

9. Liston, *The Anointed Church*, 21.

about God.'[10] While all these reasons for adopting a Third Article Theology methodology are valid and important, it is perhaps the contextual imperative that is the most particularly pertinent when considering the relationship between the church and the kingdom, and the church's transformation towards this coming future. In a world where good and evil dwell side by side, and where discerning the distinction and difference between each is becoming increasingly challenging, a Third Article Theology that focuses on neither universal continuity nor discontinuity can 'enable the Christian community both to socially and intellectually affirm some and yet contradict other aspects of the age we live.'[11] Such nuance is particularly necessary as the church collectively discerns what it means to live faithfully in a world which is rapidly changing and where the collective historical conscience of Christendom is becoming less prevalent.

Emerging several decades ago, Third Article Theology appropriately began with the development of a Spirit Christology.[12] It was in this pivotal doctrinal area that a detailed understanding of how to go about prioritizing pneumatology was first explored and where the first significant insights arising from this approach became evident. Over the course of these Spirit Christological investigations, three key methodological characteristics of Third Article Theology emerged as particularly pertinent.[13] First, and unsurprisingly, Third Article Theology starts with the Spirit. What this meant for Spirit Christology is that theologians intentionally viewed 'Christ as an aspect of the Spirit's mission, instead of (as is more usual) viewing Spirit as a function of Christ's'.[14] Second, Third Article Theology looks *through*

---

10. Killian McDonnell, 'A Response to D. Lyle Dabney', in *Advents of the Spirit: An Introduction to the Current Study of Pneumatology*, ed. Bradford E. Hinze and D. Lyle Dabney (Milwaukee: Marquette University Press, 2005), 264.

11. Dabney, 'Starting with the Spirit', 25–6.

12. Representative works include Ralph Del Colle, *Christ and the Spirit: Spirit Christology in Trinitarian Perspective* (Oxford: Oxford University Press, 1993). Also David Coffey, 'Spirit Christology and the Trinity', in *Advents of the Spirit: An Introduction to the Current Study of Pneumatology*, ed. Bradford E. Hinze and D. Lyle Dabney (Milwaukee: Marquette University Press, 2005), 315–38. And Myk Habets, *The Anointed Son: A Trinitarian Spirit Christology* (Eugene: Pickwick Publications, 2010). More recently, see Frank D. Macchia, *Jesus the Spirit Baptizer: Christology in Light of Pentecost* (Grand Rapids: Eerdmans, 2018). Also, Leopoldo A. Sánchez M., *T&T Clark Introduction to Spirit Christology* (London: T&T Clark, 2021).

13. Habets has outlined a list of ten key methodological theses. See Habets, 'Prolegomenon: On Starting with the Spirit', 14–19. I have given my own more detailed explanation about each of these in Liston, *The Anointed Church*, 23–33. Choosing three of these ten theses to focus on in this abbreviated introduction is primarily for brevity's sake. But note that the three criteria briefly explained here most strongly distinguish Third Article Theology from other methodological approaches.

14. Clark H. Pinnock, *Flame of Love: A Theology of the Holy Spirit* (Downers Grove: IVP Academic, 1996), 80.

the Spirit rather than looking at it. In terms of developing a Spirit Christology, that meant Jesus Christ and his work (as opposed to pneumatology) were the core subjects being focused upon. Pneumatology was the lens; Christology was the subject being investigated. Third and most significantly, Third Article Theology complements and does not compete with First and Second Article Theologies.[15] For Christology, what this meant is that theologians utilizing the methodology of Third Article Theology did not endeavour to replace a traditional Logos Christology with the newly emerging Spirit Christology but rather saw the two as complementary.

Applying these methodological theses to the doctrine of Christology led to significant developments in theological understanding. Two primary insights are noted here. The first is the Spirit's foundational role in understanding Christ's divinity. If Christ's divinity is only understood through the Logos, and no reference is made to the Spirit (what is sometimes termed an *exclusive* Logos Christology), this inevitably leads to a docetic and therefore inadequate Christology. Jesus' divinity needs to be understood through the twin categories of Logos and Spirit. Overemphasizing one or the other always leads to a deficient Christology.[16] Second, a nuanced comprehension of Christ's growth as a human also emerged. Emphasizing the role of the Spirit in Christ's life enabled 'the humanity of Christ to be considered apart from its once-for-all assumption by the Logos'.[17] Being human intrinsically means change and growth, and the role of the Spirit in gradually conforming Christ's human will to his divine will as he grew in wisdom and stature was an important development.

Given the profound and significant insights arising from the exploration of Spirit Christology, theologians have more recently begun to utilize the methodology of Third Article Theology to examine other loci. Doctrines explored in this way include the Trinity, ecclesiology, Scripture, anthropology and public theology.[18] A notable

---

15. This third criterion has been the subject of some debate, although consensus appears to be coming down on the side of those theologians who argue for a complementary approach. See, for example, Ralph Del Colle, 'Spirit Christology: Dogmatic Issues', in *A Man of the Church: Honoring the Theology, Life, and Witness of Ralph Del Colle*, ed. Michel René Barnes (Eugene: Pickwick Publications, 2013), 3–19.

16. For more details on the relationship of the Logos and the Spirit within Jesus, see Gregory J. Liston, 'A "Chalcedonian" Spirit Christology', *Irish Theological Quarterly* 81, no. 1 (2016): 74–93.

17. Gary D. Badcock, *Light of Truth and Fire of Love: A Theology of the Holy Spirit* (Grand Rapids: Eerdmans, 1997), 146 See also Habets, *The Anointed Son*, 118–87.

18. For an early example, see Pinnock, *Flame of Love*. More recently, specific examples include Cheryl M. Peterson, *Who Is the Church? An Ecclesiology for the Twenty-First Century* (Minneapolis: Fortress, 2013). Also Liston, *The Anointed Church*. Of particular note are the scholars who utilize a pneumatological focus as part of a broader Pentecostal approach. Examples include Amos Yong, *Beyond the Impasse: Toward a Pneumatological Theology of Religions* (Grand Rapids: Baker, 2003).

exception is the application of a Third Article Theology approach to eschatology, which to date has received very little scholarly attention. The development of some key features of a Spirit eschatology is an early objective of this volume, given that it is necessary to develop a pneumatological understanding of eschatology before the implications of that understanding can be applied to ecclesiology.[19] The question that arises for all of these doctrines, though, is how does one go about extending Third Article Theology beyond Spirit Christology to other doctrines? In a previous work I have argued that the dialogical approach adopted by Nicholas Wolterstorff in his profound and concise masterpiece, *Reason within the Bounds of Religion*, is eminently suitable for this task.[20] Given that this present volume extensively utilizes the terminology and logic of Wolterstorff's approach, it is necessary to briefly explain it and how it applies to Third Article Theology.[21]

Wolterstorff argues (*together* with much postmodern thinking) that there is no indubitable, foundational knowledge. He also asserts (*against* much postmodern understanding) that humans can nevertheless approach a true understanding of an objective and independent reality. This can occur through the interchange of background beliefs, data beliefs and control beliefs. Using the simple illustration of an astronomer measuring a star's position in the sky, Wolterstorff labels the star's position as the data belief (the reality being determined), the telescope's features as the control belief (the basis on which the exploration rests) and everything else that is not within the purview of the experiment (such as Newton's laws of motion) are labelled as background beliefs. The insightful simplicity of Wolterstorff's approach is that he recognizes that what scientists and other scholars regularly do is to swap the positions of the data, control and background beliefs. So, in another experiment, the astronomer will assume the workings of the telescope (background) and measure a star's position (control), in order to test Newton's laws of motion (data). By regularly swapping background, control and data beliefs, a scientist can ensure that all knowledge is coherent and consistently related to other knowledge. In this way, a true understanding of reality can be approached without any one aspect being considered as indisputable and foundational.

Also Veli-Matti Kärkkäinen, *Toward a Pneumatological Theology: Pentecostal and Ecumenical Perspectives on Ecclesiology, Soteriology, and Theology of Mission* (Lanham: University Press of America, 2002). And Frank D. Macchia, *The Spirit-Baptized Church: A Dogmatic Inquiry* (London: T&T Clark, 2020). Primarily, a recent dogmatic volume gives a good overview of the burgeoning interest in this approach across denominational streams: Myk Habets, ed., *Third Article Theology: A Pneumatological Dogmatics* (Minneapolis: Fortress Press, 2016).

19. The development of a Spirit eschatology is particularly addressed in Chapters 3 and 4 of this volume.

20. Nicholas Wolterstorff, *Reason within the Bounds of Religion* (Grand Rapids: Eerdmans, 1976).

21. A more detailed explanation of which the following is a summary, application and extension can be found in Liston, *The Anointed Church*, 71–7.

Consider the application of this dialogical approach to Third Article Theology and (to make it even more specific and applicable) to the development of a Third Article Ecclesiology. Applying Wolterstorffian terms to this pursuit, ecclesiology can initially be labelled as the data belief. Even a cursory examination of this data belief of ecclesiology through the lens of the Spirit, however, shows that it cannot be viewed in isolation. For example, it is the Spirit that forms the church as *Christ's* body (1 Cor. 12.13). Consequently, the constituent features emerging from applying Third Article Theology to ecclesiology are illuminated best by looking through the lens of the Spirit *from the vantage point* of other theological loci (or control beliefs). This has three implications. First, a variety of doctrinal vantage points (or control beliefs) are necessary. Ecclesiology should be viewed not just from the perspective of Christology alone but also from other perspectives such as the Trinity, eschatology and other doctrines. Second, analogical connections need to be made between each of the doctrines being used as vantage points and ecclesiology or between the control beliefs and the data belief. So, for Christology, the church is understood (at least in part) as Christ's body and bride. For the Trinity, the church participates (to an extent) in Christ's communion with the Father. For eschatology, the church is (to a certain degree) the proleptic anticipation of the kingdom. An analogical continuity exists between each of these control beliefs and the data belief of ecclesiology. The connection between the doctrines is genuine but not exact, however. (e.g. the church's identity is related to, but is not equated with, Jesus' identity.) Determining the limits to which the analogy can be taken is pivotally important in faithfully conducting the investigation. Finally, and most significantly here, the analogical connection between the doctrines is always pneumatologically enabled. For Christology, as noted, it is the Spirit that forms the church as Christ's body. For the Trinity, it is through the Spirit that the church participates in the Son's relationship with the Father.[22] For eschatology, it is the Spirit that makes the church the proleptic anticipation of the kingdom.

Summarizing this approach using the Wolterstorffian terminology that has been introduced, Third Article Theology determines the constituent features of a coherent and complete Third Article Ecclesiology as follows. There are background beliefs: Holy Scripture and the Creeds. These are crucial reference points but not the focus of this project. There are a series of control beliefs: Christology, Trinity, eschatology, among others. These are the vantage points from which the examination of ecclesiology analogically occurs, through the lens of the Spirit. Finally, there is a data belief: ecclesiology. This is the doctrine being examined. The varying perspectives of this data belief gained from the vantage points of each of the control beliefs need to be integrated and refined together to determine a coherent and complete Third Article Ecclesiology.

While the development of such a Third Article Ecclesiology is the ultimate goal of this particular theological assignment, it does not represent the end of the

---

22. See, for example, James B. Torrance, *Worship, Community and the Triune God of Grace* (Downers Grove: IVP Academic, 1996), 31.

Wolterstorffian epistemological programme. For the Third Article Ecclesiology developed (or even just the insights arising from individual parts of it) can then be used as control beliefs from which other doctrines can be explored. For example, an *eschatological* Third Article Ecclesiology[23] could be used as a control belief from which to examine a portion of Scripture – what is often termed a theological interpretation of Scripture. Or the combined understandings from all three vantage points (a *Christological* Third Article Ecclesiology, a *Trinitarian* Third Article Ecclesiology and an *eschatological* Third Article Ecclesiology) could be used as control beliefs to inform the data belief of missiology.[24] From Wolterstorff's perspective, all aspects of our understanding – theological doctrines, biblical interpretation and even beyond this to science, literature, arts, humanities and every other area of human knowledge – all of these are to be used as control, background and data beliefs, so that our entire system of knowledge is consistent, coherent and always developing.

Some initial steps along this Wolterstorffian path of developing a complete and coherent Third Article Ecclesiology have already been taken. The next section briefly outlines the approach adopted and some insights that emerged when the data belief of ecclesiology was examined through the lens of the Spirit from the vantage points (or control beliefs) of Christology and the Trinity, respectively.

1.2 Third Article Ecclesiology

The following two subsections outline the ecclesiological understandings that emerge when the church is viewed through the lens of the Spirit, from the vantage points of Christology and the Trinity respectively. So, for these explorations, in Wolterstorffian terms, ecclesiology is the data belief, Christology and Trinity are the control beliefs and all other doctrines are background beliefs. While each vantage point yields significant insight, for brevity the following sections merely summarize the overarching view that is gained of ecclesiology from each vantage point and then note two key features of the ecclesiological landscape revealed.[25] In particular, the Christological vantage point illuminates the mark of the church as

---

23. This is a shorthand expression referring to the ecclesiological understanding that emerges when this doctrine is viewed through the lens of the Spirit from the perspective of eschatology.

24. Note that these examples are not chosen randomly. The application of an eschatological Third Article Ecclesiology to Scripture, and particularly to 1 Corinthians, is undertaken in Chapter 7 of this volume. And the beginnings of an application of each of the developed Third Article Ecclesiologies to the doctrine of mission is then developed in Chapter 8.

25. For more details, see Liston, *The Anointed Church*, Sections 2 and 3. Section 2 develops a *Christological* Third Article Ecclesiology, and Section 3 develops a *Trinitarian* Third Article Ecclesiology.

one and the sacrament of baptism, while the Trinitarian vantage point illuminates the mark of the church as catholic and the 'sacrament' of fellowship.

1.2.1 A Christological Third Article Ecclesiology

Two premises inform the development of a Third Article Ecclesiology when viewed from the vantage point of Christology. The first is that significant insight into the ontology of the church can be gained through comparing it with the ontology of Christ. This analogical understanding was compellingly derived and worked out by Karl Barth with his utilization of the 'Chalcedonian pattern'.[26] The second is that this correspondence cannot be adequately examined without giving the Spirit prominence, for it is the Spirit that forms the church as Christ's body. This is a point that Barth often overlooks. As Badcock argues, 'The church as the body of Christ cannot be considered apart from [the Spirit's presence], for the ecclesiastical "body" is something that is mediated by the work of the Spirit, and cannot exist without the Spirit.'[27] Pneumatological insights into how the eternal Son became human inform our understanding of how the perfect Christ indwells an imperfect church. As Veli-Matti Kärkkäinen asserts: 'the only way to construe a viable pneumato-ecclesiology is to reflect very carefully on the relationship between Christ and the Spirit on the one hand, and on the relation of the Spirit to the church on the other hand, and then try and see these three as mutual entities that inform each other.'[28]

Prioritizing the pneumatological connection between Christ and the church reveals an important ecclesiological tension to navigate. Ecclesiologies traditionally aim for an appropriate balance between the divine and the human aspects of the church. Ecclesiologies that do not achieve such balance are labelled as ecclesial Docetism (if they overemphasize the church's divinity at the expense of its humanity) or ecclesial ebionism (if they do the reverse). Using Spirit Christology as a vantage point from which to explore ecclesiology reveals that it is equally important for the Son and the Spirit's ecclesial involvement to be balanced – both must be logically distinguished without being existentially separated. The Son's ecclesial involvement must not be subsumed into or subordinated below that of the Spirit, and the Spirit's ecclesial involvement must not be subsumed into or subordinated below that of the Son. This insight directly parallels the similar recognition noted earlier in the development of Spirit Christology. Just as Jesus' divinity needs to be understood through the twin categories of Logos and Spirit and overemphasizing one or the other leads to a deficient Christology, so Christ's

---

26. See, for example, George Hunsinger, *How to Read Karl Barth: The Shape of His Theology* (New York/Oxford: Oxford University Press, 1991), 185.

27. Gary D. Badcock, *The House Where God Lives: Renewing the Doctrine of the Church for Today* (Grand Rapids: Eerdmans, 2009), 85.

28. Kärkkäinen, *Toward a Pneumatological Theology*, 93.

indwelling of the church as his body needs to be understood as occurring through the interrelated missions of the Son and the Spirit.

Such ecclesiological balance is best achieved by exploring the pneumatologically inspired parallels that exist between Spirit Christology and Third Article Ecclesiology:

- The Spirit conceives (Christ and the church)
- The Spirit sustains the communion (of Christ and the church)
- The Spirit conforms (Christ and the church)
- The Spirit directs and empowers (Christ and the church)
- The Spirit is displayed and mediated (by Christ and the church).

Examining ecclesiology in such a parallel manner enables the balance, coherence and consistency gained in Spirit Christology to be equally applied to the church.

On the basis of these parallels we are justified in characterizing the church as the *sequel* of the incarnation. Like a movie sequel's relationship with its original, the church has a clear continuity with the incarnation. Many of the same characters emerge and similar themes are explored. But (also like a sequel) the church is not simply a continuation or repetition of the incarnation. Just as disaster awaits attempts to make a movie sequel too similar to its original, so disaster awaits attempts to identify the church too closely with Christ. The church cannot add to or replicate Christ's already completed work – in attempting to do so it becomes not more but less than it should be. Finally, there is a necessary asymmetry. Just as there is no movie sequel without an original, there is no church without Christ. Jesus is God's Son become human independent of what the church is or does. In contrast, the church is Christ's or it is not the church at all.

Exploring in detail the Spirit-inspired parallels arising from the church being the sequel of the incarnation allows some very fundamental questions to be asked and answered, such as the following. What is the church? The church is the Spirit-enabled union that exists between the incarnate Christ and the human community. Who is in the church? The church consists of those humans who have been united by the Spirit to Christ. How is a church recognized? A church can be identified by having both a Christ-centred orientation and an overall momentum towards Christlikeness. What does the church do? The church is cruciform in shape, missional in purpose, narrative in character and relational in identity. The examination of each of these parallels and their accompanying insights provides a rich, full and – most importantly – balanced view of the church as seen from the vantage point of Christology through a pneumatological lens.

Perhaps most significantly, the Christological perspective utilized illuminates the church's indivisibility: the historical church is one. This ecclesiological insight is derived and follows directly from Christ's uniqueness. One Christ means one church. It is insufficient, though, to say that the historical church is one merely because of Christ. One Christ without the ontologically establishing presence of the Spirit within the present state of fallen humanity leads inexorably to a logically and practically divided church. The reverse is also true. One Spirit without the separate otherness of Christ as a distinct and separate eschatological goal requires a present perfection that simply doesn't exist. The historical church is one because there is one Christ and one Spirit, in whom we as one church participate in Christ's one relationship of Sonship with his one Father.

The pneumatologically enabled oneness also leads to the recognition of the church's unique context: having a relationship with Jesus and being a part of the church cannot be distinguished. The argument here is not for precedence but for equivalency. When a person is united to Christ by the Spirit, then that uniquely occurs through the transformation of that person into the church, the body and bride of Christ. As Gunton puts it, 'the Spirit works in the church: his is a churchly rather than an individual sphere of activity.'[29] The church consists of individuals who are pneumatologically united to Christ. To express this differently, the church is precisely identifiable as the human community of the baptized, those who have been baptized into Christ's body by the Spirit, leading to union both with Christ and with other believers. Consequently, baptism is the ecclesial sacrament most clearly illuminated in a Christological Third Article Ecclesiology. Viewed through a pneumatological lens, baptism refers to both that of Spirit and water. Indeed, Third Article Theology illuminates their complementarity. Beyond simply not emphasizing water baptism over Spirit baptism or vice versa (which could be characterized as ecclesial ebionism or ecclesial Docetism respectively) a Christological Third Article Ecclesiology also balances two other tendencies that are in fact more common errors in contemporary ecclesiology. First, it avoids ecclesial Eutychianism, which through overemphasizing the Spirit's ecclesial role at the expense of the Son merges Spirit baptism and water baptism and consequently regards baptism as dangerously magical, essentially putting the church in control of the Spirit. Second, it avoids the opposite error of ecclesial Nestorianism, which overemphasizes the Son's ecclesial role at the expense of the Spirit. Such an understanding values both Spirit baptism and water baptism but views them as separate and (more importantly) separable. In contrast to all these various errors, viewing the church through the lens of the Spirit from the perspective of Christology (and Spirit Christology in particular) illuminates a balanced view, where water baptism becomes the appropriate corresponding action to and analogy of Spirit baptism: the human counterpart of a divine action.

1.2.2 A Trinitarian Third Article Ecclesiology

While the end result is equally rich, viewing ecclesiology from the control belief of the Trinity through the lens of the Spirit is more complex and requires significantly more nuance than the previous situation where Christology was used as a control belief. The reason for the increased complexity and nuance required is that in the former situation, both entities being discussed 'included' divinity and

---

29. Colin Gunton, 'Baptism: Baptism and the Christian Community', in *Father, Son and Holy Spirit: Toward a Trinitarian Theology* (London: T&T Clark, 2003), 213.

humanity. In comparing the Trinity and the church, however, this similarity no longer holds. One entity is entirely divine, while the other is partially (and perhaps predominantly) human. Consequently, utilizing the analogy between the Trinity and ecclesiology requires determining the answers to two pertinent questions. The first question is 'Which Trinity?' Not that there are many Trinities, but there are many doctrines of the Trinity, as evidenced in the disagreements about the *filioque*. The second question is exactly whether and how the Trinity can be analogically related to ecclesiology.

Regarding the first question, many of the pioneers who applied Third Article Theology to Christology have also explored its Trinitarian implications. These scholars have convincingly argued that 'Spirit Christology provides our best mode of access to the theology of the Trinity'.[30] While there is still some debate on the implications of this assertion,[31] I align myself with the many proponents of Third Article Theology who maintain that Spirit Christology implies a 'reconceived' understanding of the Trinity where

> the Father begets the Son in or by the Holy Spirit [and] the Son is begotten by the Father in the Spirit and thus the Spirit simultaneously proceeds from the Father as the one in whom the Son is begotten. The Son, being begotten in the Spirit, simultaneously loves the Father in the same Spirit by which he himself is begotten (is Loved).[32]

In this understanding, championed by Thomas Weinandy and Myk Habets among others, the immanent identities of the Son and the Spirit have three key features. First, both the Son and the Spirit originate from the Father in one single action with two distinguishable parts. Just as in human speech, breath and word are logically distinguishable but existentially inseparable, so too is the Father's Spirit-enabled breathing of the Word. The immanent identities of the Son and Spirit are thus logically and chronologically synchronous. Second, each of the Trinitarian persons is truly personal, with an active and constitutive role in the Godhead. So, the Father (the originating person) persons the Son (the personed person) by the Spirit (the personing person). What this leads to is a nuanced understanding of Trinitarian *perichoresis*, which is identified as the very begetting or spirating by which the *hypostases* are personed. And third, this personing is not a once-off

---

30. Coffey, 'Spirit Christology and the Trinity', 315.

31. For example, there is debate about which understanding of the Trinity Spirit Christology most clearly points towards. For more detail, see Liston, *The Anointed Church*, 191–232.

32. Thomas Weinandy, *The Father's Spirit of Sonship: Reconceiving the Trinity* (Edinburgh: T&T Clark, 1995), 17. See also Habets, *The Anointed Son*, 224. Habets has also extended his formulation of Weinandy's understanding. See Myk Habets, '*Filioque? Nein*: A Proposal for Coherent Coinherence', in *Trinitarian Theology after Barth*, ed. Myk Habets and Phillip Tolliday (Eugene: Pickwick Publications, 2011), 161–202.

activity but an ongoing reality. This final feature of the 'reconceived' understanding of the Trinity means there is no distinction between what the Trinity is and how the Trinity came to be; God *in fieri* (in the act of becoming) is God *in facto esse* (in the nature of his essence). In every moment of eternity, the Godhead is constituted and subsists as a relational ontology *through* the Father begetting the Son in the Spirit and the Son returning the love of the Father through the Spirit of Sonship given to him.

Regarding the second question of how the Trinity is analogically related to ecclesiology, Third Article Theology adopts a significantly different approach from the well-known reflective method utilized by Miroslav Volf (among others) and heavily critiqued by Kathryn Tanner (again, among others).[33] Volf's approach considers Trinitarian characteristics one by one and determines to what extent each of these characteristics can also be considered to apply to the church. The alternative approach utilized by Third Article Theology proceeds, in Gunton's words, by replacing 'a logical conception of the relation between God and the world with a personal one'.[34] So, rather than looking at how the church is *like* the Trinity, this approach examines the implications of the church being pneumatologically *in* the Trinity, participating in its very life. In this approach, then, the continuities between the Spirit's immanent identity and his ecclesial role are utilized to inform our ecclesial understanding. Moreover, the community of believers' pneumatological union with Christ enables a comparison between his identity as Son and our participatory filial role in the Trinity. The analogical connection developed between the Trinity and the church is therefore both Christologically conditioned and pneumatologically enabled.

The development of a Trinitarian Third Article Ecclesiology thus proceeds by first determining the Trinitarian understanding that is most faithful to the biblical revelation, as discussed earlier. Next, that understanding of the Trinity is applied to the economy by observing how the immanent identities of the Son and the Spirit are reprised on a series of expanding stages, Christologically in the hypostatic union between the human and divine natures of Christ, soteriologically in the mystical union between Christ and the church, and finally and most pertinently ecclesiologically in the ecclesial relation between individual church members. The underlying logic of utilizing the Trinitarian vantage point, therefore, is that the Spirit's immanent identity (as 'personing person') and the Son's immanent identity (as 'personed person') are reprised in each of these spheres. In the hypostatic union, Christ is the personed person and the Spirit is the means by which the

---

33. For Volf's reflective approach, see, for example, Miroslav Volf, *After Our Likeness: The Church as the Image of the Trinity* (Grand Rapids: Eerdmans, 1998). For Tanner's critique of such an approach, see Kathryn Tanner, *Christ the Key* (Cambridge: Cambridge University Press, 2010), 207–46. For a detailed justification and discussion of the alternative approach derived from Third Article Theology, see Liston, *The Anointed Church*, 233–72.

34. Colin Gunton, 'The Church on Earth: The Roots of Community', in *On Being the Church*, ed. C. Gunton and D. Hardy (Edinburgh: T&T Clark, 1989), 60.

Son is personed as a human. To express this in other words, the Son is incarnated as Christ by the Spirit, an action that reflects in time the Father's immanent and ongoing personing of the Son by the Spirit in eternity. In the mystical union (the next expanding stage), the church is 'personed' as Christ's mystical body by the Spirit: Christ is embodied in the church by the Spirit. Finally, and most pertinently here, in the ecclesial union, the Spirit constitutes believers as 'ecclesial persons' by enabling them to share in Christ's ecclesial consciousness: Christ is formed in each believer through the Spirit.

The understanding arising from this perspective is rich and full. The central feature that emerges from viewing ecclesiology from the vantage point of the Trinity through the lens of the Spirit is that the church itself can be characterized as existing in any and all relationships where, by the Spirit, the love of Christ is offered and returned. The implication is that fellowship between church members has an intrinsically sacramental nature. It is through pneumatologically enabled fellowship, both with Christ and with others, that Christ is 'personed' or formed in each believer. It is in offering Christ's love to others by the Spirit that we share his mind and become ecclesial persons. Such an insight leads to an important clarification of the Reformation doctrine of the 'priesthood of all believers'. In contrast to the (mis)understanding that interprets this phrase as believers all having their own individual access to God, a Trinitarian Third Article Ecclesiology argues that our means of approaching the Father is not merely through Christ but also through each other. The mind of Christ is formed in us as we genuinely fellowship together, so that rather than having *no one* 'stand in the gap', it asserts that participating in Christ, *all believers* 'stand in the gap' mediating God to each other.

A related consequence is a nuanced understanding of catholicity. Given that believers are personed not just by Christ alone but also by Christ through others, then each of us has a role in constituting other believers as ecclesial persons in Christ. There are two significant aspects to be aware of here. First, given there is one mind of Christ that we share by the Spirit, each person, however isolated, is intimately connected with others as one universal, *catholic* church. This catholicity is secure and unchangeable, rooted in the church's pneumatological union with Christ. But the church is not just catholic but being *catholicized*. Our intrinsic catholicity has to be increasingly realized for the mind of Christ to be fully formed in us. Geographic barriers need to be crossed, sociological differences need to be bridged, separate ecclesial gatherings need to genuinely interact, and this needs to happen precisely so that by the Spirit, the love of Christ can be offered and returned, in order that the mind of Christ be more fully formed in us. We are catholic through the Son and the Spirit, and so we must be increasingly catholicized in both practice and form.

Christology and the Trinity were chosen as the initial control beliefs for the development of a Third Article Ecclesiology primarily because they are the Third Article Theology doctrines that have been most significantly advanced to this point. As evidenced in even the brief and summarized explanations given earlier, the view of ecclesiology afforded from each of these vantage points is rich and full. But

Christology and the Trinity are not the only doctrines that are pneumatologically linked with ecclesiology. Among the others, the vantage point of eschatology is perhaps the most important of those that have not yet been considered. Through the Spirit, the church is the proleptic anticipation of Christ's coming kingdom. Given that the primary purpose of this volume is to develop such an *eschatological* Third Article Ecclesiology, the next section turns to an exploration of eschatology and how eschatology can and should be used as a vantage point from which to pneumatologically examine ecclesiology.

1.3 The grammar of eschatology

If the development of a Trinitarian Third Article Ecclesiology required a more nuanced and complex approach than that for a Christological Third Article Ecclesiology, then the development of an eschatological Third Article Ecclesiology is still more complex and nuanced again. At least partly this is due to the intrinsically challenging nature of eschatological study. Theologians can only speak provisionally of the coming kingdom. 'Eschatology can deliver no more than a preliminary understanding of "the end" that always stands in need of revision and supplementation.'[35] Eschatological descriptions are intrinsically preliminary. An added complication is that, unlike both Christology and the Trinity, an explicitly Third Article Theology application to eschatology is a subject that no scholar has yet addressed. For example, Habets' edited volume of dogmatic developments in Third Article Theology contained sections and articles on Christology, Trinity, soteriology, ecclesiology, anthropology and public theology (among others) but none at all focused on eschatology.[36]

The challenge of using eschatology as a vantage point should not be overstated, however. As Robinette notes, 'Imagination strains and language buckles in the attempt to speak of the *eschaton*. But then all talk of God shares the same situation. Every subdiscipline in theology, whether it is anthropology, ecclesiology, Christology, or sacramental theology, etc., ultimately flows from the same holy mystery.'[37] The way we apprehend eschatological knowledge, then, closely aligns with the way we gain all theological understanding, through leaning on the Scriptures, tradition, reason and experience, and primarily in the normative revelation of Jesus Christ understood through all of these theological sources. As Green asserts, 'This name focuses the Christian imagination; it is the seed around

---

35. Scott MacDougall, *More Than Communion: Imagining an Eschatological Ecclesiology* (London: T&T Clark, 2015), 143.

36. Habets, ed., *Third Article Theology*. Private communication with the editor confirms that he wasn't aware of anyone utilizing a Third Article Theology methodology to explore eschatology up to the point of publication.

37. Brian D. Robinette, *Grammars of Resurrection: A Christian Theology of Presence and Absence* (New York: Herder & Herder, 2009), 365.

which the myriad imagery of the Bible crystalizes into a dazzling and multifaceted whole.'[38] Applying this specifically to the eschatological vision of the future, he helpfully summarizes:

> Imagining the future Christianly requires a double act of imaginative trust: we imagine the world to come by trusting the imagination of St. John of Patmos (among others), who in turn trusted that the angelic Revelation really did bear witness to Jesus Christ (Rev 1:1). . . . The paradigmatic imagination, by which religious people imagine another world, is *analogical*, for we are able to grasp that which is not present only by means of its *likeness* to something familiar, available, or at hand. For Christians, because their paradigm is Jesus Christ, the likenesses are necessarily historical. Christians envision the world to come by analogy with the past – a very specific past, contained in Holy Scripture. We imagine the future by imagining its likeness to this past: as new creation, heavenly Jerusalem, the return of Jesus Christ.[39]

The specific historical point around which our imagination of the future most coherently adheres is the resurrection of Jesus, the eschatological event par excellence. As the most obvious and central point where the coming kingdom has broken into our present time, our analogical understanding of the future crystallizes around this occurrence. MacDougall perhaps exaggerates when he claims that 'Jesus' resurrection must provide the analogical basis for all eschatological utterances'.[40] But he exaggerates an important and necessary recognition, that Jesus' resurrection provides a coherent grammar for eschatological speech and understanding. The implications of this for how we are to speak faithfully of the future are significant. The following paragraphs outline four significant syntactic rules regarding eschatology, which combine to form a very brief grammar of eschatological speech. These grammatical understandings will be extensively utilized and expanded in the following constructive work.[41]

First, eschatology is essential but not exhaustive. The resurrection of Jesus Christ is central to Christian belief and understanding. The apostle Paul claims that if Jesus has not been resurrected, then both Paul's preaching and our faith are useless (1 Cor. 15.14). In short, no resurrection; no Christianity. The same is

---

38. Garrett Green, 'Imagining the Future', in *The Future as God's Gift: Explorations in Christian Eschatology*, ed. David Fergusson and Marcel Sarot (Edinburgh: T&T Clark, 2000), 77.

39. Ibid., 79.

40. MacDougall, *More Than Communion*, 149.

41. These four grammatical principles have been collated and synthesized from the work of several scholars, but see particularly Robinette, *Grammars of Resurrection*. Also helpful was the much briefer summary in MacDougall, *More Than Communion*, 146–9. Each of these will be worked out in much more detail in the chapters to come (particularly Chapters 3 and 4) so their introductions here should be considered as merely indicative.

true of eschatology. Christian theology without eschatology is not just deficient, it is purposeless, devoid of truth, life, hope or power. Paul says that if it is only for this life that we hope in Christ, then we deserve nothing but pity (1 Cor. 15.17). But just as the resurrection (and the cross that precedes it) is not the entirety of Jesus' incarnate life, so eschatology does not represent the totality of our Christian assurance. Our Christian lives amount to much more than just waiting in hope. In this research, I will argue that the relationship between the church's journey through time and our coming resurrection can be viewed analogously to the relationship between Jesus' earthly life and his resurrection.

Second, eschatology is supra-historical but envelops history. In Jesus' resurrection 'the absolute future *of* history has been made present *within* history'.[42] So it is insufficient to speak of eschatology as either entirely future based or entirely realized. Even more than this, it is not even sufficient to speak of eschatology as an appropriate combination of these two. The familiar 'now but not yet' terminology that is so often used is not only incorrect but also not complete. Through the incarnation, and even more dramatically and permanently in the resurrection and ascension, Jesus has united creaturely time with divine eternity. So, to speak eschatologically is to speak of the present moment, the future, eternity and also of a parallel time running concurrently with the fallen time that we presently experience, a redeemed time that the resurrected and ascended Jesus indwells which unites eternity and time together. Eschatology is thus a reality that is more than historical but one that incorporates history within it.

Third, eschatology is material but not merely materialistic. The resurrection of Jesus was a bodily resurrection (cf. Lk. 24.39). The strong and consistent witness of Scripture is that our coming resurrection will conform our bodies to his (cf. Phil. 3.20-21). When we speak eschatologically, then, we cannot speak of a non-corporeal or merely 'spiritual' reality that is to come. Talk of Jesus being resurrected into structures, institutions, memory or practice is not merely emotionally unsatisfying but grammatically insufficient. Consequently, the eschatological future of the church cannot be considered in isolation from the future of creation and its intrinsic physicality. '"Body" and "world" are inextricably bound, so that what we say of the eschatological future of one inextricably pertains to the other. . . . We miss the meaning of the resurrection, and fatally so, if we do not account for this "objective" reality.'[43] Such recognition of our material future cannot be reduced to mere materialism, though. Jesus' post-resurrection body was not identical with his pre-resurrection body. There is discontinuity as well as continuity to consider in our eschatological grammar. In his death and resurrection, Jesus' humanity experienced an ontological transformation. As has been discussed at length in the development of Spirit Christology, during Jesus' incarnation the Spirit continuously and increasingly conformed his human nature to the divine.[44]

---

42. Robinette, *Grammars of Resurrection*, 8.
43. Ibid., 22.
44. See, for example, Liston, *The Anointed Church*, 136–45.

This process was completed in a discontinuous ontological transformation at his resurrection. Our eschatological outlook is similar. Our future will be the same as now but different. And the different aspect particularly involves our receptivity and conformity to the Spirit of God within us. This is an idea which Paul captures well in his (superficially oxymoronic) declaration that we look forward to having 'spiritual bodies' (1 Cor. 15.44). It also points to the crucial and non-negotiable role that pneumatology plays in forming a clear understanding of eschatology.

Fourth, eschatology is incomprehensible, but also intrinsically transformational. Jesus' resurrection clearly exceeded the limits of the disciples' understanding. Their reactions were a 'saturated' amalgam, mixing confusion and misunderstanding together with worship and wonder. While there was no doubting the reality of what they experienced, those early witnesses struggled greatly in attempts to grasp or explain it. Whatever their level of comprehension, what is without doubt, however, is that Jesus' resurrection was transformational for these disciples. It changed how they perceived God and the world, noetically. It changed their fundamental relationship with God and the world, ontologically. And in terms of their *telos*, it changed their ultimate purpose and future. Our eschatological grammar should reflect this transformation. While our language and descriptions will always struggle to grasp its full breadth, the end result of encountering such eschatological truth should be noetic, ontic and telic transformation. Indeed, it is the intrinsically transformative nature of this eschatological grammar that this volume aims to explore.

Perhaps the core, overarching principle of eschatological grammar, as evidenced in each of these syntactical rules, is its concurrent continuity and discontinuity. In reference to the grammatical starting point of Jesus' resurrection, Robinette explains this well:

> The risen Jesus has not been transposed into a reality completely discontinuous with his embodied history, as though his humanity were only the penultimate stage. . . . His resurrection is not a disembodiment but the admission of his total historical-embodied humanity into eschatological fullness. The empty tomb tradition makes this point abundantly clear. That we are instructed to speak of a continuity in the midst of discontinuity is evident in the narratives' insistence on the familiarity and tactility of the risen Jesus, in ways that even include the identifying marks of his death.[45]

This continuity amid discontinuity is seen in each of the points earlier. The church is both continuous and discontinuous with the coming kingdom. This broad recognition will be the launching point for our discussion of the development of an eschatological ecclesiology in Chapter 2.

Having established some introductory grammatical rules for speaking eschatologically, how then can we begin to construct an eschatological Third

---

45. Robinette, *Grammars of Resurrection*, 104.

Article Ecclesiology? There are, in brief, two stages involved. The first is to determine the core features of Spirit eschatology: an understanding of eschatology where the pneumatological perspective is viewed as pivotal and primary. Such an understanding is obtained primarily through analogy with a Spirit Christology and particularly (as noted earlier) in analogy with Christ's resurrection as the eschatological event par excellence. The next stage is to explore how this understanding of Spirit eschatology impacts our understanding of ecclesiology: How is the church currently being transformed given its eschatological future and direction?

It is worthwhile hinting, even at this early point and in very general terms, about the reason for pursuing such a pneumato-eschatological approach to an exploration of ecclesiology.[46] Typically, theologians have introduced a pneumatological ecclesiology to counteract a purely Christological understanding of the church. Such a Christological emphasis can lead to an ecclesiology which is excessively institutionalized or hierarchical, as if the church simply *is* what it *is* and what it *does* or how it goes about doing what it does is of minimal importance. The problem is that a reactive and excessively pneumatological ecclesiology often trends too far in the opposite direction, where the church's identity is tied too closely to the specific activities occurring within the church, as if what the church *does* is all that matters and the church has no existence or independent reality outside of its actions. Similarly, a purely Christological understanding of the church can lead to an ecclesiology that is too triumphalistic, one which emphasizes the church's *eternal* existence and neglects to focus on its chronological journey through time, one where the discontinuity between our present existence and the coming kingdom is overly exaggerated. Such theologies often include an eschatological component in that the present reality of the kingdom is acknowledged, but all too often the church's present transformational journey through time is neglected. Reactive responses aim to focus on the purposes of the kingdom of God here and now, but unfortunately often end up simply replacing an eternal, Christologically focused ecclesiology with a timebound approach, where the continuities between the church and coming kingdom are dramatically overemphasized, and minimal recognition is given to the church's current sinful and fallen state.

The approach taken in this volume is distinguished from these unhelpful tendencies sometimes seen in Christological ecclesiologies in two distinct ways. First, rather than attempting to develop an understanding of ecclesiology that deliberately contrasts with the Christological ecclesiologies that have previously been developed, it intentionally utilizes and retains the great benefits they have achieved. In other words, the methodological approach adopted in this volume goes *through*, and not *around*, these Christological ecclesiologies. It builds on and complements their great strengths, in the same way that a Spirit Christology

---

46. Note that the very generalized explanation of the next two paragraphs is given needed nuance and specificity in Chapter 2 where the particular ecclesiologies of Barth and Hütter are considered as illustrative case studies.

properly construed builds on and complements the great strengths of a Logos Christology. Second, rather than simply developing an isolated pneumatological ecclesiology or an isolated eschatological ecclesiology, this volume deliberately ties both alternative approaches together, intentionally developing a *pneumato-eschatological* approach to ecclesiology, where eschatology is the vantage point from which ecclesiology is observed and pneumatology is the lens utilized to connect the two doctrines. Such a connection between eschatology and pneumatology is both biblically and traditionally justified. From a biblical perspective, for example, Jesus explicitly viewed the work of the Spirit as a clear and unambiguous sign of the kingdom's presence (Mt. 12.28, Lk. 11.20).[47] And from a traditional perspective, both eschatology and pneumatology were intentionally combined together within the Third Article of the Creed.[48] There is quite some reason, therefore, for expecting a pneumato-eschatological approach to ecclesiology that goes through and not around previous Christological ecclesiologies to reap significant rewards in terms of developing an insightful, nuanced and balanced understanding of ecclesial transformation. The following section outlines how the development of this argument will proceed through the chapters of this volume.

1.4 Constructing an eschatological Third Article Ecclesiology

The broad and overarching thesis being developed in this volume is that exploring the relationship between church and kingdom through the lens of the Spirit enables the construction of a nuanced and balanced account of the church's ongoing transformation, an *eschatological* Third Article Ecclesiology. This final section outlines the structure of the rest of the book, explaining how the argument justifying and expanding this thesis unfolds.

The discussion begins with an examination and critique of two existing formulations that connect eschatology and ecclesiology, those of Karl Barth and Reinhard Hütter. The detailed examination of these two understandings as outlined in Chapter 2 provides both a helpful framework from which to examine the relationship between eschatology and ecclesiology, and effective foils with which the *eschatological* Third Article Ecclesiology emerging in later chapters can be contrasted. Recognizing (along with T. F. Torrance) that a Chalcedonian-like relationship exists between kingdom and church, this chapter argues that an appropriate ecclesiological understanding will balance between an excessively static or an overly optimistic view of church transformation. While acknowledging the many positive eschatological and ecclesial insights contained in Barth and

---

47. For a more detailed biblical analysis of the connection between pneumatology and eschatology, see Section 2.2.

48. See Jaroslov Pelikan and Valerie Hotchkiss, eds, *Creeds and Confessions of Faith in the Christian Tradition: Early, Eastern and Medieval* (New Haven: Yale University Press, 2003), 669.

Hütter's accounts, it is argued that Barth's understanding leans towards a static understanding, with too great a discontinuity between church and kingdom. Hütter's understanding, in contrast, is too optimistic, tying the Spirit's work and church practices together too closely.

Chapter 3 is where the development of the overarching thesis begins in earnest. Dividing into two parts, the first section outlines the development of a Spirit eschatology and the second its application to ecclesiology. In Wolterstorffian terminology, the first half uses Spirit Christology as a control belief and eschatology as a data belief, while the second half uses Spirit eschatology as a control belief and ecclesiology as a data belief. Through applying the methodology of Third Article Theology to the doctrine of eschatology, an understanding of the church's transformational journey through time naturally emerges. Just as Spirit Christology has revealed insights into Christ's humanity and growth, similarly a Spirit eschatology informs an understanding of the church's transformation and development. Such a Spirit eschatology complements rather than replaces the more common Christologically focused eschatologies (developed in the works of Barth and T. F. Torrance, for example), painting a picture of the Spirit working through but not being beholden to the church, leading us in cruciform lives that echo Christ's overarching metanarrative. Moreover, the understanding of the church's pneumatological transformation developed here avoids the imbalances of the eschatological ecclesiologies examined in Chapter 2.

Chapter 4 deepens this approach through articulating an eschatological understanding of the *munus triplex*. Most examinations of Christ's threefold offices explore how his earthly session impacts us at our current moment in ecclesial time. Exploring the doctrine of eschatology through the lens of the Spirit enables a complementary understanding of the *munus triplex* to be developed. The discussion of the *munus triplex* is pertinent here because the church's present existence can be best understood through its participation in Christ's ongoing eschatological offices. While recent attempts to partially employ the *munus triplex* into the service of eschatology reveal considerable advances with regard to Christ's prophetic and priestly offices, it is particularly the constructive and to date relatively unexplored aspect of Christ's kingly office that offers the most insight into the question of the church's transformation through time. By the Spirit, the kingdom realities that define our future are drawn back to become (in part) characteristics of our present ecclesial existence.

Based on the previously developed material, Chapter 5 argues that the church is not just the community historically instituted by Christ, nor merely the community in whom Christ presently dwells, but in addition to these common characterizations the church is also the community in which through the Spirit Christ's coming kingdom presently exists in and impacts the world. It goes on to explain how the Spirit is gradually and continuously transforming the church into the image of the kingdom through the interplay of imagination, presence and practice. Focusing particularly on a detailed examination of the eucharist as an illustrative example, this chapter notes how in the eucharist and through the Spirit we *imagine* our future, one where we are truly and completely united with Christ through the Spirit; we *experience* Christ's presence, for he is with us by his Spirit; and we *practise* for our coming future through our worshipful and Spirit-empowered *practices*, thereby preparing ourselves for Christ's kingdom. This transformational framework of imagination, presence and practice is contrasted with the eschatological ecclesiologies of Barth and Hütter and their respective understandings of the eucharist. It is noted how through either under- or overemphasizing the Spirit both approaches minimize the reality of ongoing ecclesial transformation.

Chapter 6 contains a broader and briefer account of several other church practices, namely prayer and praise, and gospel proclamation. It similarly and comparatively outlines how through the same three intertwined realities of imagination, experienced presence and enacted practice, the Spirit uses the full range of the church's activities to mark the church out as holy and so to prepare it for its coming future. In other words, the Spirit sets us apart through imagination, presence and practice for (and from) the future, as the kingdom's proleptic anticipation within this world and at this time. Put together, Chapters 5 and 6 outline the detailed framework of an eschatological Third Article Ecclesiology, with a particular focus on how the Spirit transforms the church. An overarching summary of its key features is outlined at the end of Chapter 6.

To this point in the volume, using Wolterstorffian terminology, the control belief has been Spirit eschatology, and the data belief has been ecclesiology. Scripture and the Creeds have been background beliefs. The particular perspective that has been developed through this approach is an eschatological Third Article Ecclesiology, an understanding of the church when viewed from the vantage point of eschatology through the lens of the Spirit. In Chapter 7 this newly developed understanding is utilized as a control belief to examine the Scriptures and in particular Paul's first epistle to the Corinthians. So Chapter 7 examines this epistle from the perspective of an eschatological Third Article Ecclesiology and argues that viewing the text in this way enables its overall structure and intricate details to be viewed insightfully and clearly. Two overarching conclusions emerge. First, the key themes that feature in the development of an eschatological Third Article Ecclesiology also feature heavily throughout 1 Corinthians. These include the empowering role of the Spirit, the ongoing experience of transformation, the illuminating vantage point of eschatology, the immediate transformational implications for morality and holiness, the present experience of crucifixion and resurrection as the means of effecting our transformation and the interplay of practice, presence and imagination as the practical way that present transformation occurs. Second, the fact that this perspective provides a coherent lens on the epistle, one that informs the arguments that Paul is making throughout, provides confidence that the ecclesiological understanding constructed in this volume is itself biblical and systematic.

The final substantive chapter, Chapter 8, undertakes another Wolterstorffian exercise, one that pushes the exploration of Third Article Theology into new territory. In the chapters preceding, all of the exploration has been specifically focused on the church and its inner transformation. The important question of the relationship between the church and the world has been put to one side. This chapter outlines a way that this question can be addressed. Taking all the interrelated ecclesiological perspectives gained from the vantage points of Christology, the Trinity and eschatology, it explores what happens when these three understandings are used as control beliefs to examine the data belief of missiology. This approach contrasts with and complements the more common approach where missiology is seen as determinative of ecclesiology. Initially arguing that ecclesiology and missiology are mutually informing doctrines, this chapter develops a dialogical and pneumatological approach for viewing missiology from the vantage point of ecclesiology. The final and major section of this chapter sketches out the panoramic vision of the church's mission that arises when it is viewed from each of these vantage points, particularly when the Spirit's role is seen as primary and constitutive.

The church, as pictured in this volume, is the proleptic anticipation of the coming kingdom. Through enabling Christ's kingly presence, the Spirit draws back to the present church characteristics of the coming kingdom. This enriches, influences and transforms the present church towards its intended *telos*. The final chapter explores how this new understanding adds to and complements the previous ecclesiological understandings gained from other vantage points, outlining how all the various perspectives combine to result in a coherent and more nearly complete picture of the church. It also explores and demonstrates the inherent practicality and applicability of an eschatological Third Article Ecclesiology, before looking forward to the next steps that could be taken in developing a complete and consistent Third Article Ecclesiology.

Chapter 2

TWO CONTRASTING ESCHATOLOGICAL ECCLESIOLOGIES

Before launching into the development of an eschatological Third Article Ecclesiology, it is instructive to explore two eschatological ecclesiologies that have already been developed in detail. An examination of these alternative understandings provides both a helpful framework from which to begin an examination of the relationship between eschatology and ecclesiology, and effective foils through which the *eschatological* Third Article Ecclesiology emerging in later chapters can be contrasted. This chapter chooses the eschatological ecclesiologies of Karl Barth and Reinhard Hütter to analyse. While there is great insight in both approaches, it is argued that Barth leans towards a static understanding, with too great a discontinuity between church and kingdom. Hütter's understanding, in contrast, is too optimistic, tying the Spirit's work and church practices together too closely. Prior to the analysis of these eschatological ecclesiologies, an important preliminary discussion is needed that outlines the nature of time in both divine and human perspectives and provides a terminological backdrop through which both Barth and Hütter's understandings can be characterized.

2.1 Eschatological and teleological tensions

The initial insight undergirding and launching this theological analysis is that the church's connection with the coming kingdom involves both continuity and discontinuity. A range of possible correlations exists between these two realities. At one end is their virtual equivalency, a position held, for example, by the Roman Catholic Church prior to Vatican II.[1] This view sees the relationship between the church and the coming kingdom as primarily continuous. At the other end of the continuum is the not uncommon Protestant position that views the pair as entirely separate entities, with the church impoverished as merely a present 'holding pen'

---

1. John Haughey, 'Church and Kingdom: Ecclesiology in the Light of Eschatology', *Theological Studies* 29, no. 1 (1968): 73. More recently, McKnight has argued somewhat similarly. See Scott McKnight, *Kingdom Conspiracy: Returning to the Radical Mission of the Local Church* (Grand Rapids: Baker Publishing Group, 2014).

for believers, strongly distinguished from the kingdom which awaits it.[2] This view sees the relationship as primarily discontinuous. But neither extreme adequately represents the nuanced relationship between church and kingdom described in the Scriptures, where both significant continuities and necessary discontinuities exist.

There are three clearly outlined biblical connection points between the kingdom and the church – noetic, ontic and telic – each of which evidences both continuity and discontinuity. Noetically, our realization that the awesome characterizations of the coming kingdom describe our ultimate reality means we eagerly look forward to that time. Our knowledge is partial and not complete, however, thus exhibiting continuity and discontinuity. Ontically, we anticipate the kingdom in our ecclesial being. More than just a longing, the church's present existential reality and active shape are caused by the future to which it looks forward. In a curious temporal inversion, the church is (in part and not completely) formed by what is to come. Finally, there is a telic connection, as we move towards the kingdom. While a necessary discontinuity will occur when the kingdom comes in fullness, the church is nevertheless also being continuously transformed towards this future reality.

The presence of both continuity and discontinuity in the relationship between the church and the coming kingdom leads to the suggestion of a 'Chalcedonian' relationship between the two. Perhaps, in a manner analogous to Christology, the kingdom and the church are related 'inconfusedly, unchangeably, indivisibly, inseparably'.[3] Such an understanding is well explained by Thomas Torrance. Torrance argues that a 'Chalcedonian' analogy can be utilized between church and kingdom because eschatology can and should be characterized Christologically. He writes that 'eschatology is nothing but a thoroughgoing expression of the doctrine of grace as it concerns history, so that the important word is not *eschaton* (the last event) but *Eschatos* (the last one)'.[4] Similarly, 'Eschatology properly speaking is the application of Christology to the Kingdom of Christ and to the work of the Church in history.'[5]

The gains made through this comparison are significant. Launching from what Torrance labels the primary eschatological insight of the twentieth century – Barth's realization that the Word became a spatiotemporal being (becoming 'time'

---

2. Haughey, 'Church and Kingdom', 74. Haughey sees a 'large proportion of Protestant Christianity' as having this predilection and references Barth as an exemplar.

3. Pelikan and Hotchkiss, eds, *Creeds and Confessions of Faith in the Christian Tradition*, 181.

4. Thomas F. Torrance, *Incarnation: The Person and Life of Christ* (Downers Grove: InterVarsity Press, 2008), 309.

5. Thomas F. Torrance, *Royal Priesthood: A Theology of Ordained Ministry* (Edinburgh: T&T Clark, 1993), 43.

in the same way he became 'flesh'⁶) – Torrance draws out the implication that there are three 'times' to be considered: 'old' time (what humans currently experience in their fallen condition), eternity (God's time) and 'new' time (redeemed time in reconciliation and union with eternity). To express the relation between these three positively, he turns to Chalcedon:

> Just as in Christ God and man are united in such a way that there is neither fusion on the one hand nor yet separation on the other, without any diminishing of the completeness or perfection of deity or of humanity, so here too we may think of there having taken place in the Incarnation as it were a hypostatic union between the eternal and the temporal in the form of new time.[7]

The incarnational analogy is not sufficient alone, though:

> We must go a step beyond Chalcedon, and . . . carry the hypostatic union in our thought through the Cross to its perfection in the Resurrection. We must think . . . of fallen time as having perfected itself through the Cross and resurrection into the abiding triumph of a perfection in God which both consummates the original purposes of creation and crowns it with glory.[8]

The result is that there are two tensions to be considered, an 'eschatological' tension between 'new' (redeemed) and 'old' (fallen) time, and an ultimate 'teleological' tension between the eternal and temporal.[9] For Torrance, the first is equivalent to the tension between the new creation and the fallen world, while the second is equivalent to the holiness/sinfulness tension.[10]

Perhaps the clearest illustration of this 'Chalcedonian' eschatology is in the sacraments. Torrance sees the twin sacraments of baptism and eucharist as corresponding to the 'eschatological' and 'teleological' tensions, respectively.[11] Baptism signifies that we are 'in Christ'. Through baptism we become a 'bodily

---

6. See, for example, Karl Barth, *Church Dogmatics*, trans. Geoffrey W. Bromiley and Thomas F. Torrance (Peabody: Hendrickson, 2010), III.2 437–42.

7. Thomas F. Torrance, 'The Modern Eschatological Debate', *Evangelical Quarterly* 25 (1953): 224. See also Torrance, *Incarnation*, 334–6. And Thomas F. Torrance, *Space, Time and Resurrection* (Edinburgh: T&T Clark, 1976), 98–9.

8. Torrance, 'The Modern Eschatological Debate', 224–5.

9. The term 'eschatological' is problematic here, as Torrance uses it to refer specifically to the tension between new and old time, whereas many others use it to refer to the overarching subject of the church's ultimate purpose, future and direction. I have chosen to retain Torrance's use of eschatological and teleological as described previously and will note when another author uses 'eschatological' in a way that could cause confusion.

10. This is because Torrance argues Christ assumed a *fallen* human nature.

11. Thomas F. Torrance, 'Eschatology and the Eucharist', in *Intercommunion*, ed. D. M. Baillie and J. Marsh (London: SCM, 1952), 312.

church', incorporated into Christ as part of the new creation. It is consequently a once-only, unrepeatable action and, as such, corresponds to the eschatological tension. The eucharist in contrast is repeatable, grounded in the flow of time and thus corresponds to the ongoing and developing teleological tension between time and eternity. The eucharist emphasizes the church's incorporation into Christ as an ongoing temporal reality.[12]

Many, if not most, theological analyses of the church's journey through time overemphasize either the eschatological or teleological tension. To illustrate, and as preparatory work for the constructive development to come, this chapter explores in detail two contrasting theological proposals concerning how God transforms the church towards its ultimate goal. The first (exemplified in Barth's work) overemphasizes the eschatological tension. The root cause is that Barth's theological analysis does not sufficiently recognize the Spirit's distinctive ecclesial mission, with the result that he makes too much of the discontinuity between church and kingdom. The second (exemplified in Hütter's work) overemphasizes the teleological tension. The root cause is that church and Spirit are too closely aligned, with the result that the continuity between church and kingdom is overstated. Having examined these two imbalanced alternatives, the following chapters will demonstrate how a Third Article Theology can lead to a more balanced and nuanced understanding of the church's journey through time.

2.2 Barth and the eschatological tension

Torrance's 'step beyond Chalcedon' framework rightly suggests that an appropriate understanding of the relationship between eternity and time will balance the 'eschatological' and 'teleological' tensions. The question this section addresses is whether Barth's characterization of the church's journey through time adequately reflects that balance. The contention argued here, in line with several other commentators, is that while Barth's analysis of the relationship between time and eternity is profound, his corresponding explanation of the church's growth and development is imbalanced, overemphasizing the eschatological tension. Further, the primary cause for this imbalance is that the Spirit's ecclesial mission is not sufficiently recognized, being subsumed to some degree into the Son's mission.[13] The analysis here initially leverages the explanatory work of Hunsinger about

---

12. Stanley S. Maclean, *Resurrection, Apocalypse, and the Kingdom of Christ: The Eschatology of Thomas F. Torrance* (Eugene: Pickwick Publications, 2012), 143. See also Torrance, 'Eschatology and the Eucharist', 327.

13. Note that the underlying belief here about the Trinitarian persons is that they have distinct but clearly interrelated and inseparable missions and agencies, but nevertheless reveal a single *ousia* and will. The processions are the basis of these missions, and the missions reveal the processions. See, for example, Weinandy, *The Father's Spirit of Sonship*, particularly chapter 4.

CD I/II and Langdon about *CD* III/IV to explain Barth's understanding of time, eternity and the church's place within them,[14] before turning to explain and justify the critique of Barth overemphasizing the eschatological tension.

Barth's understanding of eternity and time is complex and nuanced. The most significant interpretive key is that Trinitarian doctrine is its formative basis. For Barth, eternity is not the milieu in which God exists but rather it is interpreted through God's intrinsically triune nature. Consequently, in contrast to previous attempts defining eternity in contrast to time *via negativa*, Barth maintains a distinction between eternity and time while including core temporal aspects such as dynamism and immanence within God's eternal existence. Utilizing this interpretive tool, and focusing firstly on *CD* I, Barth's understanding of the relation between eternity and time begins with three main aspects of God's reality: God's being (*ousia*), God's modes of being (*hypostases*) and God's becoming (*perichoresis*). God's *ousia* correlates with his Lordship as one acting subject. God's *hypostases* correlate with his internal concrete relatedness, his mutual self-giving communion of love. And God's *perichoresis* (or becoming) correlates with God's dynamism and vitality, which occur independently of any relationship he has with the world.

In *CD* II Barth explores the relationship between eternity and time by outlining a similar threefold description of 'pure duration', 'beginning, middle and end', and 'simultaneity'. Hunsinger argues that for Barth these three concepts correspond, 'roughly speaking', to the Trinitarian descriptions of *ousia*, *hypostases* and *perichoresis*. In the same way that the three aspects of God's being interrelate and cohere simultaneously and dynamically, so do the three aspects of God's eternity. As such, eternity is 'the mutual coinherence of three concrete temporal forms [beginning, middle and end], distinct but not separate, that exemplify an undivided duration, identical with the *ousia* of God'.[15] This identification allows Barth to distinguish between time and eternity. In eternity, the three temporal forms – beginning, middle and end – exist simultaneously (just as the *hypostases* exist perichoretically within each other) while in time they are not simultaneous. Created time, in Barth's view, lacks the unity and simultaneity of eternity, while eternity has everything that time has. Because of this, 'God has time because and as he has eternity.'[16]

Barth sees Christ as time and eternity's mediator. In Christ, eternity becomes time without ceasing to be eternal, just as in Christ, God becomes human without ceasing to be God; and similarly, in Christ time becomes eternal without ceasing to

---

14. The following descriptive paragraphs utilize the discussion in George Hunsinger, '*Mysterium Trinitatis*: Karl Barth's Conception of Eternity', in *Disruptive Grace: Studies in the Theology of Karl Barth* (Grand Rapids: Eerdmans, 2000), 186–209. And then similarly, the discussion in Adrian Langdon, *God the Eternal Contemporary: Trinity, Eternity and Time in Karl Barth* (Eugene: Wipf & Stock, 2012).

15. Hunsinger, '*Mysterium Trinitatis*', 198.

16. Barth, *Church Dogmatics*, II.1 511.

be temporal, just as in Christ, humanity participates in God's internal life without ceasing to be human. Here Barth's commonly used Chalcedonian pattern of unity, distinction and asymmetry is applied to time and eternity's relationship. In Christ, eternity and time are related without separation or division (unity), without confusion or change (distinction) and with eternity having a logical precedence over time (asymmetry).[17] Hunsinger summarizes the mediation by noting two movements and a resultant union. First, there is the downward vector, where in Christ, God enters time and takes time into himself. Second, there is an upward vector, where God, in taking time into himself, heals time of its imperfection.[18] Barth says that Christ 'masters time. He recreates it and heals its wounds, the fleetingness of the present, and the separation of the past and the future from one another, and from the present.'[19] The resultant union is where simultaneity and sequence come together. God consequently has a threefold relationship to time through Christ's mediation. First, Christ is pretemporal (before all beginnings). Second, he is supratemporal (not just above time but pervading it from within). Finally, he is post-temporal (the end of all endings). These three forms of God's eternity in time, in analogy with the Trinitarian hypostases, must be equally emphasized. They coexist together in union with time, giving eternity a real simultaneity together with genuine sequence and dynamism.

How does Barth's understanding of time and eternity impact upon our present ecclesial time and the church's ongoing journey? This requires delving into Barth's understanding of time and eternity in *CD* III and IV.[20] In analysing these sections, Langdon, similar to Hunsinger (and others), utilizes the Trinity as the primary interpretive key. Barth develops what Langdon terms an *analogia trinitaria temporis*: an analogy between God's eternal being and his creative activity within time. The first locus is the Father's work in creating and preserving time. Just as the Father is the origin and source of the divine life, so there is an analogous link to the Father's creating and preserving of time to enable a relationship with humanity.[21] For Barth, time is the 'theatre for covenantal activity and relations'.[22] Even though humanity has rejected this purpose, the Father sustains creatures within time so that relationship may be restored, and time itself may be recapitulated and fulfilled. The Son, as the second locus of the analogy, is associated with the anticipation, recapitulation and fulfilling of time. The Son anticipates (pretemporal), recapitulates (supratemporal) and then fulfils (post-temporal) time, enabling eternity to exist within time and time to exist within eternity. This is Torrance's

---

17. For more detail, see the description in Hunsinger, '*Mysterium Trinitatis*', 202.

18. Note that that this 'healing' is not equivalent to salvation, as time's limitations were inherent in God's original creation.

19. Barth, *Church Dogmatics*, II.1 617.

20. The following paragraphs utilize the discussion in Langdon, *God the Eternal Contemporary*, 85–186.

21. See, for example, Barth, *Church Dogmatics*, III.1 49 and III.3 28–9.

22. Langdon, *God the Eternal Contemporary*, 191.

eschatological tension, connecting fallen time with Christ's 'healed' time. Of particular note within this is the emphasis that Barth places on the resurrection, which is not just Christ's unveiling as divine but also Christ's inauguration as 'contemporaneous with all subsequent times and history'.[23] Indeed, Christ is more than just contemporaneous but actually present through the Spirit. He cannot be absent, or his presence would require being mediated through the sacraments, and the ecclesial role would go beyond witness, which for Barth it simply cannot do.[24] Barth certainly makes a close connection between the resurrected Christ and the Spirit in his ecclesiological language – a virtual identity.[25] For example, in *CD* IV.3.1, Barth directly identifies the Holy Spirit twice as 'Jesus Christ himself in the power of his resurrection'.[26] This leads to the final locus of the analogy, which is the ecclesial time of the Holy Spirit. Langdon argues that this is the time between the ascension and the eschaton we currently experience, where the Holy Spirit reveals the new reality already found in Jesus-history. 'As the self-attestation of the Son, the Spirit awakens believers to the fact that their histories are enclosed within and correspond to the history of Jesus Christ.'[27] Just as the Spirit in eternity is the bond of love between the Father and the Son, so the Spirit in time is characterized as the 'bond of salvific contemporaneity'.[28] The Spirit (internally) gathers and builds up the community, and (externally) sends her out as witness to Jesus' completed salvific work. Langdon notes, however, that this appropriation of ecclesial time to the Spirit within Barth's work is 'contentious' and that Barth 'leaves one wanting more in terms of describing ecclesial time'[29] – a point that will be expanded further.

Even granting Langdon's appropriation of ecclesial time to the Spirit within *Church Dogmatics*, what is immediately clear is that in Barth's voluminous discussion of eternity and time, when his attention turns to ecclesial time, the emphasis is very much on the eschatological tension. The focus is on the Spirit (the 'stretched out arm' of Christ[30]) bringing forwards Christ's work to us, rather than the Spirit's distinctive mission transforming the church and the believer towards the coming kingdom. There are several pieces of evidence pointing towards this conclusion. The first, and perhaps the most obvious, is that for all the insight of Barth's analysis, his exploration of eschatology characterizes it as peripheral to a study of the *last things*: humanity's future resurrection, heaven, hell

---

23. Ibid., 136.
24. When the church attempts to become more than a witness, it ironically becomes less. See, for example, Barth, *Church Dogmatics*, IV.1 657. Also, Kimlyn J. Bender, *Karl Barth's Christological Ecclesiology* (Aldershot: Ashgate, 2005), 179.
25. His Trinitarian explanations, in contrast, always recognize the Son and the Holy Spirit as distinct 'modes of being'. See, for example, Barth, *Church Dogmatics*, I.1 348-83.
26. Barth, *Church Dogmatics*, IV.3.1 352-3.
27. Langdon, *God the Eternal Contemporary*, 192.
28. Ibid.
29. Ibid.
30. Barth, *Church Dogmatics*, IV.2 323.

and particularly our current movement towards these realities.³¹ Barth describes the Spirit as conveying Christ's objective salvation to the current church – a noetic revelation rather than a mediated ontic participation or transformation. Because Barth's emphasis is on the relationship between Christ's past work and the church's present reality, its future orientation – the teleological tension – becomes minimized. Consequently, the present continuous transformational journey the church is on becomes eclipsed by the reality of what the church already is and even more so by what Christ has already achieved. This imbalance is seen as much by what is missing from Barth's work, as by what is emphatically there. This is a point that even sympathetic observers of Barth recognize. For example, Hunsinger acknowledges that Barth could have made more room for 'gradual or cumulative regeneration within the spiritual life of the believer . . . it seems undeniable that in Barth's soteriology this aspect is underdeveloped and excessively diminished'.³² For Barth, there is insufficient consideration of the development and growth of the church, resulting in what some (exaggeratedly) term a tendency towards a *disembodied* church:³³ 'Barth divides the true church from the ongoing history of the community'.³⁴ The minimization of such development requires a massive discontinuity before the kingdom can come in its fullness. For example, Barth claims that in the new creation time itself is done away with, a speculative insight which creates 'too much discontinuity between the present state of creation and the new creation to come'.³⁵ Overall, for Barth, the 'without confusion' relationship of new and old time is emphasized significantly more than their 'without separation' aspect, and, consequently, the teleological tension is subordinated to the eschatological tension.

The underlying cause of this imbalance is the insufficient distinguishing between the ecclesial missions of the Son and the Spirit.³⁶ Barth leans towards a situation where the Spirit's mission towards the church is to some degree a subset of the Son's mission. Many scholars have recognized a correlation between the limited role of

---

31. Maclean makes a similar (although less pronounced) judgement about Torrance's eschatological explanations. See Maclean, *Resurrection, Apocalypse, and the Kingdom of Christ*, 195.

32. Hunsinger, 'The Mediator of Communion', 167–8.

33. See, for example, Reinhard Hütter, 'Karl Barth's "Dialectical Catholicity": Sic et Non', *Modern Theology* 16, no. 2 (2000): 147–52. Also Nicholas M. Healy, 'The Logic of Karl Barth's Ecclesiology: Analysis, Assessment and Proposed Modifications', *Modern Theology* 10, no. 3 (1994): 258–9, although Healy later softened his more exaggerated critiques. See Nicholas M. Healy, 'Karl Barth's Ecclesiology Reconsidered', *Scottish Journal of Theology* 57, no. 3 (2004): 287–99.

34. Langdon, *God the Eternal Contemporary*, 47.

35. Ibid., 204.

36. Elsewhere, this has been labelled as ecclesial Spirit-Eutychianism. See Liston, 'A "Chalcedonian" Spirit Christology', 85–8. More specifically about Barth, see Liston, *The Anointed Church*, 95–107.

the Spirit and the consequently limited scope of his teleological ecclesial vision. Colin Gunton, for example, writes 'the weakness of Barth's doctrine of the Spirit is that it gives rise to an underdetermination of the eschatological dimensions of theology'.[37] Gunton argues that Barth tends to assign to the Son actions that are more naturally pneumatological.[38] The Spirit simply applies the objective salvation of Christ's incarnation to the present-day believer, meaning the Spirit is limited to being Christ's action towards us: 'Jesus Christ himself in the power of his resurrection'.[39] Further, according to Gunton, Barth places much less emphasis on the present relationship of the believer with Christ, mediated through the church: 'More weight is placed upon the miraculous transfer of what happened *then* to ourselves *now*, less on the relation mediated in the present by the Spirit of Christ through his body, the church.'[40] Torrance himself critiques Barth on this point, arguing that in *CD* IV.3 'the humanity of the risen Jesus appeared to be displaced by what he called "the humanity of God" in his turning toward us'.[41] The end result, Gunton claims, is that Barth ends up with 'effectively a realised eschatology of revelation',[42] where the teleological tension is underemphasized compared to the eschatological tension and more particularly to salvation's objective reality already Christologically achieved.[43]

Gunton's argument that Barth's impoverished pneumatology results in a restricted teleological focus closely relates to another claim of excessive separation between the human and divine. Gunton argues that Barth has a 'rather non-participatory conception of knowledge' and would prefer he spoke of *participation* in Christ's body rather than merely *encountering* another history.[44] A similar but more detailed account offered by Bender draws a similar conclusion. Recognizing the common critique that Barth's work is underdetermined by pneumatology, Bender notes first that Barth himself acknowledged this tendency. He similarly recognizes some validity in the critique that Barth considers redemptive history complete at the cross, leaving little for the Spirit or the church to do. While he rightly rejects the mistaken conclusion that Barth leaves no place for human

---

37. Colin Gunton, *Being and Becoming: The Doctrine of God in Charles Hartshorne and Karl Barth* (London: SCM Press, 2001), 240. Gunton is using 'eschatological' more broadly than Torrance's 'eschatological' tension here.

38. See Gunton, *Being and Becoming*, 235.

39. Barth, *Church Dogmatics*, IV 3.1 352–3.

40. Colin Gunton, 'Salvation', in *The Cambridge Companion to Karl Barth*, ed. John Webster (Cambridge: Cambridge University Press, 2000), 152.

41. Thomas F. Torrance, *Karl Barth. Biblical and Evangelical Theologian* (Edinburgh: T&T Clark, 1990), 134.

42. Colin Gunton, 'The Church and the Lord's Supper: "Until He Comes." Towards an Eschatology of Church Membership', in *Father, Son and Holy Spirit: Toward a Trinitarian Theology* (London: T&T Clark, 2003), 217.

43. For more details, see Gunton, *Being and Becoming*, 235–40.

44. Gunton, 'Salvation', 152.

agency (referencing Barth's rich notion of correspondence), Bender notes that 'Barth often speaks of a parallelism of action, rather than an embodied action. . . . The point might be illustrated by asking whether Christ comes to us through the proclamation of the Church or alongside of it.'[45]

Balthasar's critique follows a similar line. He claims that Barth has removed all interaction between God and humanity from the 'fallen' time we currently inhabit, as the entire history of God's interaction with humanity has been completed in Jesus. Our interaction is noetic rather than ontic, as Jesus' work is conveyed to us in a way that we merely encounter. Balthasar writes, perhaps exaggeratedly, that for Barth all of history is transferred

> back into a pretemporal eternity, where sin is ever the past and justification is ever the future. He [Barth] avoids all talk of growth and progress and all talk of relapses into sin and loss of faith. In short, he avoids all talk about those things that would provide for a real ongoing history between man and God in the sphere of the temporal and the relative. Thus we cannot help but feel that nothing really happens in his theology of history, because everything has already taken place in eternity.[46]

Balthasar's argument is that Barth's emphasis on the church's creatureliness, finitude and sinfulness has resulted in a radical separation between God's self-communication and the church's ongoing journey, with the consequence that the Spirit's transformational mission (and consequently the teleological tension) is eclipsed.

In his monograph-length treatment of Barth's understanding of time, Langdon also locates Barth's overemphasis on the eschatological tension to his tendency to suppress the role of the Spirit. He concludes that Barth does 'not do full justice to the work of the Spirit in the ecclesial time',[47] claiming that he 'dissolves the agency of the Spirit into the Son's, thereby limiting the role of the Spirit'.[48] In response, Langdon explicitly reads the Spirit back into Barth's understanding.[49] Utilizing such an approach, he suggests that the Spirit's work *ad extra* is analogically related to his work *in se*. The Spirit is the bond between Christ and his body (*ad extra*), just as he is the bond between Father and Son (*in se*). And therefore, the Holy Spirit joins current ecclesial time with the 'new' or 'redeemed' time of Christ as a '*vinculum* of contemporaneity'.[50] This may be interpreted as the Spirit's role in the 'eschatological' tension. The Holy Spirit is subjectively imparting Christ's

---

45. Bender, *Karl Barth's Christological Ecclesiology*, 280.
46. Hans Urs von Balthasar, *The Theology of Karl Barth*, trans. John Drury (New York: Holt, Rinehart and Winston, 1971), 277.
47. Langdon, *God the Eternal Contemporary*, 169.
48. Ibid., 165.
49. Ibid., 168–70.
50. Ibid., 169.

reconciliation to believers as 'the form and power in which the Son makes his completed work manifest to humanity'.[51] This is the Spirit's 'continuous, dynamic, particular, and unifying'[52] role. Even on this generous reading (and Langdon recognizes it as such), the Spirit's role in Barth is still essentially limited to taking Jesus' past work and making it available to us today. But what of the church's future direction and hope? Vondey perhaps exaggerates, but he locates a clear tendency in Barth's pneumatologically underdetermined eschatology by writing: 'Barth can speak of the "Spirit in history" but he does not know the "Spirit of history".'[53]

Such minimization of the teleological role of the Spirit is problematic. Particularly when the Spirit's involvement in the kingdom–church correspondence is so biblically prominent. Each of the three correlations previously noted (noetic, ontic and telic) is intrinsically pneumatologically enabled. From a noetic perspective, we only 'remember' the future through the Spirit. It was 'in the Spirit' that John had a vision of the coming kingdom (Rev. 1.10), and it is of course the Spirit that leads us into all truth (Jn 16.13) (which is not limited to but includes eschatological truth). Ontically, it is the Spirit that takes future kingdom truths and makes them present ecclesial realities. Indeed, Jesus virtually equated the working of the Spirit with the anticipatory presence of the kingdom in his own ministry (Mt. 12.28), as well as in the lives of believers (Jn 3.5). And Paul makes a similar connection for the church (Rom. 14.17). Finally, from a telic perspective, it is the Spirit who leads the church towards her future reality (2 Cor. 3.18). If the Scriptures so strongly emphasize the pneumatological connection between the church and the kingdom, then a coherent theological understanding of how the church anticipates and is connected with the coming kingdom simply cannot be formed without significant reference to the Spirit. As Lemmer says, 'the triad, eschatology, pneumatology and ecclesiology, are ineluctably and reciprocally linked; without any one of these elements, the others totally lose their significance and become non-existent.'[54]

Through a tendency to subsume the ecclesial role of the Spirit into that of the Son, Barth's ecclesial understanding overemphasizes the eschatological tension, excessively distinguishes between divine and human aspects, and cannot adequately describe the church's journey through time. While these critiques cannot be applied simplistically to others, Barth is certainly not alone in trending in this direction. Some have recognized a similar (although greatly less pronounced) tendency in Torrance's theology itself. For example, at the end of an exhaustive and largely affirming exploration of Torrance's eschatology, Maclean argues that even though Torrance's framework outlined earlier explicitly aims for a balance between the eschatological and teleological tensions, in his development

51. Ibid., 165.
52. Ibid., 173.
53. Wolfgang Vondey, 'The Holy Spirit and Time in Contemporary Catholic and Protestant Theology', *Scottish Journal of Theology* 58, no. 4 (2005): 398.
54. H. R. Lemmer, 'Pneumatology and Eschatology in Ephesians: The Role of the Eschatological Spirit in the Church' (PhD diss., University of South Africa, 1988) summary.

'the balance appears to tip in favour of the eschatological end'.[55] Maclean notes that the theme of hope is lacking in Torrance's eschatology, which is surprising given its prominence during the latter decades of Torrance's career. And Maclean has a familiar diagnosis for this imbalance – a relative neglect of the Holy Spirit's ecclesial mission.[56] He argues that Torrance's 'eschatology is *Christologically overdetermined*. Even its pneumatological aspect is determined strongly by the person and work of Christ.'[57] On those few occasions when Torrance does address the topic of hope, it is the objective, Christological side – the 'anchor of our soul', rather than the subjective aspect – the 'hope that is in us'.[58] While it is overreaching to say of Torrance (as one might of Barth) that the role of the Spirit is primarily restricted to bringing to the believer Christ's past work, it is perhaps fairer to suggest that Torrance underappreciates the Spirit's perfecting role in bringing the reality of Christ's future to bear on our present ecclesial existence.[59]

For all its profundity, then, through a tendency to subsume the ecclesial role of the Spirit into that of the Son, Barth and perhaps others have constructed an ecclesial understanding that overemphasizes the eschatological tension and consequently cannot adequately inform the ongoing journey of the church through time. How can this imbalance be corrected, and a coherent and nuanced understanding of the church's journey be constructed? Mangina suggests: 'The way beyond Barth at this point, it seems to me, lies in the direction of a "concrete" pneumatology that is able to recognise the Spirit as a salvific economy in its own right – a demand that Eastern theologians have consistently made of their Western counterparts.'[60] The next section examines the possibilities and potential problems with this suggestion.

2.3 Hütter and the teleological tension

Can a theological account of the church's journey through time that adequately balances the eschatological and teleological tensions be developed? Some theologians suggest that the solution is to essentially turn Barth's vertical relationship between church and kingdom on its side to create a horizontal (or perhaps chronologically oriented) relationship that intrinsically includes development, transformation and hope in its eschato-ecclesial account. The pivotal aspect of this alternative approach is that the Spirit works in and through

---

55. Maclean, *Resurrection, Apocalypse, and the Kingdom of Christ*, 197. As also noted earlier.
56. Ibid., 198.
57. Ibid., 199.
58. Ibid., 198.
59. For more details on this, see the discussion in Chapter 4 on the *munus triplex*.
60. Joseph L. Mangina, 'Bearing the Marks of Jesus: The Church in the Economy of Salvation in Barth and Hauerwas', *Scottish Journal of Theology* 52 (1999): 301.

the church (or its core practices) to continuously transform the church towards its teleological goal. The question, however, is whether in placing such a high priority on the transforming work of the Spirit and therefore correcting the challenge of Barth's work, such an approach loses what Barth gained? Has an imbalanced lean towards the eschatological tension been replaced by a substantial slide towards the teleological? Unfortunately, it often has. Where Barth's understanding overemphasized discontinuity and the eschatological tension, viewed the church as excessively static and subsumed the Spirit's ecclesial role into the Son's, this alternative approach does precisely the opposite, correcting the flaws while not retaining its advantages. Nevertheless, as a counterpart to Barth's understanding, a precursor to how it can potentially be extended and a caution about the balance tipping too far towards the teleological tension, a detailed examination of this alternative framework is valuable. The work of Reinhard Hütter will be utilized as an exemplar.[61]

Although his ultimate focus is on the means by which theological understanding is developed, Hütter provides a nuanced and detailed account of how the Holy Spirit draws the church towards its fulfilment through the community's central practices. At its core, Hütter's prime motivation is a realization that rather than the church *serving* the individual subject, the church is the *end* of the subject. The consequence is that both Hegel's approach to theology (participating by speculative reason in God's self-knowledge) and Barth's approach (distinguishing between God and God's self-communication) are viewed as subject-focused and therefore inadequate. In the former, the distinction between creator and creature is erased; in the latter, the Holy Spirit's identity and economy are reduced to actualization of the divine–human relationship but not having a distinct mission of his own. Hütter's alternative response is to develop an intrinsically ecclesiological understanding of doctrine. He writes, 'Knowledge of God is achieved in and through the reception of the gospel proclaimed and taught (*doctrina evangelii*), which takes place via the church's constitutive practices and via doctrine (dogma; *doctrina definita*).'[62] He

---

61. Other possible examplars include Moltmann, Pannenberg, Jenson and Zizioulas, among others. See, for example, the critique of Jenson in Michael Mawson, 'The Spirit and the Community: Pneumatology and Ecclesiology in Jenson, Hütter and Bonhoeffer', *International Journal of Systematic Theology* 15, no. 4 (2013): 454–9. Or the critique of Moltmann and Zizioulas in Liston, *The Anointed Church*, 107–19, 210–17. Clearly, there are significant differences between the eschatological ecclesiologies of these examples, and (like Hütter) they all contain insights of significant value. The justification for grouping them is that they all replace Barth's overemphasis on the eschatological tension with an overemphasis on the teleological tension.

62. Reinhard Hütter, 'The Church: The Knowledge of the Triune God: Practices, Doctrine, Theology', in *Knowing the Triune God: The Work of the Spirit in the Practices of the Church*, ed. James J. Buckley and David S. Yeago (Grand Rapids: William B. Eerdmans, 2001), 32. Hütter's approach appears very similar to Roman Catholicism. Indeed, McCormack notes this, arguing that Hütter's achievement is not so much Eastern

draws heavily on Eastern theologians to develop a detailed understanding of how the Spirit works through the core practices of the church to orient the church to its *telos* and sustain it as a visibly distinctive community.

There are several pivotal ideas that need explanation for Hütter's thesis to be understood. The first and most central pair of concepts are captured in Hütter's usage of the terms *pathos* and *poiesis*. In contrast to its normal use referring to affections or emotions, Hütter utilizes *pathos* to describe a passive reception that determines identity. *Pathos* means we become what we are because of the action of another, which we experience or 'suffer'.[63] Studebaker helpfully illustrates Hütter's ideas here using the example of children receiving a love of fishing from parents who take them on trips. While the children are active, their love of fishing is ultimately and entirely due to the action of the parents.[64] The action of the parents (*poiesis*) produces a response in the children which passively forms their identity (*pathos*). Hütter utilizes this idea of passive identity reception both within the Godhead and within creation. In the Trinity, he draws on the work of Eastern theologians such as Zizioulas and Nissiotis to argue that the divine persons receive their identities in such a way. 'The personal being of each person thus resides in its *reception* of identity through the other two; that is, it is *pathically* constituted.'[65] In creation, the Holy Spirit acts (*poiesis*) through the core practices of the church to draw believers as a community into the life of the Trinity. In this way, the Spirit determines the church's identity (pathically) by leading and guiding the church to the Spirit's desired *telos*. Specifically, the Spirit acts (*poiesis*) through the church's core practices to create theological convictions within the church, which is an aspect of the church's identity (*pathos*).

Hütter uses the overarching term *doctrina* to describe these theological convictions. He divides *doctrina* into two key aspects, forming the second pair of key ideas. The first is *doctrina evangelii*, which is the gospel at its core, Christ's own presence in his promise. The second is *doctrina definita*, which is dogma – what the church teaches. While the two need to be kept distinct, Hütter maintains they cannot be isolated from each other, for 'Christ's saving presence cannot be separated from the Spirit's sanctifying mission as enacted through his

---

as 'hyper-Catholic'. He notes that Hütter did indeed become Roman Catholic some years after *Suffering Divine Things* was written. See Bruce L. McCormack, 'Witness to the Word: A Barthian Engagement with Reinhard Hütter's Ontology of the Church', *Zeitschrift für Dialektische Theologie. Supplement Series* 5 (2011): 76.

63. Hence the title of his key work: *Suffering* Divine Things (italics added).

64. Steven M. Studebaker, 'The Pathos of Theology as a Pneumatological Derivative or a Poiemata of the Spirit?: A Review Essay of Reinhard Hütter's Pneumatological and Ecclesiological Vision of Theology', *Pneuma* 32, no. 2 (2010): 272.

65. Reinhard Hütter, *Suffering Divine Things: Theology as Church Practice*, trans. Doug Scott (Grand Rapids: Eerdmans, 2000), 117.

2. Two Contrasting Eschatological Ecclesiologies 39

particular works, the church's core practices'.[66] In this way, Hütter is recognizing two aspects of the Holy Spirit's role in the church.[67] The first is that as *Spiritus Creator*, the Spirit transcends linear history to create the church as the body of Christ, an event or act (*poiesis*) where the church receives its life through the Spirit from the triune God (*pathos*). Following Zizioulas, Hütter asserts that it is through the Spirit that the church is 'hypostatized' to become Christ's body. Where Christ instituted the church, the Spirit now constitutes it. But second, the Spirit is acting simultaneously as the teleological Spirit, guiding the church as a concrete institution or being towards its ultimate end. 'It's being always remains dependent on the presence and activity of the Holy Spirit', says Hütter, but 'at the same time, as the work of the Holy Spirit, it is also characterized by duration, concreteness and visibility. . . . In this way the work of the Spirit acquires its own, eschatological extension "in time".'[68] Again, following the example of some Eastern theologians, Hütter argues that the church does not just anticipate the forthcoming kingdom but actually participates in it. He argues that the Lord's supper, for example, 'is not the "anticipation" of something yet to come, but the pneumatic manifestation of the eschaton'.[69] In other words, for Hütter, the church does not just proleptically anticipate the kingdom, but in some instances and performing some activities (the core practices), the church actually is the kingdom.

This leads to the final set of key ideas in Hütter's work to be examined in this analysis, again contained in two unusually utilized theological terms. These are the *enhypostatic* relationship between the Spirit and church practices, and the suggestion that the church is the Spirit's *public*. Regarding the former, Hütter writes, 'The salvific-economic mission of the Holy Spirit is thus realized not "spiritualistically" in the immediacy of the in-spiration of the Spirit into individual religious consciousnesses, but in the form of concrete church practices.'[70] What he means is that the Spirit fulfils his sanctifying mission not by working directly on the individuals involved in some mystical manner but through their participation in the core practices of the church.[71] He argues that when the core practices are

---

66. Hütter, 'The Church', 37. There is a third concept here, *dogmatics*, which is identified as 'a particular consensus of teaching at a particular time' and distinguished from both *doctrina evangelii* and (more particularly) *doctrina definita*. So, the writings of the Cappadocian fathers would be dogmatics, while the creeds arising from the Constantinople council would be *doctrina evangelii*, or similarly the writings of Barth would be dogmatics, while the Barmen declaration would be *doctrina evangelii* (see Hütter, 'The Church', 37-8). This distinction is not crucial in this analysis.

67. See particularly Hütter, *Suffering Divine Things*, 118-20.

68. Ibid., 119.

69. Ibid., 120.

70. Ibid., 127.

71. Hütter utilizes Luther's list of church's constitutive marks to describe these core practices: proclamation (including reception), baptism, the Lord's supper, office of the keys and ordination. See Hütter, 'The Church', 34. Also, Hütter, *Suffering Divine Things*, 128-31.

not seen specifically, clearly and exclusively as the Spirit's work, this results in the Spirit being seen and accessed 'everywhere and nowhere' so that invoking the Spirit becomes an 'empty expression'.[72] Consequently, the 'core church practices are essential if the Holy Spirit is to lead the church to perfect truth'.[73] In describing how the Spirit's work and church practices are related, Hütter utilizes the descriptive theological term *enhypostatic*. By this he means that in an analogous way to how the divine person of the Logos indwells Jesus' human nature so that Christ truly is and acts as the Son, so the Spirit indwells the core practices of the church. So, for Hütter, the core practices of the church truly are the work and being of the Spirit.[74] Both the Spirit and the practices together can be seen as divine activity (*poiesis*) through which the church passively receives its identity (*pathos*) and through which its development and growth occur. It is in the Spirit's ecclesial work that the Trinitarian communion binds itself to the ecclesial *koinonia* and thereby constitutes the church's nature. The end result of this is that the Spirit is the church's *public*.[75] Drawing from the sociological work of Hannah Arendt,[76] Hütter defines a 'public' as a particular set of normative convictions, embodied in constitutive practices and directed towards a distinctive *telos*.[77] By utilizing such a descriptive term, Hütter is arguing that the church is the public presence of the Holy Spirit in the world. The church as a 'public' is characterized by a set of core beliefs that the Spirit has led it to and by a set of core practices through which the Spirit acts and exists in the church. Through this set of beliefs and practices, the Spirit transforms the church towards its soteriological *telos*.

Summarizing, then (and avoiding uncommon terminology), Hütter's thesis is that the church grows and develops through time because the Spirit exists in and works through the church's core practices. It is through the Spirit indwelling these practices that the church passively receives her identity, establishes the truth of her beliefs both propositionally and experientially, and is not just drawn towards but actively participates in the future kingdom that is her *telos*.

There is a great deal to affirm in Hütter's work, as reviewers regularly comment. For example, Rae notes that 'There is no doubt . . . that Reinhard Hütter's *Suffering Divine Things* is an important book'. He finds 'Hütter's theological proposals to be both theologically coherent and persuasive'.[78] Dorrien accurately describes the book as 'an important antidote to the conception of theology as individualistic

---

72. Hütter, *Suffering Divine Things*, 127.
73. Ibid., 128.
74. See the description in Ibid., 132-3.
75. See Ibid., 125-6.
76. Hannah Arendt, *The Human Condition* (Chicago: University of Chicago Press, 1998).
77. Hütter, 'The Church', 40.
78. Murray Rae, 'Suffering Divine Things (Review)', *Modern Theology* 17, no. 3 (2001): 398.

self-expression and construction'.⁷⁹ Certainly, the claim that theology is impossible outside the context of the church is one that is both necessary and timely, and in developing his understanding, Hütter provides an interesting response to some of Barth's excesses. Perhaps his pendulum has swung too far to the other extreme, however. There are significant challenges with his proposal, particularly in the extremely close connections posited between the Spirit and the church's practices, and between the sacraments and the coming kingdom.

In terms of the former, Hütter's claim that the church's core practices are enhypostatically works of the Spirit is problematic. Mawson, for example, questions whether this understanding essentially institutionalizes the Spirit, not properly allowing for 'the freedom and priority of the Spirit's work with respect to the church'.⁸⁰ Specifically, Mawson suggests that 'Hütter's account of the church as receiving the Spirit through its core practices, at least by itself, does not seem sufficiently to acknowledge how the Holy Spirit might be at work *even in spite of* the church and its practices'.⁸¹ To further emphasize the point, he questions how, in Hütter's understanding, the church could ever be recognized as sinful. By binding the Spirit's work and the church's practices together 'enhypostatically', the church's practices can never be so sinful that no connection between the Spirit and the church's core practices takes place. Following this theme, Healy accurately diagnoses Hütter's proposal's underlying flaw: 'The Spirit not only works within the church's traditions and practices, but also apart from them and even, at times, over against them, so as to destabilize what is settled and secure.'⁸² It is questionable whether Hütter's thesis can adequately account for such 'external' pneumatological movement.

The same kinds of challenges exist with the identification Hütter makes between the eucharistic sacrament and the future kingdom. Volf's critique of Zizioulas (who Hütter follows here) can be equally applied. Identifying the two removes any sense of ecclesial progression, as the future is completely experienced in the present eucharist.⁸³ This identification thus ironically seems to remove the very advantages of ecclesial growth and development that Hütter's formulation originally promised. Similarly, it is questionable how such elevating of present human activity recognizes and acknowledges our innate sinfulness. Human actions simply don't justify such confidence.

---

79. Gary J. Dorrien, 'Suffering Divine Things (Review)', *Pro Ecclesia* 11, no. 1 (2002): 105.

80. Mawson, 'The Spirit and the Community', 461.

81. Ibid.

82. Nicholas M. Healy, 'Practices and the New Ecclesiology: Misplaced Concreteness?', *International Journal of Systematic Theology* 5, no. 3 (2003): 299.

83. Volf, *After Our Likeness*, 101.

At the core of both overidentifications lies the root cause that in Hütter's formulation Christ has been subsumed into the Spirit's ecclesial mission.[84] By collapsing the ecclesial involvement of the Son into that of the Spirit, the Spirit cannot be identified as a distinct person within the church leading us into the (logically distinguishable) life of the Son. Rather the Spirit is simply the risen Christ who is drawing us gradually to himself. With only one active participant, there is only one place the Spirit can act (within the church and its practices) and only one dimension along which the church can be transformed (continuously towards its future teleological reality). Without the separate and distinct pole of Christ to balance, in the present time, the developing, growing and currently sinful reality of the church, the close identification of the church with the Spirit and the church with its teleological future, with all of their consequent problems, are not merely unfortunate side effects but logical necessities of the system that Hütter has constructed. As Healy concludes, in Hütter's system, 'the church's stability and authority comes at the expense of a theologically (and sociologically) thin account of the church and of the Spirit'.[85]

Interestingly, Hütter's conception of the ecclesial journey through time is almost precisely the opposite of Barth's. Where Barth's understanding leans towards emphasizing discontinuity and the eschatological tension, viewing the church as static and unchanging, and subsuming the Spirit's ecclesial mission into that of the Son, Hütter does the opposite, emphasizing continuity and the teleological tension, tying the Spirit exclusively to the church and subsuming the Son's ecclesial role to that of the Spirit. Certainly, Hütter gives a prominent place to the Spirit, but in doing so he appears to have lost the substantial ground that Barth and others have gained. The obvious conclusion is that a complete and nuanced account of the church's temporal journey, together with its relationship to the coming kingdom, cannot be developed without an awareness of the full and complementary missions of both the Son and the Spirit, where both are seen as integrally related to and involved in the growth of the church but in differing ways. A nuanced understanding of the church's journey through time will need to realize that the Son's and Spirit's ecclesial missions are logically distinct but existentially inseparable. The overall contention of this research is that such a nuanced understanding of the church's growth and development through time can be obtained through examining the loci of eschatology through the methodology of Third Article Theology. It is to the development of such an understanding that we now turn.

---

84. See, for example, McCormack, 'Witness to the Word', 74. Using terminology developed and explained elsewhere, Hütter makes the error of ecclesial Spirit ebionism. See Liston, 'A "Chalcedonian" Spirit Christology', 74–93.

85. Healy, 'Practices and the New Ecclesiology', 299.

Chapter 3

THE CHURCH'S JOURNEY THROUGH TIME

As noted in Chapter 1, Third Article Theology is a recently developed methodology which intentionally views reality through the lens of the Spirit.[1] Initially, theologians pursuing this approach focused on the development of a Spirit Christology. Among the many insights arising were the Spirit's foundational role in understanding Christ's divinity and a nuanced comprehension of Christ's growth and development as a human. Following this progress, the methodology of Third Article Theology has been applied to a variety of other doctrines, including ecclesiology, Scripture, anthropology and public theology. One loci that has not yet been as rigorously examined through the lens of the Spirit as others, however, is eschatology. As previously mentioned, this is well illustrated in that a recent and comprehensive edited volume of dogmatic developments in Third Article Theology contained sections and articles on Christology, Trinity, soteriology, ecclesiology, anthropology and public theology (among others), but none focused on eschatology.[2]

Just as Spirit *Christology* has enabled a more nuanced understanding of Christ's growth and development as a human to emerge, so a pneumatologically focused Spirit *eschatology* enables the development of a nuanced understanding of the church's situation and journey through time. Consequently, this chapter investigates the value arising from exploring the doctrine of eschatology through the methodology of Third Article Theology and particularly its implications for and connection with our current ecclesiological journey. Initially, it determines how Third Article Theology can be applied to eschatology, making the Spirit's foundational role in eschatology explicit. This leads to an even more pivotal investigation exploring how a Spirit eschatology provides a nuanced picture of the church's growth and development through time. As Yong comments, 'the more important matter . . . concerns how eternity's beckoning cuts into each present

---

1. At various points in this chapter, comments made in the previous two chapters are reprised in order that the flow of the argument is, to some approximation, self-contained.

2. Habets, ed., *Third Article Theology*. Private communication with the editor confirms that he wasn't aware of anyone utilizing a Third Article Theology methodology to explore eschatology up to the point of publication.

moment of existence.'³ The resulting portrait is one where the Spirit guides the church on its journey towards its future *telos* through its suffering obedience – its cruciform shape and actions.

3.1 Constructing a Spirit eschatology

Virtually all proponents of Third Article Theology recognize two key methodological criteria, namely (1) Third Article Theology starts with the Spirit, and (2) Third Article Theology looks through the Spirit rather than at it.[4] While there are continuing discussions about other aspects of this methodology,[5] increasing numbers of scholars argue that a third criterion should be added: (3) Third Article Theology complements and does not compete with First and Second Article Theologies.[6] Such a complementary approach is adopted here. Consequently, this section argues that just as Spirit Christology complements Logos Christology in demonstrating the Spirit's foundational role in Christ's incarnation, so a Spirit eschatology complements a Christologically focused eschatology by explicitly

---

3. Amos Yong, *Renewing Christian Theology: Systematics for a Global Christianity* (Waco: Baylor University Press, 2014), 55.

4. These are the first two criteria listed by Habets in Habets, 'Prolegomenon: On Starting with the Spirit', 14–16. See also the discussion in Section 1.1.

5. See, for example, the contrasting approaches of the two prolegomena articles in Habets' edited dogmatics. Both of these can be compared with the overlapping approaches of a distinctly Pentecostal approach to theology with its prioritization of a pneumatological lens. See, for example, Amos Yong, 'Introduction: Pentecostalism and a Theology of the Third Article', in *Toward a Pneumatological Theology: Pentecostal and Ecumenical Perspectives on Ecclesiology, Soteriology, and Theology of Mission*, ed. Amos Yong (Lanham: University Press of America, 2002), xiii–xx. The area where these Pentecostal approaches overlap with a Third Article Theology approach to eschatology is particularly noted in this first section.

6. First and Second Article Theologies explore reality through the lenses of the Father and Son, respectively. Habets lists Third Article Theology's complementarity with these approaches as his fourth criterion. See Habets, 'Prolegomenon: On Starting with the Spirit', 16. Theologians whose pneumatologically focused proposals explicitly reject such a complementary approach include Roger Haight, Norman Hook, Hendrikus Berkhof and James Dunn, among others. See, for example, Roger Haight, 'The Case for Spirit Christology', *Theological Studies* 53 (1992): 257. For further details and critiques of this non-complementary or replacement approach to Third Article Theology, see Habets, *The Anointed Son*, 30–40, 194–200. Also Philip J. Rosato, 'Spirit Christology: Ambiguity and Promise', *Theological Studies* 38 (1977): 423–9. More recently, Liston, 'A "Chalcedonian" Spirit Christology', 76–8.

acknowledging the Spirit's foundational eschatological role.⁷ The next section extends this discussion by exploring how, just as Spirit Christology enables a nuanced comprehension of Christ's growth and development, a Spirit eschatology enables a dynamic understanding of ecclesial time to emerge. In other words, a Spirit eschatology moves beyond a static to a dynamic view of the church: an understanding that clearly accounts for ecclesial growth and development.⁸

The theological approach of exploring the eschatological relationship between eternity and time through a Christological lens without significant reference to the Spirit can be labelled 'Logos eschatology' (paralleling the terminology of Logos Christology). The pivotal insight of Logos eschatology is (through analogy) to see eternity as corresponding to Christ's divine nature and time as corresponding to his human nature, so that eternity and time can be related in a similar manner to Christ's divine and human natures. Such a Second Article Theology approach is exemplified in the work of Barth and T. F. Torrance among others and has proved to be exceedingly fruitful.⁹ Many argue, however, that it undervalues the Spirit's role and consequently results in an excessively static account of ecclesial development. For example, as noted in the previous chapter, Balthasar argues (perhaps a little exaggeratedly) that Barth 'avoids all talk about those things that would provide for a real ongoing history between man and God in the sphere of the temporal and the relative . . . nothing really happens in his theology of history, because everything has already taken place in eternity'.¹⁰

---

7. Similarly to the situation in the Christological loci, there are scholars who seek to replace a focus on the Son with a focus on the Spirit within other fields. Examples include Robert Jenson, John Zizioulas and Reinhard Hütter, among others. For example, as discussed in the previous chapter, Hütter describes the relationship between the Spirit and the church's core practices as *enhypostatic*. See Hütter, *Suffering Divine Things*, 132–3. Such a move subsumes the Son into the Spirit's ecclesial mission (See McCormack, 'Witness to the Word', 74). Further, it essentially institutionalizes the Spirit to the church. See Mawson, 'The Spirit and the Community', 453–68. For a broader overview of the challenges arising from identifying the Spirit too closely with the church and church practices, see Healy, 'Practices and the New Ecclesiology', 287–308.

8. See, for example, the detailed exploration of Pentecostal eschatologies in dialogue with Moltmann's work in Peter Althouse, *Spirit of the Last Days: Pentecostal Eschatology in Conversation with Jürgen Moltmann* (London: T&T Clark International, 2003). While none of these Pentecostal eschatologies (nor Moltmann's) are focused only on the development of a Spirit eschatology specifically (as defined in this chapter), they all include aspects of this approach in their broader outworking.

9. Many resources expound the fruitfulness of this approach. See the discussion in Section 2.2, for example. Or for Torrance, see Maclean, *Resurrection, Apocalypse, and the Kingdom of Christ*.

10. Balthasar, *The Theology of Karl Barth*, 277. These are common critiques of Barth and won't be expanded further For a more extended discussion, see Langdon, *God the Eternal*

T. F. Torrance's eschatology provides a mature and developed example of a Second Article Theology approach to the subject. The following discussion uses Torrance's work as an exemplar to not just demonstrate the strengths and weaknesses of Logos eschatology but also construct a complementary Spirit eschatology that corrects its weaknesses without losing these strengths.[11] Recognizing the presence of both continuity and discontinuity in the relationship between the church and the coming kingdom, Torrance argues for a 'Chalcedonian' relationship between the two, helpfully suggesting that the kingdom and the church are related 'inconfusedly, unchangeably, indivisibly, inseparably'.[12] Torrance argues that a 'Chalcedonian' analogy can be utilized between church and kingdom because eschatology can and should be characterized Christologically. He writes, 'eschatology properly speaking is the application of Christology to the Kingdom of Christ and to the work of the church in history.'[13]

From a Third Article Theology perspective, Torrance's approach here is accurate yet incomplete. For Christ's incarnation itself (let alone its eschatological application) cannot be understood except through the lens of the Spirit. If we affirm the Chalcedonian Definition's understanding that in Christ divine and human natures are hypostatically united, this requires an equal affirmation that this union happens through the Spirit. As has been demonstrated elsewhere, 'Our Lord Jesus Christ is fully and uniquely the person of the Son *and fully and uniquely anointed by the Spirit*.'[14] Any explanation of the hypostatic union that does not explicitly include the Spirit's mission leads to a flawed Christological understanding, for it is through the Spirit that the divine and human are united in Christ.[15] Just as a simplistic understanding of Christology without pneumatology will end up imbalanced, a simplistic application of Christology to eschatology without acknowledgement of the Spirit's constitutive role will end up equally imbalanced.

Contemporary. Also, Vondey, 'The Holy Spirit and Time in Contemporary Catholic and Protestant Theology', particularly 397-8. And Gunton, 'Salvation', 143-58.

11. Given that Torrance's characterization of eschatology is utilized only at a high level in the first section of this chapter, it is described without significant critique. For a helpful and critical analyses that goes into more depth, see Andrew Purves, 'The Advent of Ministry: Torrance on Eschatology, the Church, and Ministry', in *Evangelical Calvinism: Volume 2*, ed. Myk Habets and Bobby Grow (Pickwick, 2017), 95-127. Also, Maclean, *Resurrection, Apocalypse, and the Kingdom of Christ*, 190-203.

12. Pelikan and Hotchkiss, eds, *Creeds and Confessions of Faith in the Christian Tradition*, 181.

13. Torrance, *Royal Priesthood*, 43.

14. Liston, 'A "Chalcedonian" Spirit Christology', 76. Italics added. For a full justification of this point, see Liston, 'A "Chalcedonian" Spirit Christology', 74-93.

15. See, for example, Macchia, *Jesus the Spirit Baptizer*, 11-14. Also, Leopoldo A. Sánchez M., *Receiver, Bearer and Giver of God's Spirit* (Eugene: Pickwick, 2015), 86-109.

Utilizing this Chalcedonian analogy and launching from what Torrance labels the primary eschatological insight of the twentieth century – Barth's realization that the Word became a spatiotemporal being (becoming 'time' in the same way he became 'flesh'[16]) – Torrance draws out the implication that there are three 'times' to be considered: 'old' or 'fallen' time (what humans currently experience in their fallen condition), eternity (God's time) and 'new' or 'redeemed' time (the time Christ experiences, which reconciles 'old' or 'fallen' time in union with eternity). The relationship between these three can be expressed through a Christological analogy. 'Here too we may think of there having taken place in the Incarnation as it were a hypostatic union between the eternal and the temporal in the form of new time.'[17]

The application of a Third Article Theology approach to Torrance's original chain of logic leads beyond this to the recognition that eternity and time are joined *through the Spirit*. Certainly, it is 'in' Christ that time and eternity are intertwined, but the point that is often neglected in a Logos eschatology, and that is explicit and foundational in a Spirit eschatology, is that this happens 'through' the Spirit. The relationship between time and eternity is Christologically situated, as Torrance ably notes, but it is also pneumatologically enabled. Eternity indwells time in Christ *through the Spirit*, and time is taken up into eternity in Christ *through the Spirit*. This is precisely why (with nuanced qualifications) the Spirit can take the past reality of Jesus' work and apply it to our present situation. But it is also precisely why (again, with nuanced qualifications) the Spirit can take the future benefits of Jesus' coming kingdom and apply them to our current reality. Through the Spirit (and in Christ), all times are this time. Just as through the Spirit (and in Christ), all places are this place. As Yong comments, 'Not only does Luke say that the *time* of the last days has begun with the coming of the Spirit, but he also says that the *place* of the kingdom is now being redeemed by the Spirit.'[18]

But Torrance, of course, is concerned not just with the relationship between time and eternity but also with the relationship between old (fallen) and new (redeemed) time. 'We must think ... of fallen time as having perfected itself through the Cross and resurrection into the abiding triumph of a perfection in God which both consummates the original purposes of creation and crowns it with glory.'[19] The result is that there are two tensions to be considered, an 'eschatological' tension between 'new' (redeemed) and 'old' (fallen) time, and an ultimate 'teleological' tension between the eternal and temporal. For Torrance, the first is equivalent to the tension between the new creation and the fallen world, while the second is equivalent to the holiness/sinfulness tension. Torrance essentially envisions time

---

16. See, for example, Barth, *Church Dogmatics*, III.2 437–42.

17. Torrance, 'The Modern Eschatological Debate', 224. See also Torrance, *Incarnation*, 334–6. And Torrance, *Space, Time and Resurrection*, 98–9.

18. Amos Yong, *In the Days of Caesar: Pentecostalism and Political Theology* (Grand Rapids: Eerdmans, 2010), 331 (italics added).

19. Torrance, 'The Modern Eschatological Debate', 224–5.

as two separate lines running in parallel (new and old time), both of which are positioned within the constant background and framework of eternity, with new time being the Christological union of old time with eternity.

But here again, we need to recognize not just the reality of what has been achieved in Christ but the pneumatological manner through which it was achieved – for both the cross and the resurrection occurred *through the Spirit*. Not only was Jesus' life pneumatologically empowered, but it was through the Spirit that he offered himself to God on the cross (Heb. 9.14), and it was by the Spirit that he was raised from the dead (Rom. 8.11).[20] If, then, we think of fallen time as having perfected itself through the cross and resurrection (as Torrance says) we ought to also think of the means through which this happens – through the Spirit. It is in the Spirit that we who exist in fallen time participate in Christ's new redeemed time, and it is in the Spirit that Christ's past, present and future in this new redeemed time are brought to bear on our present reality.[21] Essentially, what happens is that through the Spirit, all times in Christ's new time are brought to bear on the single moment we currently inhabit in old time.

It is at this point that the value of adopting a *complementary* approach to Spirit eschatology becomes particularly clear. The alternative of *replacing* a focus on the Son with a focus on the Spirit fundamentally alters the understanding of new and old time running in parallel that was developed through a Logos eschatology.[22] When the ecclesial mission of the Son is subsumed into that of the Spirit, the Spirit cannot be identified as a distinct person within the church leading us into the (logically distinguishable) life of the Son. Rather, the Spirit is simply the risen Christ drawing us gradually to himself. With only one active participant, there is only one place the Spirit can act (within the church and its practices) and only one dimension along which the church can be transformed (continuously in fallen time towards its future teleological reality). The result is that, in direct contrast to the Logos eschatologies of Barth and Torrance that undervalue the church's development through time, these replacement Spirit eschatologies essentially merge new and old time together, giving our present experience of fallen time an undeserved precedence. Such an approach ignores the ontological separateness of Christ from the Church, confusing and merging the two.

A complementary Spirit eschatology, in contrast, does not alter the broad framework connecting time and eternity developed through a Logos eschatology approach. Redeemed and fallen time are still understood as existing and evolving

---

20. See, for example, Steven M. Studebaker, *From Pentecost to the Triune God: A Pentecostal Trinitarian Theology* (Grand Rapids: Eerdmans, 2012), 80–7.

21. See particularly the detailed discussion of the interaction between God's time and our time in Matthew K. Thompson, *Kingdom Come: Revisioning Pentecostal Ecclesiology* (Dorset: Deo Publishing, 2010), 109–27.

22. This tendency can be seen in several eschato-ecclesial approaches that replace a focus on the Son with a focus on the Spirit. The description of Hütter's eschatological ecclesiology in Chapter 2 provides one clear example.

in parallel. In addition to these insights arising from a Logos eschatology, however, a complementary Spirit eschatology also enables a dynamic understanding of the church's transformation within fallen time (as explored in the next section). Further, it ensures that the full interaction between the two times is considered. Using a complementary Third Article Theology approach, all of redeemed time, from its beginning with Christ's resurrection through to its culmination in the coming kingdom, interacts with the present moment we exist in within fallen time. Looking through the lens of the Spirit ensures that we do not minimize the relationship between the two parallel times by restricting it to just bringing forward Christ's past work or just acknowledging the presence of Christ with us through the Spirit. But through the Spirit, the past, present and future reality of Christ in new time impacts us at the present moment we are experiencing in ecclesial time. Christologically focused attempts to connect fallen and redeemed time often focus on specific aspects of redeemed time and neglect other aspects, rather than pneumatologically looking across the entire spectrum of Christ's existence in new time and its relevance to us now. Barth's analysis, for example, focuses on bringing forward to us Christ's past work and has a noetic focus. This aspect can be likened or appropriated to Christ's prophetic role, bringing forward the knowledge of our salvation in Christ through the Spirit. Torrance, without losing Barth's noetic understanding, has an ontic focus, exploring Christ's present heavenly session and how we participate through the Spirit in Christ's present and ongoing vicarious humanity. This can be likened or appropriated to Christ's priestly role, effecting our salvation through standing in the gap between humanity and divinity, and between time and eternity. But what Barth and Torrance both arguably undervalue (to differing degrees) is the telic aspect, the Spirit's role in bringing back to us (in part) the reality of Christ's future kingdom, a connection that can be likened or appropriated to Christ's kingly role. This understanding is analysed in detail in Chapter 4.

Such a complementary approach to eschatology also enables apparent dichotomies to move towards resolution. For example, there is some debate in Pentecostal scholarship over whether priority should be given to eschatology or Spirit baptism. Faupel and Land, for example, argue for eschatology being Pentecostalism's 'overarching and dominant distinctive'.[23] In contrast, Macchia and Studebaker maintain that, remaining true to Pentecostal history, Spirit baptism

23. As described in Frank D. Macchia, *Justified in the Spirit: Creation, Redemption, and the Triune God* (Grand Rapids: Eerdmans, 2010), 94. For more detail, see particularly D. William Faupel, *The Everlasting Gospel: The Significance of Eschatology in the Development of Pentecostal Thought* (Sheffield: Sheffield Academic Press, 1996), 42–3. Also, Steven J. Land, *Pentecostal Spirituality: A Passion for the Kingdom* (Sheffield Academic Press, 2001), 62–3. For an overview of eschatological perspectives in Pentecostal scholarship, see Larry R. McQueen, *Towards a Pentecostal Eschatology: Discerning the Way Forward* (Dorset: Deo Publishing, 2012), 5–59.

should be primary.[24] Studebaker adopts the latter position because 'the alternative confuses cause and effect'.[25] I would argue that this dichotomy emerges, at least in part, from understanding time as having a single dimension, which in turn arises from the subtle tendency existing in some Pentecostal theologies to overemphasize the Spirit at the expense of the Son. If, in contrast, eschatology is viewed in dual dimensions – not just as the future end of time but as an ongoing interaction between eternity, Christ's redeemed time and fallen time – then Studebaker's cause-and-effect logic does not necessarily hold. Adopting an approach that recognizes both a Logos eschatology and a complementary Spirit eschatology, the eschatological reality and Spirit baptism can be seen as mutually reinforcing, two sides of the same coin. Spirit baptism leads the community towards the coming eschatological reality, and the already existing eschatological reality enables Spirit baptism.[26]

While significantly more can and should be said about the broad sweep of this pneumatological connection between old and new time, the previous discussion adequately reveals the foundational role of the Spirit in the relationship between time and eternity, together with some of its immediate implications. But the gains of applying a Third Article Theology methodology to eschatology go well beyond these affirmations of the Spirit's foundational eschatological role. The second promised aspect (if the parallel with Spirit Christology is pursued and similar advantages are gained) is that a Spirit eschatology will reveal a dynamic understanding of the church's journey through time.

3.2 The pneumatological journey of the church through time

Exploring the pneumatological journey of the church through time requires theological analysis of the analogical connection between two relationships. The first is the relationship between Christ's existence before and after the resurrection. The second is the relationship between the church's existence in old and new time.

---

24. See, for example, Macchia, *Justified in the Spirit*, 93–5. Frank D. Macchia, *Baptized in the Spirit* (Grand Rapids: Zondervan, 2006), 38–48. Also, Studebaker, *From Pentecost to the Triune God*, 75–6.

25. Studebaker, *From Pentecost to the Triune God*, 75.

26. Dempster, for example, is one Pentecostal scholar who by adopting a multi-faceted understanding of eschatology draws it together with Spirit baptism, effectively leveraging their combination towards a Pentecostal social ethic. See Murray W. Dempster, 'Eschatology, Spirit Baptism, and Inclusiveness: An Exploration into the Hallmarks of a Pentecostal Social Ethic', in *Perspectives in Pentecostal Eschatologies*, ed. Peter Althouse and Robert Waddell (Eugene: Pickwick, 2010), 160–7. See also the comments on Macchia's position in Peter Althouse, 'Pentecostal Eschatology in Context: The Eschatological Orientation of the Full Gospel', in *Perspectives in Pentecostal Eschatologies*, ed. Peter Althouse and Robert Waddell (Eugene: Pickwick, 2010), 221–3.

The second relationship can be understood to some degree as analogous to and driven by the first. This section observes this connection through a pneumatological lens to see what insight it gives about the journey of the church through old (or fallen) time towards its telic consummation.[27]

As was noted in Chapter 1, there are five pneumatological parallels between a Spirit Christology and a pneumato-ecclesiology, namely that (1) the Spirit conceives (Christ and the church); (2) the Spirit sustains the communion (of Christ and the church); (3) the Spirit conforms (the church to Christ's likeness); (4) the Spirit directs and empowers (Christ and the church); (5) the Spirit is displayed and mediated (by Christ and the church). Exploring these enables the church to be metaphorically viewed as the incarnation's sequel, having aspects of continuity (because the church is united with Christ), discontinuity (because the church does not repeat the incarnation) and a clear asymmetry (for the existence and function of the church depend entirely on the existence and function of Christ). A detailed theological analysis of the aspects of continuity, discontinuity and asymmetry that exist for each of the five pneumatological parallels between Christ and the church can be constructed. While the other parallels are important, this chapter's focus on the church's eschatological direction means that parallels three and four, which directly explore Christ's and the church's journey towards their respective (but intertwined) futures, are the most pertinent.

With regard to the third aspect, a comparison of Christ and the church recognizes that just as Christ developed and grew as a human, so the church develops and grows. That is, the church has a pneumatologically enabled *Christotelic* momentum. There are, of course, discontinuities between the two growth journeys. Before the church begins its quantitative and communal conformation (the journey that parallels Christ's), we undergo a qualitative and individual transformation that enables us to be in Christ.[28] Further, our growth and development even after this transformation are not perfect as Christ's was, what McFarland calls the 'fundamental disanalogy between the incarnation and the life of the church'.[29] But, as Gary Badcock argues, if we have a 'thick' understanding of the Spirit (one that recognizes the Spirit's intentional bridging role between a holy God and sinful humanity), then even the church's sinfulness does not stop his

---

27. The following work leverages off and extends previous research that used a Third Article Theology approach to explore the analogical relationship between Christ and the church. See Liston, *The Anointed Church*, 121–54. Also Gregory J. Liston, 'Towards a Pneumato-Ecclesiology: Exploring the Pneumatological Union between Christ and the Church', *Colloquium* 44, no. 1 (2012): 31–58.

28. In this sentence our qualitative and individual transformation (wherein we become new creatures in Christ) is contrasted with Christ and the church's quantitative, gradual transformation which happens degree by degree as we mature. For more detail, see Liston, *The Anointed Church*, 136–45.

29. Ian A. McFarland, "The Body of Christ: Rethinking a Classic Ecclesiological Model', *International Journal of Systematic Theology* 7, no. 3 (2005): 245.

conforming presence. Just as on the cross when Christ was 'full of sin', the Father and Son were united by the Spirit, so the Spirit continues to be present with the church even in our sinfulness, conforming the church towards her future.[30]

The fourth parallel explores how this conformation happens, based on the insight that in the life of both Christ and the church, it is the Spirit that directs and empowers. This is seen in the parallels between the direction (and perhaps compulsion) of the Spirit in Christ's life (e.g. Mk 1.12) and the direction (and perhaps compulsion) of the Spirit in the life of the early church (e.g. Acts 8.39). The crucial point to recognize here is the centrality of obedience and suffering. Just as the Spirit guided Christ to learn obedience in suffering, and to suffer in obedience (e.g. Heb. 5.5-8), so the Spirit similarly guides the church. 'The Spirit conforms the church into the image of Christ, therefore, as she suffers and obeys, or better, as she suffers in obedience.'[31] Unfortunately, the church does not always suffer obediently (a clear point of discontinuity), but when she does, that is when conformation occurs. In this way, the church is cruciform in shape. It is through our Christlike suffering and obedience that we are moulded and conformed to Christ's image.

Putting these two parallels together, we gain a picture of the Spirit guiding the church towards its ultimate fulfilment and continuing to do so even when we fall and fail.

> The Spirit enabled Christ to grow into who he was as his human nature developed. As he surrendered himself in obedient submission, the Spirit led him down the path of suffering and into glory. Similarly, the church as a whole, unified, historic institution grows into what it is over its history, and this growth happens through obedient submission to the Spirit that leads us along the same path of suffering and into glory.[32]

Recognizing and extending on these pneumatological parallels between Christ and the church's journey, and utilizing the insight about the connection between Christ (pre and post resurrection) and the church (in old and new time), allow several insights to be drawn.

The first is the relatively obvious but nevertheless important observation that the church's journey from old time through to new time is guided and enabled by the Spirit. Just as it was through the Spirit that Christ was directed to the cross and through the Spirit that he was raised up after his death, so it is through the Spirit that the church journeys through old time and through the Spirit that together we as a church will eventually be raised up in Christ in our own resurrection to participate fully and completely in new time. The church should therefore

---

30. See Badcock, *The House Where God Lives*, 194–209. Or for a summary and application, see Liston, *The Anointed Church*, 142-4.

31. Liston, *The Anointed Church*, 147.

32. Ibid., 150.

endeavour to be highly conscious of and receptive to this leading. For example, Land comments that among the early Pentecostals, 'The vivid presence of the Spirit heightened expectation, propelled into mission, enlivened worship and increased consecration for the appearance of the Lord of the harvest.'[33]

The second insight is that this guiding, enabling Spirit is distinct from the church and cannot be identified with it. The Spirit works in and on the church, but the Spirit is not the church (contra Jenson for example) nor should he be identified or 'hypostatically' united with the church's practices (contra Hütter). Equating Christ's person with the *hypostasis* of the Spirit is precisely the error that 'replacement' Spirit Christologies make when exploring the life of Jesus, and similarly equating the church's being and activity with the person of the Spirit is precisely the error the 'replacement' Spirit eschatologies make when considering the church's ongoing journey. The parallel between Christ and the church's journey suggests, however, that the Spirit is more accurately viewed as a *hypostasis* who is distinct from, but closely related to, the church, just as the Spirit is distinct from, but closely related to, the Logos within Christ. This enables the Spirit to act within the church, guiding, leading and enabling, but at the same time remaining separate from it, able to work outside of and even at times against the church.

Further, the analogy between Christ and the church, and particularly the distinct existence of both the Logos and the Spirit within Christ's incarnation, points towards the idea of a communal ecclesial spirit – something that is the analogical equivalent in the church of the Logos in Christ. This is reminiscent of Bonhoeffer's idea of the church's objective spirit, which is a communal spirit that is distinct from the Holy Spirit's ecclesial presence.[34] The church's objective spirit is perhaps most easily seen as the church's 'body', in a related sense to Christ being the church's 'head'. The Holy Spirit joins the objective spirit (the body of the church) with the head (who is Christ), thereby forming the *totus Christus*, the 'pneumatologically enabled union that exists between the incarnate Christ and the human community of the church.'[35] But the Spirit also *forms* the church as Christ's body (1 Cor. 12.13). Bonhoeffer argues that the church's objective spirit is generated through the pneumatologically guided interaction of the members of the Christian community, writing that the 'Holy Spirit uses the objective spirit as a vehicle for its gathering and sustaining social activity in spite of all the sinfulness and imperfection of the individuals and of the whole.'[36]

The question naturally arises from this discussion: How does this body of the church, united as she is through the Spirit to Christ who is her head, grow and develop over time? The third insight arising from the pneumatological parallel

---

33. Land, *Pentecostal Spirituality*, 72-3.

34. This is a concept Bonhoeffer developed in his published doctoral dissertation *Sanctoro Communio*. Dietrich Bonhoeffer, *Sanctorum Communio*, trans. Reinhard Krauss (Minneapolis: Fortress Press, 1998).

35. Liston, *The Anointed Church*, 156.

36. Bonhoeffer, *Sanctorum Communio*, 215.

being explored here suggests that just as the Spirit enabled Jesus to 'learn obedience through the things that he suffered' (Heb. 5:8) we are similarly conformed to Christ's image as we suffer in obedience. Torrance, for example, points in this direction by recognizing that Christ's image is *seen* in the church through her suffering obedience, arguing that 'wherever the Church shows forth His death until He comes and presents its body a living sacrifice, there the image of Christ is to be seen and His Body is to be discerned in the Church'.[37] The contention here certainly incorporates this profound point but goes beyond it. Through suffering obedience and cruciform actions the church does not just *display* the image of Christ (as Torrance argues), but even further it is as the Spirit guides the church through cruciform actions of suffering obedience that the church is *conformed* to the image of Christ. In other words, it is through suffering obedience, through its cruciform shape and actions, that the Spirit guides the church on its journey through time towards its future *telos*. Increasingly, charismatic and Pentecostal scholars are seeing the centrality of such suffering obedience as not merely compatible with a belief in the transformational power of the Spirit but indeed biblically and theologically integrated with it.[38] As the biblical scholar Michael Gorman comments, 'Paul clearly suggests that transformation into glory begins in the present and advances by degrees into the eschatological future. . . . Somehow, in the midst of suffering and cruciformity, transformation into the image of the glorified Christ is taking place.'[39]

What this leads to is a picture of the relationship between eternity and time where, through the Spirit, the eschatological tension (the vertical relationship between new and old time) and the teleological tension (the horizontal or chronological relationship between old time and eternity) come together and reinforce each other. Because, through the Spirit, the church is participating in Christ's life, we have a fundamentally new way of being where the old rules of before and after do not simplistically apply anymore. Rather, our new existence is intrinsically cruciform as in Christ and through the Spirit we are constantly and

---

37. Thomas F. Torrance, 'Atonement and the Oneness of the Church', *Scottish Journal of Theology* 7, no. 3 (1954): 259.

38. See, for example, the helpful comments on this subject in Kärkkäinen, *Toward a Pneumatological Theology*, 176–8. Also Peter Althouse, 'In Appreciation of Jürgen Moltmann: A Discussion of His Transformational Eschatology', *Pneuma: The Journal of the Society for Pentecostal Studies* 28, no. 1 (2006): 30–2. Althouse also comments that an appropriation of Moltmann's theology of the cross would enable Pentecostal scholarship to draw a deeper and richer connection between the eschatological kingdom and its potential to impact and transform oppressive sociopolitical structures. See, for example, Althouse, *Spirit of the Last Days*, 186–92, particularly p. 192.

39. Michael J. Gorman, *Cruciformity: Paul's Narrative Spirituality of the Cross* (Grand Rapids: Eerdmans, 2001), 35. Note that Gorman sees this transformation as intrinsically communal. 'Fundamentally, cruciformity means community, and community means cruciformity.' Gorman, *Cruciformity*, 366.

simultaneously experiencing the reality of death and resurrection in our day-to-day lives.[40] This reality is available to us because of the eschatological tension in which through the Spirit, the entirety of Christ's new time is brought to bear on the current moment in which we exist in old time, but it feeds our conformation process in the teleological tension. The Spirit takes Christ's past (a prophetic declaration of our salvation through his suffering), Christ's present (a priestly enabling of a filial relationship) and Christ's future (a kingly manifestation of our future glory) and brings them all to bear on the church's present reality. It is precisely because of this simultaneously experienced reality that the church is increasingly conformed to Christ's image as we journey through time. We are living moment by moment and day by day, a communal and yet intensely personal experience of life in death, of joy in suffering, of self-giving love. But as we live in this reality, through the Spirit we are being conformed more and more to the image of Christ for whom this cruciform, self-giving way of being is simply the way he was and is. We are learning to be Christlike. We are learning it by the same process that he learned it, by giving up our rights to self-determination and allowing the Spirit to guide us. And in this way, we are not just reliving Christ's story as he is in us, but we are practising, preparing, hoping for and being transformed towards the time when our ongoing mini-deaths and mini-resurrections will lead us like him to an actual physical death and a full, final, complete and communal resurrection by the Spirit. The small stories and experiences that we experience contribute to the larger community and time-stretching story of which we are a part

This insight is well illustrated by the mathematical concept of a fractal. A fractal is a curve or geometrical pattern, each part of which has the same character as the whole. If you focus in or magnify just a small portion, you see the same shapes as exist in the overall pattern. Scientists use fractals to understand structures like snowflakes, where similar patterns occur at smaller and smaller scales, and each of these smaller patterns adds together to contribute to the bigger picture.[41] The final insight from this Third Article Theology examination of eschatology is that for the community of the church the shape of time has an intrinsically fractal-like character. The master-story of birth, death and resurrection is not just the overarching story of divinity and humanity seen through the broad expanse of time, but it gets lived and repeated over and over again, at successively smaller scales.[42] It gets repeated because we participate by the Spirit in Christ, who continues to live

---

40. Note that death and resurrection here (and following) do necessarily refer not only to our final death and resurrection which will lead to our participation in Christ's kingdom but also to the regular challenges and rewards that we experience in our day-to-day lives, both individually and communally as the church.

41. See, for example, K. J. Falconer, *Fractals: A Very Short Introduction* (Oxford: Oxford University Press, 2013).

42. Thompson beautifully expresses a complementary idea by utilizing the language of the cosmic Pentecost and the symbol of glossolalia as an eschatological sacrament. See Thompson, *Kingdom Come*, 128–43.

his cruciform life in and through us. We see the story repeated in the lives of the worldwide church community,[43] in the lives of particular church communities, in our individual lives through time (from birth to death to resurrection), in the day-to-day lives of our families and as individuals in our day-to-day lived experiences as well. We are always learning what it means to die and rise again. Cruciformity is the shape of time, of our communities, of our overall lives and of each individual portion of them. Each cruciform pattern is not independent, however, but joins together with other cruciform moments to create in the overall journey of the church a growth, development and movement towards a fundamental and final self-giving, cruciform reality.

So 'the past "work" of God's Son, embodied on the cross, has become the present work of the Spirit of God's Son, embodied in the believer and in the community'.[44] What this means for us can be expressed through the commonly used Pauline framework of faith, hope and love. Faith and hope are the past and future tense of trust. Looking backwards we trust that the story of Jesus has become our story. Through the Spirit who defines and empowers us, the cruciform gospel is being lived again in our experience. Looking forwards we trust that God's promises already fulfilled in Jesus will also be fulfilled in us. Through the Spirit we will together as a church community share the resurrection life and enjoy in full the new time that Christ presently experiences. And love is the centre of our story right now. It is the present reality of our self-giving lives, as through the Spirit we enjoy continual and ongoing deaths and resurrections. These smaller fractal images describe our present existence, but the Spirit works through each of them to conform us into Christ's image, so that each of the smaller images echo and illustrate the larger picture, enabling it to increasingly be the defining image of our lives. Through each of these fractal sub-images, we learn experientially what it means to live a genuinely ongoing cruciform existence. Such an approach avoids the error of an isolated Logos eschatology, which leads to a static understanding of time where 'sin is ever the past and justification is ever the future'.[45] It also avoids the error of a replacement Spirit eschatology that understands time as having just a single dimension, and so too closely ties the Spirit to the work of the church, and doesn't 'sufficiently acknowledge how the Spirit might be at work *even in spite of* the church and its practices'.[46] In contrast to both, it provides a dynamic understanding of the church's journey through time, where the existentially interrelated but logically

---

43. Examples of the worldwide church community experiencing 'death' and 'resurrection' moments need to be identified and analysed with careful historical nuance but could potentially include the early Roman persecutions and subsequent growth of the early church or, more recently, perhaps the 'demise' of the mainline Western church and the rise of Pentecostalism in the Global South over the last century.

44. Gorman, *Cruciformity*, 58.

45. Balthasar, *The Theology of Karl Barth*, 277.

46. Mawson, 'The Spirit and the Community', 461.

distinct missions of the Son and the Spirit in the church are both acknowledged and contribute to the cruciform shape of our ongoing experience.

3.3 Conclusion

Applying the approach of Third Article Theology to eschatology has not just demonstrated the foundational eschatological role of the Spirit but also illuminated nuanced insights into the church's journey through time. A Spirit eschatological approach has revealed the church's intrinsically pneumatological nature, how the Spirit acts within the church while not being identified with it (through an understanding of the communal or 'objective' spirit of the church), the pivotal role of obedience and suffering in the conformation of the church, and the intrinsically fractal-like character of time, where the church's eschatological tension enables it to experience cruciformity in its teleological existence and so continuously be transformed into the image of its cruciform-shaped God. In an analogous way to how a Spirit Christology has complemented the more traditional Logos Christology, bringing to it both an increased recognition of the foundational role of the Spirit in the incarnation and a more nuanced understanding of Christ's growth and development as a human, so a complementary 'Spirit' eschatology works together with the more established Christologically focused eschatologies, enabling the Spirit's fundamental role in uniting time and eternity together in Christ to be acknowledged and, furthermore, illuminating the development of a nuanced understanding of the church's journey through time.

Chapter 4

AN ESCHATOLOGICAL *MUNUS TRIPLEX*

As noted in Chapter 3, applying the methodology of Third Article Theology to the doctrine of eschatology enables us to see the full breadth of Christ's pneumatological interaction with humanity across the expanse of time. Through the Spirit, Christ's past, present and future reality in new time impacts us at the present moment we are experiencing in ecclesial time. The implication is that the traditional Reformed understanding of Jesus Christ as prophet, priest and king, and of *Christian* participation in this *munus triplex*, can be refined, complemented and extended through viewing this theologoumenon eschatologically. The Spirit takes Christ's past (a prophetic revelation of our salvation through his suffering and exaltation), Christ's present (a priestly enabling of a filial relationship) and Christ's future (a kingly manifestation of our future glory), and brings them all to bear on the church's present reality. Viewed through the lens of the Spirit, all aspects of Christ's existence in the new, redeemed time he currently experiences impact us at our current moment of existence in present, fallen time. Exploring this eschatological understanding of Christ's *munus triplex* and the church's participation in it enables the account of ecclesial transformation developed in the previous chapter to be significantly expanded.

Consequently, this chapter, after offering an outline of the traditional Reformed usage of the *munus triplex*, initially examines several recent attempts to partially employ this theologoumenon into the service of eschatology. Such examination reveals considerable advances in how Christ's threefold offices can be employed as an eschatological heuristic. Karl Barth emphasized Christ's prophetic office – bringing forward a revelatory encounter of Christ's reconciliatory work and presence. Thomas Torrance speaks of Christ's priestly role – ontologically effecting our salvation through vicariously bridging the gap between humanity and divinity. The examination also reveals a lacuna that needs to be addressed. For these eschatological perspectives can be extended still further with a detailed exploration of Christ's kingly office – the proleptic reality of God's coming kingdom. This is an eschatological aspect of the *munus triplex* that to date has been undervalued in the Reformed tradition. A detailed exploration of Christ's kingly role and our participation in it insightfully informs how the Spirit transforms the church in its journey through time.[1]

4.1 A timebound view of the munus triplex

It is not a new claim to recognize Christ's threefold office as prophet, priest and king. Justin Martyr gives an early indication of it in CE 150: 'He Himself received from the Father the titles of King, and Christ, and Priest, and Angel [Messenger].'[2] A century later Eusebius specifically connected Christ's threefold office with the Spirit, recognizing that 'all [three titles] refer to the true Christ, who is the only High priest of the universe, the only King of all creation, and the only Archprophet of the Father'.[3] In the following centuries, many others, including Peter Chrysologus in the fifth century and Thomas Aquinas in the thirteenth century, utilized the *munus triplex* framework.[4] The most common association, however, particularly within the Reformed context, is Calvin's outworking in the Geneva Catechism (1542), together with his detailed explanations in the *Institutes*.[5] While the framework existed before him, Calvin's utilization of the *munus triplex* was significantly more systematic and detailed than previous outworkings, and his influence can be clearly discerned in numerous Reformed expressions that followed.[6] In most of these expressions, and particularly in the Reformed catechisms, the focus is

---

1. While the prominence of the *munus triplex* framework within the Reformed tradition makes it natural to develop and explore this proposed revision to its traditional interpretation in direct dialogue with this historical perspective, the implications of this newly developing understanding are not limited in any way to merely Reformed perspectives. The implications noted in this and the following chapters are intentionally and clearly ecumenical.

2. Justin Martyr, *Dialogue with Trypho the Jew*, Ch. 86. Retrieved 11 March 2019, accessed from http://www.newadvent.org/fathers/01286.htm.

3. Eusebius, *The Church History: A New Translation and Commentary*, trans. Paul L. Maier (Grand Rapids: Kregel Publications, 1999), 28 (Book 1, Chapter 3).

4. For Chrysologus, see, for example, George E. Ganss, William B. Palardy, and S. A. R. P. Chrysologus, *Selected Sermons*, vol. 2 (Washington, DC: Catholic University of America Press, 2004), 226. For Aquinas, see, for example, Thomas Aquinas, *Summa Theologica*, trans. Fathers of the English Dominican Province (London: Burns Oates & Washbourne, 1920), III question 22 article 1.

5. See, for example, George W. Stroup, 'The Relevance of the Munus Triplex for Reformed Theology and Ministry', *Austin Seminary Bulletin (Faculty ed.)* 98, no. 9 (1983): 22–5. Also, Fred Guyette, 'Jesus as Prophet, Priest, and King: John Wesley and the Renewal of an Ancient Tradition', *Wesleyan Theological Journal* 40, no. 2 (2005): 91–3.

6. Examples include the Heidelberg Catechism (1563) and the Westminster Confession (1647), among many others. See, for example, Thomas F. Torrance, ed., *The School of Faith: The Catechisms of the Reformed Church* (London: James Clarke and Co., 1959).

on Christ's earthly session and its implications for us. There is, in contrast, less emphasis on Christ's heavenly session, Christ's continuing role as prophet, priest and king, and the relevance of that to our current ecclesial existence. As such, most expressions of the *munus triplex* view it within the bounds of fallen time, rather than exploring it through an intrinsically eschatologically focused framework.

Consider, for example, the Geneva Catechism. Calvin begins his development of the *munus triplex* in Q31, writing that 'By this title [Christ], His office is still better expressed – for it signifies that he was anointed by the Father to be a King, Priest, and Prophet'.[7] The catechetical questions and answers that follow outline the nature of each of these offices – his kingdom is spiritual (Q37), his priesthood involves the offering of an acceptable sacrifice (Q38) and as prophet he has given us a true and full account of the Father (Q39). These explanations lead to a parallel exposition in Q's 40–45 of the benefits that come to us through Christ having each of these roles: 'He received the Holy Spirit in full perfection with all His graces, that He may lavish them upon us and distribute them.'[8] His kingdom bestows upon us liberty of conscience and power (Q42), his priesthood offers us access to the Father (Q43) and his prophetic office enlightens us with truth (Q44). In each of these affirmations the emphasis is on Christ's earthly session and how the benefits won there apply to us now. As prophet, Christ revealed God to humanity during his earthly session, and this truth is brought forward to us through the Word and the Spirit. As high priest, Christ offers himself as a sacrifice during his earthly session, bringing forward to us the benefits of joint access as Christ's colleague. As king, Christ established his kingdom during his earthly session, and we enjoy the benefits of living under the jurisdiction of that continuing kingdom. The logic of the exposition is from then to now, from the earthly session of Jesus to the benefits it now brings to us. What is not in focus, however, are the eschatological aspects and implications of Christ's offices of prophet, priest and king.

Most recent Reformed expositions of the *munus triplex* adopt a similar approach.[9] The focus is on Christ's earthly session, particularly his death, and then as a consequence they (sometimes) go on to consider the implications of these offices for us now. The following discussion notes just a few illustrative examples.

---

7. Torrance, ed., *The School of Faith*, 10.

8. Ibid., 11.

9. While Reformed explanations of the eschatological dimensions of Christ's *munus triplex* do exist, they are normally very brief. For example, Berkhof in his influential *Systematic Theology* briefly mentions Christ's continuing offices in his heavenly session, taking less than a page to do so. This is followed by a 56-page exploration of the offices based around Christ's earthly session, in which the atonement is dealt with in detail. See Louis Berkhof, *Systematic Theology* (Edinburgh: Banner of Truth, 1939), 352–3, 56–412. This proportion is illustrative of much Reformed expositions of the offices, where the eschatological exploration of the offices is not always absent but if present it is proportionally underdeveloped. See similarly Heinrich Heppe, *Reformed Dogmatics*, trans. G. T. Thomson (London: George Allen & Unwin, 1950), 448–87.

McKim in his introduction to the Reformed faith argues that 'the biblical roles of prophet, priest, and king are ways of understanding what Jesus Christ *has done*'[10] and then describes how the confessions utilize the *munus triplex* to explain the relevance and importance of Christ's death. Migliore's textbook introduces the *munus triplex* as a way of summarizing a discussion about theories of the atonement.[11] Sherman makes a similar but more extended link between atonement theories and the offices by cautiously interrelating and associating Christ's kingly office with the *Christus Victor* atonement theory, Christ's priestly office with the theory of vicarious sacrifice and Christ's prophetic office with the 'empowering exemplar' atonement theory.[12] And finally, in an article connecting our baptism with Christ's death, Otto first explicitly recognizes the close association of the *munus triplex* with Christ's earthly session and death,[13] and then argues that the offices provide a way of seeing baptism as participating in Christ's death.[14]

As illustrated in the previous examples, Reformed theology has utilized the *munus triplex* to good effect. The examples also reveal that its usage is not as comprehensive as it could be. In addition to these timebound understandings which are based on a then-to-now logic, there is a complementary way of viewing Christ's threefold office, through an eschatological lens and not merely a soteriological one.[15] Focusing on Christ's heavenly session – and how through the anointing of the Spirit Christ continues to be prophet, priest and king for us in new, redeemed time – enables an expanded, complementary view of the *munus triplex* to be examined. The next section outlines and justifies such an eschatological approach.

---

10. Donald K. McKim, *Introducing the Reformed Faith* (Louisville: Westminster John Knox, 2001), 94. Italics added.

11. Daniel L. Migliore, *Faith Seeking Understanding: An Introduction to Christian Theology* (Grand Rapids: Eerdmans, 2004), 186.

12. See Robert Sherman, *King, Priest, and Prophet* (New York: T&T Clark, 2004), 23.

13. 'The threefold office is generally introduced in Reformed theology texts under the rubric of the death and atoning work of Christ.' Randall E. Otto, 'Baptism and the Munus Triplex', *Evangelical Quarterly* 76, no. 3 (2004): 218.

14. See Otto, 'Baptism and the Munus Triplex', 217–25.

15. There are only two detailed investigations of the *munus triplex* I have encountered to date that head in this eschatological direction. The first is that of Cornelis van der Kooi. The strong influence he places on its implications for our present Christian life means his analysis has aspects of an eschatological approach, even though his primary logic is timebound. See Cornelis van der Kooi, *This Incredibly Benevolent Force: The Holy Spirit in Reformed Theology and Spirituality* (Grand Rapids: Eerdmans, 2018), 99–123. The second is from Michael Welker, who moves from the threefold office of Christ to the threefold gestalt of Christ's reign. See Michael Welker, *God the Revealed: Christology*, trans. Douglas W. Stott (Grand Rapids: Eerdmans, 2013), 209–50. While there are some overlaps, both authors take their analyses in quite different directions from that explored in this chapter.

4.2 An eschatological view of the munus triplex

Developing an eschatological view of the *munus triplex* requires an understanding of the relationship between new, redeemed time (what Christ experiences) and old, fallen time (what we experience). This understanding emerges from an examination of the relationship between kingdom and church viewed through the lens of the Spirit, a Third Article Eschatology.[16] A Chalcedonian analogy, where time analogically corresponds to Christ's human nature and eternity corresponds to Christ's divine nature, enables the recognition that there are three times to be considered: 'old' time (what humans currently experience in their fallen condition), eternity (God's time) and 'new' time (redeemed time in reconciliation and union with eternity).[17] Time is thus envisioned as two separate lines running in parallel (new and old time), both of which are positioned within the constant background and framework of eternity, with new time being the pneumatologically enabled Christological union of old time with eternity. As T. F. Torrance says, 'we may think of there having taken place in the Incarnation as it were a hypostatic union between the eternal and the temporal in the form of new time.'[18]

The question that arises from this formulation is how new time interacts with and affects old time. And the only satisfactory conclusion is that looking through the lens of the Spirit, all of new time impacts our present moment in old time.[19] All of Christ's past, present and future in new time – the entirety of his heavenly session – impacts us in our present moment of old time. The interaction between the two times is not restricted to simply bringing forward Christ's past work or acknowledging Christ's presence through the Spirit. Through the Spirit, the past, present and future reality of new time pneumatologically impacts us in old time. It is from this perspective that an eschatological understanding of the *munus triplex* emerges. So Christ's past in new time impacts us by bringing forward the revelation of Christ's work.[20] This aspect can be appropriated to Christ's prophetic role, revealing the knowledge of our salvation effected in Christ through the Spirit

---

16. Again in this chapter, core ideas from previous chapters will be briefly restated so the argument is, to some approximation, self-contained.

17. See, for example, Torrance, 'The Modern Eschatological Debate', 224. See also Torrance, *Incarnation*, 334–6. And Torrance, *Space, Time and Resurrection*.

18. Ibid.

19. See the discussion in Section 3.1.

20. The phrase 'Christ's past in new time' cannot be taken to necessarily imply that Christ's experience of new, redeemed time is temporal and linear. 'Past' here refers to those events which are closely associated with our past in fallen time (Christ's crucifixion, resurrection, ascension, etc.); 'future' refers to those events which are associated with our future in fallen time (the final judgement, kingdom coming, etc.) and 'present' refers to Christ's activity in new time that cannot be associated with our past or our future. While my opinion is that Christ's existence in redeemed time, as well as ours in heaven, will be necessarily temporal, the analysis of this chapter is not dependent on this particular

and thus has a noetic focus. And Christ's present in new time impacts us through our participation in Christ's ongoing vicarious humanity. This can be appropriated to Christ's priestly role, effecting our salvation through standing in the gap between time and eternity, and thus has an ontic focus. Finally, Christ's future in new time impacts us by bringing back to us Christ's coming kingdom, a connection that can be appropriated to Christ's kingly role. This relationship has a telic focus, as through it we are being transformed into what we will become.

The following sections will argue that Barth's work accounts well for the noetic focus, prophetically bringing forward the knowledge of what Christ has done for us in a revelatory encounter, and that Torrance's work coherently describes the ontic focus, exploring how we participate in Christ's ongoing heavenly session as the great high priest vicariously intercedes between God and humanity. But the final section will argue that both these theologians, together with much Reformed theology, tend to neglect the telic or kingly aspect. This final section will explore some of the ways in which the future kingdom of Christ is anticipated in the church through the Spirit and the transformational impact this has even amid our current experience of living in old time.

4.3 Christ and the church's prophetic eschatological office

Barth's exploration of *The Doctrine of Reconciliation* in Volume IV of *Church Dogmatics* skilfully and creatively interacts with all three of Christ's offices.[21] Butin even argues that the '*munus triplex* provides the basic, if subterranean structure of Barth's Christology'.[22] The following section argues that while Barth insightfully utilizes all three offices, his analysis of the priestly and kingly office nevertheless retains the traditional then-to-now logic often used in Reformed theology. In treating Christ's prophetic office, however, Barth extends this approach to give it an explicitly eschatological orientation.

Barth's analysis of the three offices roughly corresponds to the three part-volumes comprising Volume IV of *Church Dogmatics*. The first part-volume deals with Christ's priestly office, exploring his humiliation – the Lord as Servant. The second part-volume deals with Christ's kingly office, exploring his exaltation – the Servant as Lord. The third part-volume deals with Christ's prophetic office – the True Witness. While recognizing the great insight and creativity in all this analysis, Barth's treatment of Christ's priestly and kingly offices in the first two part-volumes of *CD* IV retains the kind of logic previously noted in the Reformed catechisms. That is, the exposition is timebound, working from then to now. It develops from

---

understanding. For more details, see Scott Steinkerchner OP, 'Time in Heaven: From Glory to Glory', *New Blackfriars* 100, no. 1087 (2019): 264–83.

21. Barth, *Church Dogmatics*, IV.

22. Phil Butin, 'Two Early Reformed Catechisms, the Threefold Office, and the Shape of Karl Barth's Christology', *Scottish Journal of Theology* 44, no. 2 (1991): 200.

the earthly session of Jesus to the benefits his already completed work transposes to us through the Spirit. So, in terms of his priesthood, Barth sees Christ as the great high priest judged in our place. Christ sacrifices himself for us and because of that we are justified before God and gathered together as a community.[23] In terms of his kingship, Barth focuses more on the kingdom come than the kingdom coming. Indeed, despite all of Barth's emphasis on eschatology, he characterizes it as peripheral to a study of the *last things*: humanity's future resurrection, heaven, hell and our current movement towards these realities.[24] In Christ, humanity has been exalted to glory, and we live now in the light of that already achieved reality.

When Barth turns to Christ's prophetic office in *CD* IV.3, however, while his approach incorporates a timebound then-to-now logic, it extends well beyond it. Traditional approaches explain Christ's prophetic office as revealing God's truth during his earthly session, with that truth being accessible now through the written Word and the Spirit. In choosing the prophetic office as the third and final office to address, Barth rearranges the traditional *taxis* of the *munus triplex*,[25] with his explanation of the prophetic office building cumulatively on the previous two offices. Indeed, Barth is critical of the tradition's narrow exposition of Christ's prophetic office.[26] Because of the divine-to-human humiliation explored in Christ's priestly office and the human-to-divine exaltation explored in Christ's kingly office, Barth argues that we can now speak of the reconciliation of God and humanity which is prophetically revealed to us in Christ. So for Barth, reconciliation is revelation. 'Revelation takes place in and with reconciliation. Indeed, the latter is also revelation. As God acts in it, He also speaks. . . . Revelation takes place as the revelation of reconciliation, as the How of this What, as the self-declaration of this history.'[27] The eschatological extension that Barth introduces here is that the prophetic office is not just an understanding about God transferred to us by the

---

23. See particularly, Barth, *Church Dogmatics*, IV.1 274–83.

24. This comment about Barth's treatment of eschatology is quite common. See, for example, Nathan Hitchcock, *Karl Barth and the Resurrection of the Flesh* (Eugene: Pickwick, 2013), xi. For a fuller outworking, see, for example, Langdon, *God the Eternal Contemporary*, 129–58, particularly 143–50.

25. Note that the Geneva Catechism also has the prophetic office as the last mentioned, but most scholars suggest that the reason for this is that Calvin is explicitly adding the prophetic office onto the *munus duplex* for the first time. See, for example, Butin, 'Two Early Reformed Catechisms, the Threefold Office, and the Shape of Karl Barth's Christology', 197, n. 7. Virtually all expressions of the *munus triplex* since use a taxis of prophet, then priest, then king.

26. For example, Barth writes, 'The question can and must be asked, however, to what degree the meaning, importance and relevance of this newly discovered or rediscovered third problem of the doctrine of reconciliation are really grasped and brought out either then or more recently.' Barth, *Church Dogmatics*, IV.3 14. By 'third problem', Barth is referring here to the *munus Christi propheticum*, Christ's prophetic office.

27. Barth, *Church Dogmatics*, IV.3 8.

Spirit but a genuine encounter with an 'alien history' that is the truth and reality of Christ himself. Christ comes to us by the Spirit, and it is truly Christ that we encounter. In his person, he is the truth with which we engage, and in this way, Christ eschatologically fills his prophetic office. This point is pre-eminent, pivotal and central for Barth. He rejects all forms of sacramental mediation because Christ is not absent. The person we encounter is the eschatological reality of the risen Christ himself. 'The return of Jesus in this middle form, in which it takes place here and now, is His coming in the promise of the Spirit. This is His direct and immediate presence and action among and with and in us.'[28]

Barth's emphasis on Christ's prophetic office corresponds with him seeing the church's primary role as prophetic witness. For Barth, the limit of ecclesial activity is to bear witness to the divine event that reconciles us to Christ. When the church attempts to be more than a witness, it ironically becomes not more but less.[29] Through the Spirit, Christ's own prophetic self-proclamation is echoed in the proclamation of the church. This relationship can be characterized through the Chalcedonian-inspired threefold pattern of unity, differentiation and asymmetry.[30] Just as (for Barth) Christ's defining and cumulative office is prophetic, so the church's primary role is similarly prophetic (unity). The church's prophetic role is distinctly dissimilar to Christ's, however, because while Christ points to himself as the revelatory and reconciliatory truth, the church always points distinctly and deliberately away from itself (differentiation). And it is only because of Christ's prophetic ministry that the church has anything of which to prophetically point (asymmetry).

This connection between new and old time as illuminated through Barth's analysis has three key features. First, it is personally prophetic: Christ does not merely convey the truth about God during the incarnation, but he is the truth that we encounter by means of the Spirit's work. Second, it is primarily noetic. The knowledge Christ brings is the revelation of reconciliation. Indeed, some argue that this emphasis on noetic revelation leads Barth to have a rather non-participatory conception of reconciliation. Gunton, for example, critiques Barth for merely talking about encountering another history, rather than participating in Christ's body.[31] Third, it primarily connects the beginning of Christ's existence in new time with our present moment of existence. Barth's eschatological discussion

---

28. Ibid., IV.3 50.

29. See particularly Barth, *Church Dogmatics*, IV.1 657. Also, Bender, *Karl Barth's Christological Ecclesiology*, 3–4. Also, Hunsinger, *How to Read Karl Barth*, 177. Barth often illustrated this limited role for the church by likening it to John the Baptist. For example, Barth writes, 'One might recall John the Baptist in Grünewald's Crucifixion, especially his prodigious index finger. Could anyone point away from himself more impressively and completely . . .? And could anyone point more impressively and realistically than here to what is indicated?' Barth, *Church Dogmatics*, I.1 112. See also I.1 262; I.2 125; III.3 492.

30. See, for example, Bender, *Karl Barth's Christological Ecclesiology*, 4.

31. Gunton, 'Salvation', 152.

focuses more on the kingdom come than the kingdom coming, on Christ already resurrected rather than our coming resurrections.[32] And he is more focused on the objective reality of Christ's work brought forward to us than our existing and ongoing subjective telic transformation. For these reasons, Barth's analysis of the connection between new and old time could be indicatively characterized as an arrow from the start of new time (at the point of Christ's resurrection) through to our present moment in old time, an arrow labelled with the complementary but distinct terms *noetic* and *prophetic*. While this connection falls short of a complete account of the full interaction between Christ's new time and our present time, it nevertheless goes well beyond the traditional timebound explanations of the *munus triplex* that focus solely on Christ's earthly session. For Barth, the Spirit takes Christ's past (a prophetic revelation of our salvation through his suffering and exaltation) and brings it personally to bear on the church's present reality.

4.4 Christ and the church's priestly eschatological office

Like Barth, T. F. Torrance interacts with all three offices. Without losing Barth's eschatological focus on Christ's prophetic office, however, Torrance 'makes a creative attempt to go beyond Barth in expressing the reconciling work of Christ in explicit terms of the priestly office'.[33] Consequently, Christ's vicarious humanity and his priestly office are common themes throughout Torrance's writings. The following section describes Torrance's rich understanding of Christ's eschatological priestly office and through participation our correlative priestly ministry. It also argues that Torrance does not develop a similarly rich understanding of the eschatological aspect of Christ's kingly office.

For Torrance, the ascension is pivotal.[34] While in the incarnation, God in Christ existed in humanity's space, now in the ascension, humanity in Christ exists in God's space.[35] To categorize Christ's continuing activity in the ascension, Torrance turns to the *munus triplex*. Christ continues to be and acts as king, prophet and priest in his heavenly session. Torrance's explanation of Christ's continuing role as king is both brief and traditional.[36] Because of Christ's self-offering, he is installed in his ascension as the head of all humanity. And from there he reigns over the

---

32. See, for example, the rather harsh critique of Barth on this point in Hitchcock, *Karl Barth and the Resurrection of the Flesh*.

33. Butin, 'Two Early Reformed Catechisms, the Threefold Office, and the Shape of Karl Barth's Christology', 203, n. 22.

34. See, for example, Thomas F. Torrance, *Scottish Theology from John Knox to John McLeod Campbell* (Edinburgh: T&T Clark, 1996), 21.

35. See, for example, Torrance, *Space, Time and Resurrection*, 129.

36. In *Atonement* for example, Torrance's description of Christ as ascended king is less than one page (270–1) while his exploration of Christ's ascended role as priest (271–7) and as prophet (277–81) are at least seven and five pages respectively. See Thomas F. Torrance,

church and all of creation. This explanation echoes the then-to-now logic of the traditional *munus triplex* formulations. In contrast, Torrance's explanation of Christ's ascended prophetic role echoes Barth's reconceived analysis. Through his Spirit, Christ is truly present delivering a prophetic word of reconciliation.

> The ministry of the word is not separable from the ministry of reconciliation. It is the word of forgiveness. . . . That is the kind of word that is mediated to us through the blessing of Christ and the pouring out of his Spirit, a prophetic ministry in which Christ is himself its living, actual and full content, or in which Christ himself ministers to us.[37]

And, again like Barth, Christ's prophetic ministry resonates through the church's pneumatologically enabled witness.

> Primarily it is his own kerygma, his self-proclamation, which through the Spirit he allows to be echoed and heard through the preaching of the church, so that their kerygma about Jesus Christ is made one with his own kerygma. . . . In and through the preaching and teaching of the word it is Christ himself the incarnate and risen Word who is mightily at work confronting men and women with himself and summoning them to believe and follow him.[38]

Torrance significantly expands on Barth's traditional approach to the priestly office, however. He goes well beyond simply describing how through Christ's priestly sacrifice we are justified before God and gathered together as a community.[39] Torrance argues that Jesus Christ not only was but presently is humanity's ongoing exclusive language to God.[40] In his vicarious humanity, Christ intercedes for us, proclaims God's blessing on us and enables our continuing communion. So, for Torrance, Christ's priesthood is not just something he has done but something that he is continuously doing. 'The resurrection and the ascension, however, do not mean that Christ's priestly sacrifice and oblation of himself are over and done with, but rather that in their once and for all completion they are taken up eternally into

---

Atonement: The Person and Work of Christ (Downers Grove: InterVarsity Press, 2009), 270–81.

37. Torrance, *Incarnation*, 278–9.

38. Ibid., 278.

39. Apparently, Barth's response to Torrance suggesting the extension of Christ's priestly role was that Torrance should rewrite aspects of *CD* IV. See, for example, Langdon, *God the Eternal Contemporary*, 148. Also, Douglas Farrow, 'Karl Barth on the Ascension: An Appreciation and Critique', *International Journal of Systematic Theology* 2, no. 3 (2000): 141–3.

40. See Thomas F. Torrance, *Reality and Evangelical Theology* (Philadelphia: The Westminster Press, 1982), 88–9.

the life of God, and remain prevalent, efficacious, valid, abidingly real.'[41] In his ongoing priesthood, Christ stands in the gap between God and humanity. Having united himself with us during his earthly session, he now presents himself as a human to the Father in his heavenly session and moreover presents ourselves in and through him, representing us through his continued priestly self-offering. And the result of this continuing advocacy is ontological transformation. 'It is with that ontological content of his advocacy on our behalf that we are concerned here. It is an advocacy in which his word and person and act are one and indivisible.'[42] For Torrance, the ongoing priestly self-offering of Christ, and us in him, fundamentally changes the nature of who we are and what we do. Its effects are ontological and all-encompassing. 'This applies to the whole of my life in Christ and to all my human responses to God, for in Jesus Christ, they are all laid hold of, sanctified and informed by his vicarious life of obedience and response to the Father.'[43]

As in the previous discussion of Barth and the prophetic connection, Torrance's analysis of Christ's ongoing priestly office has ecclesial implications.[44] Christ's ongoing priestly office leads not just to ontological transformation or activity but even more significantly to communion. We participate in Christ's priesthood: 'While the New Testament uses priestly language to speak of the Royal Priesthood of Christ in His Word and Action, it also applies priestly language to the Church, showing that the Church is given to participate in his ministry, in word, deed, and life.'[45] Torrance sees this priestly outworking of the church through the Word and sacraments. The sacraments are priestly actions for they refer to our incorporation into Christ (baptism) and our continued renewal in that incorporation (eucharist),[46] and it is the Word that sacramentalizes the ordinances and turns them into genuine means of grace. Once again, the relationship between Christ's priestly office and the church's reality can be characterized through the threefold pattern of unity, differentiation and asymmetry. The church's priestly role echoes Christ's priestly office, for we participate in his ministry in word, deed and life (unity). Just as he stands in the gap for us, we stand in the gap for each other. There is, however, only one priestly intercessor between God and humanity. Jesus is God's exclusive language to humanity and humanity's exclusive language to God. We might intercede for each other; Jesus alone intercedes between humanity and God (differentiation). And it is only because of this intercession between God and us that we can intercede for each other (asymmetry).

41. Torrance, *Incarnation*, 273.
42. Ibid., 275.
43. Thomas F. Torrance, *The Mediation of Christ* (Edinburgh: T&T Clark, 1992), 98.
44. Torrance focuses particularly on these in his 1955 monologue, *Royal Priesthood*. See Thomas F. Torrance, *Royal Priesthood* (Edinburgh: Oliver and Boyd, 1955).
45. Torrance, *Royal Priesthood*, 21-2.
46. See Ibid., 74-5. Also, Paul D. Molnar, 'The Eucharist and the Mind of Christ: Some Trinitarian Implications of T. F. Torrance's Sacramental Theology', in *Trinitarian Soundings in Systematic Theology*, ed. Paul L. Metzger (London: T&T Clark, 2005), 185-6.

Consequently, Torrance's analysis of the priestly connection between new and old time has three key features. First, it focuses on Christ's present priesthood: Christ's intercession is not focused in the past but is present and ongoing. Second, it is primarily ontic: affecting not just our status or knowledge but our ontological reality. Through the Spirit we join the Trinitarian life, participating in Christ's filial relationship. Third, it primarily connects Christ's 'current' existence in new time with our present moment of existence in old time. This insight is primarily one of exclusion, as Christ's priestly mediation does not stem primarily from his initial ascension into new time or our future joining of him in the coming kingdom. Clearly Christ's priestly mediation is not merely bringing forward into our time the results of Christ's resurrection. Moreover, it is also not bringing back to us blessings from the coming kingdom. Indeed, Torrance's exploration of Christ's kingly role and the coming kingdom is curiously underdeveloped, as several commentators have noted. For example, Eugenio writes that 'At least in comparison to his greater and more in-depth treatments of the prophetic and priestly offices of Christ, the kingly office in Christ's incarnate economy and its implications for Christian life are noticeably less discussed. In particular, he does not elaborate the important implications of Christ's vicarious victory over sin and death for Christians now.'[47] In a more detailed examination, Baxter similarly comments that 'there is not very much emphasis in Torrance's theology upon the kingly work of Christ viewed in terms of the restoration of the whole creation and specifically the restoration of man's relation to the creation.'[48] Combining these three features, Torrance's analysis of the connection between new and old time can be characterized as an arrow from the 'middle' of new time (at some point between Christ's resurrection and the full inauguration of the coming kingdom) through to our present moment in old time, an arrow labelled as both ontic and priestly. Where Barth explored the connection of Christ's past in new time with our present in fallen time (a prophetic revelation of our reconciliation through his suffering and exaltation), Torrance combines this with a similar exploration of Christ's ongoing vicarious humanity (a priestly enabling of a filial relationship). Both of these extend the timebound logic of traditional formulations of the *munus triplex* to explore the pneumatological connection between new and old time. The question naturally arises, though: What of Christ's eschatological office as king? And what of the Christ's future in new time? In what way does Christ's (and our) future kingdom reality impact our present existence in fallen time?

---

47. Dick O. Eugenio, *Communion with the Triune God: The Trinitarian Soteriology of T. F. Torrance* (Eugene: Wipf & Stock Publishers, 2014), 139.

48. C. Baxter Kruger, 'Participation in the Self-Knowledge of God: The Nature and means of our Knowledge of God in the Theology of T. F. Torrance' (PhD Thesis, University of Aberdeen, 1989) 325. See 324–34 for more detail.

4.5 Christ and the church's kingly eschatological office

While Barth and Torrance helpfully outline the prophetic and priestly connections between new and old time, both arguably undervalue the kingly connection. This section will explore how the kingly connection complements and extends Barth and Torrance's work, and how the reality of Christ's future is brought to bear on the church's present reality. The most obvious move in doing this would be to leverage recent scholars who have intentionally adopted a future-oriented approach.[49] While there is creativity and value in this work, simplistically utilizing it to explore the kingly connection between new and old time proves intractable. First, because most often these chronologically oriented approaches do not distinguish between new and old time, and, as such, intrinsically diverge from the connections outlined earlier. In contrast, they often collapse the distinction between these two times, giving fallen time an undeserved precedence and priority. In doing so, these approaches ignore the ontological separateness of Christ from the church.[50] A second challenge is that these approaches rarely acknowledge the practical reality of the future kingdom impacting present time. As van der Kooi acknowledges,

> even where today the notion of God's kingdom is acknowledged as a holistic idea, there is still immediate hesitation, for example, if it involves healing. The theologies of Jürgen Moltmann and Wolfhart Pannenberg are examples of this position. Both scholars defend the idea that the future is already present here, but instead of becoming concrete, they remain stuck in generalities, if not obfuscations.[51]

The objective of this final section then, is to *concretely* explore how Christ's kingly reign is present in the church and how, by means of the Spirit, this impacts our current existence in fallen time. For the Spirit doesn't just prophetically bring forward Jesus' past work or in a priestly manner enable us to share in Christ's present vicarious humanity. The Spirit also draws back into our current time the coming kingdom so that it becomes a part of our present ecclesial experience. Even more, this pneumatologically transposed experience of the future kingdom drives us forward, empowering our development and transformation. This section first outlines how four interrelated characteristics of the coming kingdom – truth, life, justice and love – are pneumatologically brought back into our current time to become characteristics of our present ecclesial existence and further how the Spirit transforms the church to more completely reflect these characteristics. In Scripture, these four qualities stand out as essential and often repeated features of the eschatological life. Each of them provides a concrete data point for how

---

49. Examples include Hütter, Pannenberg, Zizioulas and Moltmann, among others.
50. For further discussion of this point, see Section 3.1.
51. van der Kooi, *This Incredibly Benevolent Force*, 16.

the future kingdom is pneumatologically anticipated in our present ecclesial experience. An examination of all four qualities allows common patterns to emerge. This section examines each of these data points in order to recognize the systematic patterns through which the coming kingdom pneumatologically impacts our present existence. The resulting picture outlines the kingly connection between new and old time.

That the coming kingdom is a place of truth, where every hidden reality is revealed and every falsehood is unmasked, is implicitly illustrated through God's ever-present revealing light (Rev. 21.23-24) and explicitly noted through the absence of misleading evildoers (Rev. 21.8, 22.15). The captivating descriptions in Revelation 21–22 paint a picture where every remnant of falsehood and darkness has been swept away by God's all-encompassing truth and light. There is an ultimate connection between truth and holiness here, for the unalloyed presence of truth and righteousness necessarily means the holy removal of error and evil. Truth reigns in the coming kingdom because Christ reigns and Christ is the truth (Jn 14.6). But the Spirit, in part, brings that kingdom reality of truth back to become a reality in our ecclesial existence now. For not only has Christ's kingdom truth been revealed to us in the Spirit (1 Cor. 2.9-12) but the Spirit is the Spirit of truth (Jn 16.13), who continuously leads us into all truth (1 Jn 2.26). Empowered by the Spirit, then, the church should not only oppose all mistruths that reject Christ and keep people from knowing God (1 Cor. 10:4-5) but also proclaim Christ's kingdom truth with all the wisdom that has been given to us, relying on Christ's power present within us to do so (Col. 1:28).

Abundant life is perhaps the most insistently repeated characteristic in the depictions of the coming kingdom in the final chapters of Revelation. Its inhabitants are named in the book of life (Rev. 20.12), and two central geographic features are a river (filled with the water of life) and the tree of life (Rev. 22.1-2), whose leaves provide a healing so potent that the coming kingdom has no more death, sorrow, crying or pain (Rev. 21.3). This kingdom life goes well beyond biological existence (*bios*) to spiritual life (*zoë*) – life truly lived and lived to the fullest – a life that finds its true source in the resurrected Jesus (Jn 20.31), the lamb on the throne from which flows the water of life (Rev. 22.1). Abundant life is consequently the reigning reality in the kingdom, because Christ reigns, and Christ is life (Jn 14.6), and our life is found in him (Jn 1.4). But the Spirit, in part, brings that kingdom experience of abundant life back to become a reality in our ecclesial existence now. For not only has participation in Christ's resurrection life been given to us at the present time through the Spirit (Jn 7.37-39) but the Spirit is the Spirit of life (Rom. 8.2), leading the church towards an abundant existence and a renewed creation (Jn 6.63). Empowered by the Spirit, then, the church should not only proclaim words of physical, emotional and spiritual healing over those who are suffering (1 Cor. 12.9),[52] but we should intentionally live out abundant lives, finding in our present

---

52. See, for example, the profound discussion of healing in van der Kooi, *This Incredibly Benevolent Force*, 112–15.

existence true fulfilment and increasingly abundant joy in the pneumatological presence of the resurrected Christ (Jn 10.10).

Justice is the third characteristic of the coming kingdom, for it is a place where there is no more poverty, no more inequality and no more bondage. From its earliest precursors through to its final descriptions, justice is explicitly noted as a primary characteristic of the Son's kingdom (e.g. Isa. 9.6-7, Rev. 19.11). There is a connection between justice and liberty here, for the judge who judges justly brings freedom to all who are unjustly oppressed (Lk. 4.18-19, Jn 8.34).[53] God's coming kingdom is consequently a place where freedom reigns – freedom from tyranny and oppression, certainly, but even more than that freedom from death, decay and sin. Indeed, it is not just God's children who experience such justice and liberty but creation itself that is rightly released from its unwelcome captivity to corruption (Rom. 8.21-22). But the Spirit, in part, brings that kingdom reality of justice and freedom back to be experienced in our ecclesial existence now. For through the Spirit we have already been given a 'foretaste of future glory' (Rom. 8.23), being freed from the power of sin (Rom. 8.1) and justified through the work of Jesus (Rom. 3.21-26). That future declaration of righteousness from the final judgement has now, at the present time, been proclaimed over us, so that the justice of God in Christ might be truly seen. But the Spirit does not just declare the justice of God in our current time but grows us increasingly into becoming a just and liberated community. He is the Spirit of liberty, leading the church towards freedom, to an existence where righteousness and justice flourish, increasingly reflecting the character of our king (2 Cor. 3.17-18). For one of the primary signs through which the Spirit's presence is evident within an individual (Lk. 4.18-19) or a community (Acts 2.45, 4.32-34) is that they increasingly embrace the neglected and prioritize the poor.

The final characteristic of the coming kingdom addressed in this section is love, for all who live in God live in love (1 Jn 3.16). Just as justice pervades the descriptions of the kingdom from beginning to end, so too does love (e.g. Isa. 16.5, 1 Jn 3.1-7). Indeed, love is the greatest, most enduring and primary defining trait of the future kingdom, for God is love (1 Jn 4.8). The coming kingdom is infused with love because Christ the king loves us (Rev. 1.5) and has demonstrated this love through his sacrificial death (Jn 15.13). There is a connection between love and unity here, for Christ's loving sacrifice has broken down the dividing wall of hostility (Eph. 2.14-16), so that the future kingdom is a place where all the diversity of humanity (Rev. 8.9) and creation itself (Isa. 11.6) dwell together in loving harmony. But the Spirit, in part, brings that kingdom reality of love and unity back to be experienced in our ecclesial existence now. This is why Paul can use a pneumatological argument to demonstrate that all divisions within the

---

53. There is similarly a connection between truth and freedom (e.g. Jn 8.32), but that is perhaps more specifically seen as a freedom from evil and error, rather than a freedom from oppression. The two are clearly interrelated, as are all the characteristics of the coming kingdom.

church are theologically impossible (1 Cor. 12.13).[54] Just as the Spirit is the bond of love between the Father and Son, so too is he the bond joining Christians together in unity (Jn 17.20-26). But the Spirit does not just declare our loving unity, he leads us towards becoming a loving and united Christian community. He is the Spirit of unity (Eph. 4:4), leading the church towards love and unity. Through the Spirit our hearts are filled with love for each other (Rom. 5.5, 15.30), and as our love grows more perfect we lose our fear of judgement and look forward to the coming kingdom with longing (1 Jn 4.17-18).

All four of these examples reflect a common pattern. First, the qualities of truth, life, justice and love that characterize the kingdom do so because of Christ's kingship. It is only because Christ is king that his character is reflected so perfectly in the coming kingdom. Second, through the Spirit, these kingdom characteristics are brought back to be a part of our ecclesial reality now. Their occurrence among us can be attributed to Christ's genuine presence with us as king. In other words, Christ dwells among us as king by his Spirit, and so our communities are places of truth, life, justice and love. Of course, our ecclesial reality is not completely characterized by these qualities, because the fullness of the kingdom is still coming and has not yet arrived.

Just as Christ's prophetic and priestly connections between new and old time had present ecclesial implications, so too does Christ's kingly presence. This is the third feature in the pattern, for the Spirit leads our communities increasingly into these kingdom realities. In other words, in bringing back to us the presence of Christ the king, the Spirit leads and drives us on towards the coming kingdom, so that the presence of these kingdom qualities and Christ's kingly reign itself are increasingly apparent among us. The presence of Christ as king through his Spirit has consequences; it affects not only who we are but who we are becoming. The Spirit's work goes beyond transforming our communities, however. The fourth and final feature of the pattern is that the church becomes not just the recipient of, and characterized by, these kingly qualities but the purveyors of them. The Spirit continues his work as the Spirit of truth, the Spirit of life, the Spirit of liberty and the Spirit of love, and he does this through the church. Just as Christ the king brings truth, freedom, unity and life to the kingdom and to the church, so the Spirit uses the church to bring these qualities to the world. This is our vice-regency, as united with our king we act on his behalf. So it is an aspect of the church's mission to speak public truth, to liberate those who are oppressed, to unite people and draw them together in love, and to preserve life and bring healing to humanity and creation. These are essential parts of the church's mission, because the church's royal ministry role reflects Christ's kingly office. Once again, though,

---

54. 'This text affirms that the visible ritual of initiating diverse human beings through the power of the Spirit into a single local assembly is meant to point to the invisible bond of love by which the *Spiritus Congregator* renders them one in mind and heart as members of the universal Body of Christ.' Philip J. Rosato, 'The Mission of the Spirit within and beyond the Church', *Ecumenical Review* 41, no. 3 (1989): 391.

the relationship is not merely one of union but of differentiation and asymmetry. The difference is that our royal ministry is not intrinsic but representative – we are Christ's ambassadors (2 Cor. 5.20) who are working in enemy territory (2 Cor. 4.5) – so we have no intrinsic authority to insist or compel, only the winsomeness to persuade. And the asymmetry comes from the fact that it is only because Christ has given us truth, life, justice and love that we have the opportunity to be purveyors of these qualities to the world.

To summarize, this final connection between new and old time has three key features. First, it is a kingly connection. It is Christ's future reign as the true king of his coming kingdom that is pneumatologically anticipated in our present ecclesial communities. Second, it is a telic connection. The presence of the king transforms our communities towards our ultimate *telos*. Christ's pneumatologically enabled presence not only allows the kingly traits of truth, life, justice and love to be evident and growing among us, it encourages and enables us to act as purveyors of these traits to the outside world, not forcefully through intrinsic authority but through persuasion as kingly representatives living in a foreign land. Third, it connects the culmination of Christ's existence in new time with our present moment in old time. It denotes a connection between the coming kingdom and our present time. For these three reasons, this connection can be represented as an arrow from the culmination or 'future' of Christ's new time through to our present moment in old time, an arrow labelled as both telic and kingly. These three features do not by any means exhaust the theological richness of this kingly connection. Many questions remain to be explored.[55] They do, however, illustrate and outline its significance, and point to the truth that even beyond the already examined prophetic and priestly connections, a more detailed exploration of the kingly connection between new and old time has rich potential to enhance Reformed theology.

4.6 Conclusion

Most Reformed formulations of the *munus triplex* focus on Christ's earthly session and the impact Christ's past roles as prophet, priest and king have for us at our current moment in ecclesial time. The argument in this chapter has been that these chronologically based understandings can be refined, complemented and extended by viewing each of these offices eschatologically. Applying the methodology of Third Article Theology to the doctrine of eschatology enables the full breadth of Christ's interaction from his new time to our present moment in old time to be explored. This eschatological interaction was categorized into three aspects, corresponding to Christ's three offices in the *munus triplex*. The Spirit takes Christ's

---

55. These include but are not limited to: How does the pneumatological presence of Christ the king enable the church's growth and transformation? How does the approach to the kingly connection here compare with that of other future-oriented approaches? Aspects of these questions are addressed specifically in the next chapters.

past (a prophetic revelation of our salvation through his suffering and exaltation), Christ's present (a priestly enabling of a filial relationship) and Christ's future (a kingly manifestation of our future glory) and brings them all to bear on the church's present reality. And because of these pneumatological connections, the church itself participates in Christ's eschatological offices. During our present existence in fallen time, the Spirit makes the church prophetic (bearing witness to Christ), priestly (communally standing in the gap for each other) and royal (purveying Christ's character). Further, each of these eschatological offices has a defining character. The prophetic office is primarily noetic – Christ pneumatologically reveals the truth of reconciliation to us. The priestly office is primarily ontic – Christ transforms our relational being, drawing us into God's life. And the kingly office is primarily telic – the presence of the future kingdom gradually transforms our communities to such an extent that we become transformers ourselves. While the prophetic and priestly connections have been deeply explored by Barth and Torrance, the kingly connection has been comparatively neglected in the Reformed tradition. The previous analysis, although initiatory and indicative, points to the richness of this kingly connection. Further analysis would afford insight into the pneumatological transformation of the church, a topic that will be explored in more detail in the next chapter.

Chapter 5

EUCHARISTIC TRANSFORMATION

Building on the pneumatological, eschatological and ecclesiological insights developed in the previous chapters, the objective of the next two chapters is to construct a nuanced understanding of church life when viewed from the vantage point of the coming kingdom, through the lens of the Spirit: an *eschatological* Third Article Ecclesiology. After an initial and overall characterization of the church as the proleptic anticipation of the kingdom, the major emphasis of this chapter is to explore in detail the pneumatological and eschatological nature of the eucharist as a prototypical example of how the Spirit goes about transforming the church and moreover how we can participate in the Spirit's ongoing ecclesial transformation. Chapter 6 then extends this prototypical example to other practices, exploring how the Spirit uses all aspects of our ecclesial life together to mark us out as a holy and distinct community within the world, and to guide and empower our personal and communal transformation. Both chapters also compare the constituent features of this developed eschatological ecclesiology with Barth's and Hütter's alternative approaches as presented in Chapter 2, arguing that the understanding of ecclesial transformation emerging from an eschatological Third Article Ecclesiology avoids the core errors of overemphasizing the eschatological or teleological tensions that Barth and Hütter's work respectively exemplified.

5.1 *The church as the proleptic anticipation of the kingdom*

The primary insight emerging from the development of an eschatological Third Article Ecclesiology in Chapters 3 and 4 is that the church needs to be viewed not just as the community of people historically constituted by the life, death, resurrection and ascension of Jesus Christ, and not just as a community presently united to Christ by the Spirit, but also and equally as a communal and proleptic anticipation of Christ's coming kingdom. Viewing the church as both presently situated in fallen time and pneumatologically united with Christ who exists simultaneously across the full breadth of redeemed time means that the church's existence has both a present situation and a past as well as future orientation. This relationship between our present timebound existence and Jesus' existence in a reality which merges fallen time and eternity enables us to see God's reconciliatory work as not merely eternally realized but also and simultaneously being progressively achieved. As Gunton comments, 'Jesus does indeed do something for the whole human race; but the perfecting of that complete work continues to depend on its realization in time by the work of the Spirit who brings particular people into the community of the reconciled. Reconciliation is thus universal in intent, but not yet fully realized.'[1]

Consequently, the church has three causes or callings. It is caused or called into being through the past life, death and resurrection of Christ, whose salvation is brought forward to us through the Spirit. It is also caused or called into being through the ongoing presence of Christ with whom the church is united by the Spirit. And finally, it is caused or called into being through its pneumatological connection with Christ's coming kingdom, and, as such, it exists as that community through which Christ's completed work will be gradually perfected and fully realized. Expressing those three orientations in other words, the church lives in historical solidarity with the community instituted by Christ and maintained by the Spirit. It also exists as the community in whom Christ presently dwells through the presence of the Spirit. But, in addition to these two important characterizations, the church must also be considered as the community in which through the Spirit Christ's coming kingdom presently exists in and impacts the world.[2] We are called to live not just out of the past work of Christ, or out of our present relationship with Christ, but the church is also called specifically and uniquely to anticipate the future (and completed) reign of Christ.[3]

As has been noted on several occasions in previous chapters,[4] Barth's work focuses on the first of these characterizations (bringing forward Christ's work) and comparatively neglects the latter two aspects, with particularly little recognition of the church's pneumatological connection with Christ's coming kingdom and the gradual conforming that the church consequently experiences. In Chapter 2 this tendency was characterized as an overemphasis on the eschatological tension (between eternity and time) and a consequent underemphasis on the teleological tension (acting through time). Essentially, for Barth, the entirety of God's interaction with humanity has already been completed in and through Christ, his

---

1. Colin Gunton, *The Christian Faith: An Introduction to Christian Doctrine* (Oxford: Blackwell, 2002), 164.

2. As will be discussed later, these characterizations do not restrict the work of the Spirit to the church, but it does correctly imply that the Spirit's ecclesial role is distinct and primary compared to those roles performed outside of the church.

3. Note that each of these perspectives can also be correlated with the vantage points that have been used to view a Third Article Ecclesiology. So, the past perspective correlates most closely with the Christological vantage point. (See Part Two of *The Anointed Church*.) The present perspective correlates most closely with the Trinitarian vantage point. (See Part Three of *The Anointed Church*.) And the future perspective most closely correlates with the eschatological vantage point, which is the subject of this volume.

4. See particularly Sections 2.2 and 4.3–4.4.

5. Eucharistic Transformation

death and resurrection. The Spirit's role is primarily taking Jesus' past (or eternal) work and making it available to us today (or in time). This limited characterization lacks aspects that feed into the church's ongoing transformation and hope. Chapter 2 also noted that the root cause of this overemphasis on the eschatological tension was Barth's tendency to supress the role of the Spirit within ecclesial time and subsume it into the prior and eternal action of the Son. This results in the church's journey through time and its telic and transformational connection with the coming kingdom being downplayed. It was also noted that a similar tendency, although much less pronounced, can be recognized in Torrance's work.

Barth's overemphasis on the eschatological tension cannot be corrected with an overemphasis on the teleological tension, however.[5] Hütter (among others) minimizes the eschatological tension by closely identifying church practice with both the work of the Spirit and the future kingdom. As such he replaces Barth's overemphasis on the vertical dimension (or an eternal focus on the completed work of Christ) with an overemphasis on the horizontal dimension (or a chronological focus on the ongoing work of the Spirit). As has been noted, such an approach essentially constrains the Spirit to the church and does not adequately acknowledge human sinfulness.

The question that arises is how the great gains made by Torrance and Barth in exploring the nature of the church from an eschatological perspective can be retained, but complemented by also viewing the church as the proleptic anticipation of Christ's coming kingdom. And further what the practical and concrete implications of these insights are for church life. While it has been argued that in the work of Hütter and other teleologically focused theologians (e.g. Moltmann, Pannenberg, Zizioulas) the pendulum swings too far from the eschatological to the teleological tension and that their analysis is consequently too intrinsically timebound, their work is not therefore wholly discounted! The following analysis judiciously utilizes the insights of such theologians, together with the important and foundational considerations from Barth and Torrance on an eschatological ecclesiology, to propose a coherent and concrete understanding of the kingly, telic and future-oriented aspects of church life. Its goal is to intentionally develop an understanding that to a significant degree complements and integrates with the analysis of Barth (that focuses on the prophetic and noetic aspects of church life) and that of Torrance (that focuses on the prophetic and ontic aspects). As Kimlyn Bender comments, 'In the future, ecclesiologies are wise to not go around, but to go through Barth's doctrine of the church. They may find need to address deficiencies; they dare not ignore his lessons.'[6]

In order to make the analysis as concrete as possible, this chapter chooses one particular example of church life to focus on and explores how the Spirit works through that practice to transform the church. As the *centralis agere* in the life and transformation of the church, the eucharist is an obvious choice to prototypically

---

5. See Section 2.3.
6. Bender, *Karl Barth's Christological Ecclesiology*, 284.

inform an understanding of the Spirit's ecclesial transformation.[7] The discussion proceeds in three stages. The first section (5.2) considers in general terms how the Spirit transforms the church through the eucharist, introducing three intertwining factors: imagination, presence and practice. The second section (5.3) makes this general analysis more concrete by applying this threefold understanding of transformation to the defining features of the coming kingdom recognized in the previous chapter: unity, life, truth and justice. This section explores how, through the eucharist, the Spirit makes each of these kingdom realities increasingly present within our church communities. The third and final section (5.4) contrasts this detailed account of pneumatological church transformation with the eucharistic portrayals of Barth and Hütter.

5.2 The eucharist in ecclesial transformation

This chapter focuses on the eucharist as the prototypical example of how church practices can lead to ecclesial transformation. This is because (in contrast to baptism) the eucharistic sacrament is the central and defining aspect of the *ongoing* life and worship of the church. As Torrance characterizes it:

> the emphasis upon the once and for all union of God and man, of the eternal and the temporal falls most heavily upon the sacrament of Baptism, while in the eucharist or sacrament of holy communion we have the emphasis most upon the continuation of that in the contradictions and abstractions of fallen time. . . . If at Baptism we think of our union with Christ as *opus dei*, work of God which takes place in and for its own sake, at communion we think of the same union inserted into our flesh and blood, into time and history as by faith we partake of Christ's flesh and blood.[8]

Moltmann makes a similar assertion:

> Just as baptism is the eschatological *sign of starting out*, valid once and for all, so the regular and constant fellowship at the table of the Lord is the eschatological *sign of being on the way*. If baptism is called the unique *sign of grace*, then the Lord's supper must be understood as the repeatable *sign of hope*.[9]

So, if the eucharist is the example par excellence of church life as situated within time and history, the question being explored in this section is how the Spirit

---

7. The words *eucharist*, *Lord's supper* and *communion* are used interchangeably in this section.
8. Torrance, *Incarnation*, 339.
9. Jürgen Moltmann, *The Church in the Power of the Spirit: A Contribution to Messianic Ecclesiology* (New York: Harper and Row, 1977), 243 (italics in original).

utilizes this aspect of ecclesial life to sustain and transform the church in its journey and, further, how we can participate in that pneumatological transformation. Examining the Spirit's transformational role in the eucharist will (comparatively) inform the Spirit's transformational role in many other significant aspects of church life as well.[10]

Like the church itself, the eucharist has three aspects, relating to its past, present and future, respectively. The past aspect of the eucharist is based in the meal's remembrance of what Christ has done: 'do this *in remembrance* of me' (Lk. 22.19) (italics added). This aspect is aligned with the understanding of the church as historically constituted by the life, death and resurrection of Jesus Christ. And it corresponds to the prophetic ministry of Christ discussed in Section 4.4, for in the eucharist through the Spirit we encounter the truth of Christ himself. Through taking the bread and the cup the reality of Christ's reconciliation is revealed to us and we pneumatologically participate in the past events of Jesus' death and resurrection.

The present aspect of the eucharist is derived from it being a meal of fellowship and communion, both with God and with other believers: 'I have earnestly desired to eat this Passover meal *with you*' (Lk. 22.15) (italics added). This aspect is aligned with seeing the church as a community presently united to Christ by the Spirit. And it corresponds to the priestly ministry of Christ discussed in Section 4.5, for in the eucharist through the Spirit we are united with the Son, with all the relational and ontological changes that such a union involves. Through taking the bread and the cup we become one with Christ and pneumatologically participate in his filial relationship with the Father.

The future aspect of the eucharist is that the meal anticipates a coming celebration of the full and final union and communion between God and humanity: 'From now on I will not drink of the vine *until the kingdom of God comes*' (Lk. 22.18) (italics added). This aspect is aligned with an understanding of the church as the proleptic anticipation of Christ's coming kingdom. And it corresponds to the kingly ministry of Christ discussed in Section 4.6, for in the eucharist through the Spirit we anticipate and even (to an extent) participate in the lamb's wedding supper. Through taking the bread and the cup we are gradually transformed through our pneumatological participation in these coming events.

As often noted, it is this latter aspect of the eucharist that is most obviously underemphasized in today's (particularly Protestant) church practice. For example, Craig Blomberg writes,

> As for temporal emphases of the Lord's Supper, the church in general today seems best at stressing the backward look to the cross. The most neglected is our

---

10. The extension of this analysis to other parts of church life is discussed in detail in the next chapter.

anticipation of the heavenly banquet. Somewhere in between falls our focus on present fellowship with God and others.[11]

Further, it is this future aspect of the eucharist that most clearly and directly influences the church's transformation through the passage of time. This section broadly and briefly sketches out the overarching aspects of how a pneumatologically and eschatologically enabled eucharistic celebration empowers the church's transformation. It argues that such transformation occurs through the intersecting interplay of imagination, presence and practice.

5.2.1 Imagination

The first eschatological and pneumatological phenomenon considered in this analysis of the eucharistic celebration is the creation and stimulation of our imaginations. Through participating in the eucharist we increasingly see ourselves as people of the kingdom, foreigners living in a strange world, an exiled community whose true home is distinct from the place and time in which we currently reside (Phil. 3.20, 1 Pet. 2.11). As an anticipation of the lamb's wedding supper, the eucharist paints a picture for us of reality as it should and will be, a place and time where Christ is truly and completely king and we as the church are truly and completely united to him as his bride. Participating in the eucharist develops within our communities a foretaste, a picture and a deep desire for such a reality, and it is these aspects that give significance and meaning to our participation in the eucharistic celebration and our lives beyond it. Moreover, pneumatological transformation is enabled through this created and stimulated eschatological imagination that occurs during the eucharist, a 'renewing of our minds' (Rom. 8.2). Of course, the creation and stimulation of our kingdom-centred imagination does not occur only at the eucharist but within all aspects of the church's communal life. As MacDougall says, 'Ecclesiology is the theological articulation of an imagination of what it is to be church.'[12] But as the centre of the church's ongoing life and worship, the eucharist's role in the formation of a coherent and compelling imagination of the future kingdom is particularly evident and important.

Imagination, as the term is being used here, must be sharply distinguished from mere wishful thinking or fantasy. In contrast, it aligns with the type of construct Charles Taylor describes through the phrase 'social imaginary'.[13] Imagination in this sense provides the fundamental understanding of who we are as a community, how we relate to one another and what our common life should be like. It is the

---

11. C. L. Blomberg, *1 Corinthians* (Grand Rapids: Zondervan Academic, 2009), 238. See also I. Howard Marshall, *Last Supper and Lord's Supper* (Vancouver: Regent College Publishing, 1980), 153.

12. MacDougall, *More Than Communion*, 1.

13. See, for example, Charles Taylor, *Modern Social Imaginaries* (Durham: Duke University Press, 2004), 23–30.

framework through which we make sense of our existence and actions. While such imagination clearly has an intellectual component, it reaches well beyond this. It is pre- (and post-)cognitive, instinctual, embodied, aspirational and affective. So the theological imagination that is developed in the church through participating in the eucharist is much more than just an intellectual 'worldview'.[14] It is a way of seeing, understanding and doing life that defines and characterizes who we are.

A Christian 'social imaginary', though, does not just look forward but backward as well, for what we anticipate is determined and guaranteed by the death and resurrection of Christ and the gift of the Spirit. We have a future that has been predetermined by the past. As discussed in Chapter 3, our ongoing existence in time is conditioned by this pattern of cruciformity, which defines not just our individual and communally present lives but also our present and future as well. 'By the resurrection God has set the future inexorably in motion; the "coming" of Christ and subsequent "judgment" are inevitable corollaries, as sure as life itself.... Those sure events radicalize present Christian existence.'[15] So, given this past and future orientation, our present imagination can be labelled as *Christo/eschato-logical*. It is based on the past and our participation in Christ's death and resurrection but looks forward with certain hope to the future when those kingdom realities will be fully and not merely partially present in our own lives.

Perhaps the key word to associate with the creation and stimulation of such a Christo/eschato-logical imagination, then, is 'longing'. An 'imagination' of the future which is based on Christ's death and resurrection produces longing, and through that longing, the church community both recognizes that the future is not currently realized in its completeness (with appropriate angst and groaning [e.g. Rom. 8.29]) while simultaneously experiencing the reality that through Christ's current pneumatological presence as king the future kingdom is at least partially but nevertheless genuinely present and evident in the eucharistic feast. A church can only be the church if it both anticipates the quality of life that is planned and prepared for it in the coming kingdom, and simultaneously realizes that to a great degree that quality of life and communion currently elude it. As Neuhaus comments, 'The Biblical statements about the Church ... are either false or nonsense, unless they are understood as statements of a future hope anticipated in the present.'[16]

Closely associated with the affections that this longing represents is the profound recognition that any extent to which the church does anticipate the future kingdom occurs not through human effort but through a miraculous pneumatological and eschatological invasion. The foretaste of the kingdom comes from the outside

---

14. See James K. A. Smith, *Desiring the Kingdom: Worship, Worldview, and Cultural Formation* (Grand Rapids: Baker Academic, 2009), 63–5.

15. Gordon D. Fee, *The First Epistle to the Corinthians*, ed. Ned B. Stonehouse, et al. (Grand Rapids: Eerdmans, 1987), 157.

16. Richard John Neuhaus, 'Wolfhart Pannenberg: Profile of a Theologian', in *Theology and the Kingdom of God*, ed. Richard John Neuhaus (Philadelphia: Westminster, 1969), 42.

and not from within. 'If the all-too-human church can be considered divine, it is as the institutional community that . . . anticipat[es] in its life and ministry the dawn of the new creation.'[17] It is for this reason that the pneumatologically inspired imagination engendered through participating in the eucharist is not sufficient in itself but must be partnered with genuine experience of the divine presence.

5.2.2 Presence

For at least the last five centuries, arguments about the exact manner of Christ's presence in the elements have pervaded and consumed discussions about the eucharist.[18] While these debates are not unimportant, such sustained attention to the manner of Christ's presence has to a large degree diverted the church from the more significant truths of the reality and impact of his presence. Leithart characterizes this emphasis as having a 'zoom' like effect so that our attention is focused exclusively on functional (exactly what happens with the bread and the cup) and individualistic (what is the benefit to the individual participant) understandings of the eucharist, missing the ontological and communal aspects that are even more pivotal and significant.[19] Leithart argues that the more central and pressing issue is not the manner but the 'doctrine of the real presence. . . . The eucharist shapes the church because Christ is present at the meal by his Spirit, and therefore she is . . . changed by communion with her husband. The Supper makes the church the church because the communion that takes place at the Supper makes the church like Christ.'[20]

While my own understanding regarding the exact nature of Christ's presence at the table is closest to the Reformed perspective, I maintain that the exact manner of Christ's presence does not affect to any great degree the points made in the following discussion about the pneumatological and eschatological transformation occurring in the eucharist. What is pertinent is not the specific manner but the genuine reality of Christ's presence. The foundational truth from which the eschatological and pneumatological understanding of transformation emerges is that Christ is genuinely present in the eucharistic celebration and that our celebration of the meal together intrinsically involves genuine communion with

---

17. MacDougall, *More Than Communion*, 179.

18. See, for example, Russell D. Moore et al., *Understanding Four Views on the Lord's Supper* (Grand Rapids: Zondervan, 2007). For a more detailed history of eucharistic theology, see Paul H. Jones, *Christ's Eucharistic Presence: A History of the Doctrine* (New York: Peter Lang, 1994). Also, Gary Macy, *The Banquet's Wisdom: A Short History of the Theologies of the Lord's Supper* (New York: Paulist, 1992).

19. Peter J. Leithart, 'The Way Things Really Ought to Be: Eucharist, Eschatology, and Culture', *The Westminster Theological Journal* 59, no. 2 (1997): 159. Geoffrey Wainwright makes a similar argument. See Geoffrey Wainwright, *Eucharist and Eschatology* (London: Epworth Press, 1971), 1–2.

20. Leithart, 'The Way Things Really Ought to Be', 175.

him. This is a point upon which virtually all viewpoints concur.[21] As Armstrong argues in an essay introducing a scholarly debate on the manner of Christ's presence: 'There is room for discussion about this matter, but there seems little room for disagreement about one particular fact: in some way we fellowship with Christ himself at this meal.'[22]

While Christ's eucharistic presence necessarily includes all three of his offices of prophet, priest and king, viewed from an eschatological perspective, the emphasis falls particularly on his kingly office. The Christ with whom we commune, the Christ whose wedding supper we are anticipating, this is Christ the king – the Lord of all creation. As was noted in the previous chapter, in bringing back to us from the future the presence of Christ the king, the Spirit leads and drives us on towards his coming kingdom, so that the presence of these kingdom qualities and Christ's kingly reign itself are increasingly apparent among us. In particular, the presence of Christ as king through his Spirit has ontological consequences, fundamentally affecting who we are as people. It is Christ's presence through the Spirit that writes the laws of the king on our hearts and minds. It is his Spirit living within us that moves us to follow his kingly decrees (Ezek. 36.27).

To suggest this divine transformation happens intrinsically and automatically through partaking in the eucharist is to make the mistake of ecclesial Eutychianism, however – too greatly melding and confusing human and divine action. As Leithart comments, 'the eucharist does not shape the church and its members by ceremonial manipulation, as if repetition of the rite, by putting words in our mouths and making us go through the motions of ecclesiastical unity, performs a kind of sacred brainwashing.'[23] But we similarly cannot make the mistake of ecclesial Docetism, focusing only on divine action and ignoring, neglecting or minimizing the human aspect. Divine action from the creator needs to be complemented by human action in a manner appropriate to the creature. And so the first pneumatological phenomenon (the creation and stimulation of our eschatological imagination) and the second (the eschatological presence of Christ in us through his Spirit) must be complemented and completed by a third pneumatological phenomenon (which is empowered human practice).

5.2.3 Practice

In the eucharist, we do not merely 'imagine' the coming kingdom, and we do not merely enjoy communion with the coming king, we 'practise' genuinely being part of the kingdom. Using the vocabulary of the Spiritual Disciplines movement, in the repeated performance of communal practices we are led into the righteousness of the kingdom through 'indirection'. By doing what we can do (taking the bread

---

21. The only exception would perhaps be a hyper-extreme memorialist understanding.
22. John H. Armstrong, Introduction: Do This in Remembrance of Me', in *Understanding Four Views on the Lord's Supper*, ed. Paul E. Engle (Grand Rapids: Zondervan, 2007), 23-4.
23. Leithart, 'The Way Things Really Ought to Be', 175.

and the cup together in communion), we receive from God the resources to do what we cannot do (live virtuously as true subjects of the kingdom).[24] As we 'practise' what it means to genuinely live as if the kingdom has already come, we are gradually transformed by the Spirit to become the kind of people and the kind of community who genuinely belong and fit within that coming kingdom.[25]

The kingdom is both a present and a coming reality. The eucharist is therefore a celebration where we presently practise being a part of the coming kingdom, because (in one sense) we are already a part of the coming kingdom. 'At the Supper, we eat bread and drink wine together with thanksgiving not merely to *show* the way things really ought to be, but to *practice* the way things really ought to be.'[26] It is through acting as if the future were already here and that we are genuinely a part of it (which is partly but not completely true) that transformation occurs. In short, through the Spirit, as we take the eucharist together, we increasingly become like what we (in truth, but only in part) already are: genuine citizens of the kingdom and true and loyal subjects of the king.

In characteristically forthright and helpful fashion, C. S. Lewis outlines the essence of this concept in *Mere Christianity* by describing our practices (and practise) as 'pretending'. Focusing specifically on the ecclesial practice of prayer, Lewis notes that the very first words of the Lord's prayer are 'Our Father'. He goes on to explain:

> Do you now see what those words mean? They mean quite frankly, that you are putting yourself in the place of a son of God. To put it bluntly, you are dressing up as Christ. If you like, you are pretending. Because, of course, the moment you realise what the words mean, you realise that you are not a son of God. You are not a being like The Son of God, whose will and interests are at one with those of the Father: you are a bundle of self-centred fears, hopes, greeds, jealousies, and self-conceit, all doomed to death. So that, in a way, this dressing up as Christ is

---

24. The language in this sentence adjusts Foster's words to directly address this context. See Richard Foster, 'Foreword', in *The Spirit of the Disciplines* (London: Hodder and Stoughton, 1988), 14.

25. On this topic, see particularly Sánchez's groundbreaking work on the transformative role of the Holy Spirit, based on Spirit Christology. Leopoldo A. Sánchez M., *Sculptor Spirit: Models of Sanctification from Spirit Christology* (Downers Grove: IVP Academic, 2019). The primary distinction between his work and these chapters is that his book is focused on how *persons* are formed by the Spirit into the image of Christ, while the focus here is particularly on how ecclesial *communities* are pneumatologically transformed into Christ's image. The intentionally eschatological approach also distinguishes it from Sánchez's methodology. The two approaches are complementary, of course. For a briefer summary, see Leopoldo A. Sánchez M., 'Sculpting Christ in Us: Public Faces of the Spirit in God's World', in *Third Article Theology: A Pneumatological Dogmatics*, ed. Myk Habets (Minneapolis: Fortress Press, 2016), 297–320.

26. Leithart, 'The Way Things Really Ought to Be', 175 (italics in original).

a piece of outrageous cheek. But the odd thing is that He has ordered us to do it. Why? . . . the pretence leads up to the real thing. . . . Very often the only way to get a quality in reality is to start behaving as if you had it already.[27]

While Lewis explains the essence of this concept well for an introductory book on Christianity, there is obviously more nuance needed. When it comes to being God's sons and daughters, for example, we are living in a simultaneous state of both being and becoming sons and daughters. We are 'becoming' sons and daughters of God in the sense that as we grow and develop through time, we are increasingly transformed by the Spirit to achieve greater communion with Christ, fully realizing this potential for ontological union and identification at the eschaton. We are 'becoming' sons and daughters of God in the sense that we are being prepared for that day. But simultaneously, we already 'are' sons and daughters of God as Christ has united himself to us, with the promise of fuller and greater communion to come. Just as the 'not guilty' verdict of the final judgement is enacted 'at the present time' (Rom. 3.26), our future union with Christ and adoption as true sons and daughters of the Father is (in a nuanced sense) enacted at this moment, through the *arrabōn* (deposit) of the Spirit.[28] So the pretending is not mere pretence. But neither is it the entire reality. Being and becoming exist together.

Turning to the eucharist and its relationship with the coming kingdom, the situation is similar. Through the enacted and lived out practice of participating in communion, not only are the ways in which we are currently living a kingdom reality strengthened and solidified, but the intentional and unintentional areas in which we are *not* living out the reality of the kingdom also become increasingly clear to us. And having had these areas brought to our attention by the Spirit through our eschatological practice, we then lean on the Spirit's empowering to gradually transform us as individuals and as a community to live in a way which is more consistent with the coming kingdom which is our true home.

This relationship between presence and practice can (cautiously) be compared with the relationship between the divine and human natures of Christ, conveyed particularly clearly in the anhypostatic/enhypostatic couplet. Just as there is no human nature of Christ without the indwelling Logos (anhypostasis), all 'practice' of the eucharist is non-effectual and indeed completely pointless without the pneumatological presence of Christ in the meal. A church community and the individuals within it may determinedly practise living as if they were part of the kingdom, but without the indwelling presence this will not result in any genuine transformation. (Even in this situation, though, as noted in the forthcoming discussion, the Spirit may work apart from and against the church practices, coming with conviction and judgement.) In contrast, as the Logos becoming flesh means that Jesus is a true and genuine person (enhypostasis), the presence of Christ in the eucharistic celebration means that a church's practice is genuinely effective

---

27. C. S. Lewis, *Mere Christianity* (London: HarperCollins, 2002), 187–8.
28. See the similar discussion in Liston, *The Anointed Church*, 137–8.

and transformational. Through the presence of Christ, our frail, faltering and all-too-human attempts to truly live and act as members of the coming kingdom as we 'practise' the eucharist become significant, meaningful and effective in transformation.

The analogy being used here, while helpful and important, must be applied cautiously. In Section 2.3, Hütter was critiqued for using very similar and sometimes overlapping terminology to essentially bind the Spirit to the church's practices. The significant distinction between Hütter's understanding and that being presented here, however, is that while his understanding maintained a strong continuity between the eucharist and the coming kingdom, this presentation argues for a clear discontinuity between them as well. The church anticipates the kingdom, but it is not to be identified as the kingdom.[29] This discontinuity and distinction are illustrated particularly clearly through use of the term *imagination*. We can only *imagine* the kingdom *because* we do not completely experience it. Consequently, the eucharist is not just a *practice* (a noun describing the activity churches do) but something we *practise* (a verb describing how the activity intentionally transforms and prepares us for something different that awaits us). As is explained further in Section 5.4, it is this very distinction that provides the freedom for the Spirit to work within church practices (enhypostatically), but also enables the Spirit to work outside of and, even at times, against our church practices (anhypostatically). Rather than neglecting the church's sinfulness, the understanding here is in fact predicated on it, for it is (at least in part) our sinfulness that means the church community requires transformation.

Using the eucharist as a significant and prototypical example, then, the previous discussion has argued that the Spirit transforms the church through the interplay of imagination, experienced presence and empowered practice. Regarding the first aspect, the Spirit's work in our imaginations is primarily noetic, although this does not mean it is limited to a merely cognitive change. During the eucharist the Spirit fills our hearts and minds with a vision of the coming kingdom, a vision which promotes in us longing and wonder. And it is (in part) through this imaginative renewing of our minds that the Spirit transforms us. Regarding the second aspect, the Spirit's mediation of the presence of Christ to us is primarily ontic, although this does not mean that any change effected in us is magical, involuntary or automatic, intrinsically separated from our own creaturely actions. During the eucharist, we genuinely commune with Christ who is present to us through the Spirit. This presence is the divine empowering of the transformation we experience, as the Spirit writes the laws of the coming kingdom on our hearts and moves us to follow Christ's kingly decrees. 'This is the age . . . when by the power of the Holy Spirit, who inhabits the Church . . . all who believe in Jesus Christ may taste the powers of the age to come through sacramental incorporation into the new creation.'[30]

---

29. For example, compare this understanding with Hütter's rejection of anticipatory language in Hütter, *Suffering Divine Things*, 121–4.

30. Torrance, 'Eschatology and the Eucharist', 308–9.

Regarding the final aspect, the Spirit's work in our 'practices' is primarily telic, although that does not mean that it is only through our actions that transformation occurs. Practise, alone, does not make perfect. All three aspects – imagination, presence and practice – are interrelated and intertwined. During the eucharist we are 'practising' for the future kingdom we will inhabit while simultaneously recognizing that the future is (at least in part) already experienced as a present reality. While human 'practice' alone is completely ineffectual at implementing genuine transformation, the presence of Christ through his Spirit in the eucharist bestows our finite human actions with genuine transformational efficacy.

5.3 A concrete account of eucharistic transformation

One of the common critiques of eschatologically determined ecclesiologies is that while they defend the idea that the future is already present to some degree, they 'remain stuck in generalities, if not obfuscations'.[31] Finishing the discussion of eucharistic transformation at this point would be to make precisely this kind of error. Consequently, in order to avoid this critique, and to outline the practical and concrete implications of developing a pneumatologically inspired eschatological ecclesiology, this section intentionally explores how through the eucharist the kingly reign of Christ is pneumatologically present in and transforms the church. In what concrete ways are we being transformed? What are the tangible qualities of the coming kingdom that are most clearly and evidently imagined, experienced and practised in the eucharist? While there are many, the most obvious and significant are precisely those qualities noted in the previous chapter: love, life, truth and justice. The following four subsections therefore outline how through the empowering of the Spirit in the eucharist we imagine, experience and practise those qualities into an increasing and genuine existence within our communities.

5.3.1 Love and unity

At its most basic, the eucharist is simply a meal we share together. We join as one to eat and drink, remembering, anticipating and celebrating the things that unite us. Consequently, when we take the eucharist, we imagine, experience and practise what it means to live as the loving community that we will one day truly become. Through the interplay of all three of these aspects, the Spirit gradually transforms our community into an increasingly united fellowship.

In terms of imagination, the Bible often describes the coming kingdom through the descriptive language of feasting. Obviously, this image is central in Revelation, which compellingly describes the wedding supper of the lamb (Rev. 19.9), but there are many other allusions. John the Baptist distinguished his ministry from Jesus' ministry by referring to Jesus as the bridegroom (Jn 3.29). Jesus himself

---

31. van der Kooi, *This Incredibly Benevolent Force*, 16.

described the kingdom as being like a king inviting reluctant guests to a feast (Mt. 22.1-14). He talked of the journey many would take to eat at Abraham, Isaac and Jacob's table in the kingdom to a believing Roman officer (Mt. 8.5-13). He even explicitly told the disciples that they would eat and drink at his table in the kingdom (Lk. 22.29-30). The distinctive significance of this feasting imagery is that while you can eat alone, feasting is intrinsically social. Moreover, feasts are times of celebration, characterized by abundance, joy and most significantly here, love and unity. When we picture our future, our imagination is not of isolated, individualistic and incorporeal bliss. Rather, our minds should be filled with visions of cheerful noise, merriment and crowded bodily togetherness.

The Spirit transforms us towards this imagined future of love and unity through presence and practice. As Paul expresses it, 'And though we are many, we eat from one loaf, showing that we are one body' (1 Cor. 10.17 NLT). No doubt this is why Paul finds it almost inconceivable and thoroughly reprehensible that people should partake of the Lord's supper while being at odds with others in the church community. While his clear disappointment with the Corinthian church noted in 1 Corinthians 11 appears to be partially and perhaps even primarily because of the social injustice occurring (a topic addressed in Section 5.3.4), there is an equally pressing issue of 'divisions' that he similarly abhors. This lack of love and unity can be seen in both Paul's introduction ('First, I hear there are divisions among you when you meet as a church' (1 Cor. 11.18 NLT)) and his capstone remark ('For if you eat the bread or drink the cup without honouring the body of Christ, you are eating and drinking God's judgment upon yourself' (1 Cor. 11.29 NLT)).[32] Paul's remedy is that the Corinthian church should 'examine' themselves (1 Cor. 11.31). The clear implication is that if there are divisions or disunity among the community, then partakers of the bread and the cup should do all they can to right these divisions and restore relationship before taking the eucharist together. There are clear echoes here of Jesus' words in Mt. 5.23-24 about postponing temple offerings until reconciliation with fellow believers has been attempted.

What is being exemplified in Paul's comments about the eucharist provides a clear illustration of the transformational aspects of the church's actions. The Lord's supper is an anticipation of that future feast where there will be no divisions and love will be abundant. It is as we come together in love and unity around the eucharistic table that the genuine pneumatologically enabled joy that such unity engenders is most clearly recognized and experienced. But similarly, it is as we practise coming together, in anticipation of that future feast, that any existing divisions and recriminations among us are most clearly illuminated.[33] The Spirit

---

32. While there is debate on Paul's reference to the 'body of Christ' in this verse, and while the meaning is clearly multivalent, it certainly doesn't mean less than the fellowship of the community, which Paul goes on to immediately reference and describe further in 1 Corinthians 12.

33. One cannot help but be reminded of some Christmas gatherings where relational cracks within families become all too obviously evident.

thus works both within the practices of the church (enhypostatically) and over and against them (anhypostatically). When divisions do become apparent, we need to do all we can to repair and reconstruct deep community, so that our partaking in the eucharist models as much as is possible within the present time the coming kingdom feast we are proleptically anticipating. For such genuine transformation to occur, however, both the continuity and discontinuity between the eucharistic and eschatological feasts need to be adequately recognized. If the continuity is overemphasized, what need is there for transformation? If the discontinuity is overemphasized, what possibility is there of it?

But how can our human efforts to heal division and display love be transformative when so often deep rifts and significantly uncharitable behaviour remain? Here we must point to and continue to believe in the transformative power of Christ the king who is present through his Spirit in the elements of the eucharist. The Spirit is intrinsically relational. As was noted in the Trinitarian analysis of Third Article Ecclesiology:

> An 'individualized' Spirit is as inconceivable as a stationary photon. In the immanent Trinity, the Spirit is never merely the Father's Spirit or the Son's Spirit, but is rather the Spirit by which the Father persons the Son, and by which the Son persons the Father. . . . In ecclesial contexts, as in the Trinity, it is only as believers are giving and being given the Spirit – personing others and being personed by others through offering and returning the love of Christ by the Spirit – that believers have the Spirit. . . . The Spirit indwells the relationship, and is not localized as an individual's possession.[34]

Practice in and of itself is not sufficient to effect transformation. But just as the Spirit's actions within our eucharistic practice can alert us to the existence of division, Christ's presence through his relational Spirit can transform our meagre human efforts into something effectual. Clearly rational explanation is not sufficient at this point, and we are bridging into an unattainable aspect of mystery. Yet in faith we can and must affirm that through the Spirit, as we practise the presence of Christ in the eucharist, we can gradually become what we truly are, one body, joined together in him (1 Cor. 12.12-13).

This concrete discussion of love and unity clearly highlights a gaping weakness in ecclesial practice, however. The typical mechanics of celebrating the eucharist in many churches are more effectively designed to hide any potential disunity rather than to reveal it and so to enable reconciliation within the community. Distributing 'chewing gum-sized pellets of bread and thimble-sized shot glasses of juice'[35] portrays Christianity as merely a private affair involving God and the individual participant. If, as has been noted, practising the practice is an intrinsic

---

34. Liston, *The Anointed Church*, 31-12.
35. Moore et al., *Understanding Four Views on the Lord's Supper*, 41-2.

part of pneumatological transformation, perhaps our eucharistic celebration should more deliberately mimic the communal wedding supper it is anticipating.

5.3.2 Abundant life and joy

Given that our eucharistic celebrations intentionally anticipate the coming wedding breakfast between Christ and his church, perhaps they should also become more intentionally joyful. As noted in the previous chapter, the most insistently repeated characteristic in the depiction of the coming kingdom in the final chapters of Revelation is abundant life. But the life of the coming kingdom is not merely infinitely elongated biological existence (*bios*) but deepened quality of life (*zoë*) – life truly lived and lived abundantly and joyfully to the fullest.[36] This abundant and joyful life is evident not just in that the eucharist is a feast but in that it is a feast where we consume bread and wine. Jesus is the bread of life (Jn 6.35), and in the discourse in Jn 6.22-58, Jesus makes unambiguously clear the connection between the eucharistic consuming of his flesh and blood and the receiving of abundant life. In the eucharist, then, the reality that Jesus is our truest and greatest source of life and joy is imagined, experienced and practised.

Consider, first, how our imagination is created and stimulated through the eucharist. The specific actions we go through while partaking of the Lord's supper clearly illustrate the reality that Jesus is our one source of true and abundant life. When we eat from the loaf, for example, there are three stages. First, we destroy the food, both through intentionally breaking the bread and more thoroughly in masticating it. Second, the bread becomes a part of us. The atoms that made up the bread become intertwined and interspersed with the atoms that make up our bodies. Finally, through this destruction and ingestion, physical energy, vitality and movement are released. This progression is a symbolic representation of precisely what occurs in believers' lives spiritually. The first stage is our recognition of Jesus' destruction and our own culpability in that. Second, and precisely because of his suffering and our recognition of and participation in that, Jesus becomes intrinsically integrated within our lives. We are united together with Christ, with us becoming a part of him and Jesus becoming a part of us. Finally, the end result of these two events (Jesus' destruction and our union with him) is the release in both our communities and our individual lives a wellspring of pneumatologically enabled energy and vitality.

But in eating the bread, it is not simply our imagination that is stimulated and transformed. The point here is not merely that during the Lord's supper we thoughtfully dwell on the reality of Christ being our genuine source of abundant

---

36. While many authors make the distinction between the Greek terms *bios* and *zoë*, the terminology is particularly idiosyncratic to C. S. Lewis. See Lewis, *Mere Christianity*, 159, 77, 89. It is also important to note that in Jesus' discourse on the bread of life in John 6 (referred to in detail in this section), the term *life* which is repeatedly used is a translation of *zoë* and not *bios*.

life (although such cognitive reflection is clearly one important aspect) but even more so that we enact this truth. In communion, we 'practise' living as if Christ is our one true life source as we take the bread together. Leithart explains this well: 'Though the eucharist does not bypass the mind and conscious reflection, the effect it has is more in the realm of acquiring a skill than in the realm of learning a new set of facts; the effect is more a matter of "training" than "teaching".'[37] That in the eucharist we 'practise' finding abundant life and joy in Christ is perhaps even more obviously evident in the cup. Wine is a drink of celebration and not merely of nutrition. Moreover, wine is drunk at the end of the day and not at the beginning; when work is complete, not when there is more still to be done. Such allusions point to the reality that drinking the cup is an intrinsically eschatological action. Indeed, the fermentation of grape juice over time is a helpful symbol for the transformation and maturation of the church as it readies itself for the coming kingdom. But, again, the point here is not just imaginative or noetic. Wine does not just merely cognitively point us to the coming kingdom; it physically creates in humans an experience somewhat akin to that of the coming kingdom. Calvin alludes to this reality in question 341 of the Geneva Catechism: '341. But why does the Lord represent His body by the bread and His blood by the wine? C. . . . as wine strengthens, refreshes, and rejoices a man physically, so his blood is our joy, our refreshing, and our spiritual strength.'[38] Meyers writes similarly, 'We are not merely supposed to think about rest and relaxation at the Lord's Table, we must in some measure *experience* it. . . . The wine we drink goes down like fire-water and produces the feeling of "shalom" (peace) in our guts, which then leads the mind to give thanks and rejoice in God's gift of salvation.'[39]

Even further, though, the purpose of eating bread or drinking wine in our celebration of the Lord's supper is not merely that we imagine a joy-filled life, or that we practise it, but that we are transformed through the genuine experience of it. Through the eucharist we are to become a more joyful people. The fact that at the centre of our lived experience as the church is a practice that is intrinsically and intentionally joyful should forever put to rest any notion that Christianity is a primarily sober pursuit. 'A church that celebrates a feast of wine is being formed into a joyful community that contests the equation of Christian seriousness with prudishness.'[40] Jesus is our greatest joy, and we do not merely imagine or practise this reality at the eucharist; we experience it. The life and joy given to us in the eucharist is not merely metaphorical or aspirational. It is not simply practice or imagination; it is a lived experience, for Christ the king is genuinely present. What we are enjoying during the eucharist, therefore, is living in the reality that Jesus is our truest source of life. Once again, there is continuity and discontinuity here. Objectively, Jesus actually is our most fundamental source of life, in terms

---

37. Leithart, 'The Way Things Really Ought to Be', 175.
38. Torrance, ed., *The School of Faith*, 60.
39. Jeffrey J. Meyers, 'Concerning Wine and Beer', *Rite Reasons* 48–9 (1997): n.p.
40. Leithart, 'The Way Things Really Ought to Be', 176.

of both quantity and quality. But at this point in our ecclesial journey, we do not always subjectively appreciate that reality or live in the light of it. In the eucharist, though, we intentionally imagine, practise and (to some degree at least) experience *subjectively* living as if Jesus truly is our greatest source of life and joy. Through the interplay of these three aspects, we are transformed by the Spirit to increasingly recognize that Jesus is our true source of life.

Just as a concrete discussion of love and unity suggests our eucharistic feasts could be more communal and less individualistic, so a concrete discussion of eternal life offered to us in the bread and cup suggests that our *celebration* of communion could be more joyful. Certainly, the Lord's supper should have an air of solemnity to it. A wedding is a serious thing and 'is not by any to be enterprised . . . unadvisedly, lightly, or wantonly . . .; but reverently, discreetly, advisedly, soberly, and in the fear of God'.[41] But similarly, it would be a sad and sorry reflection on the coming marriage if a wedding was entirely and only solemn! Are not all our most meaningful occasions (births, marriages, etc.) moments when genuine solemnity and deep joy merge together? As the most profound of such occasions, our celebration of eucharist should similarly combine solemnity and joy.

5.3.3 Truth and holiness

If the eucharistic meal were merely a feast where bread and wine are consumed, it would not in any significant way be distinguished from other worldly celebrations and gatherings. What distinguishes the eucharist most clearly from these other feasts is that the bread and wine clearly and unequivocally present Christ as the foundational point around which all other reality revolves. To put it simply, the eucharist conveys truth to us. But the truth conveyed is more than mere content. The truth of the eucharist is the person of Christ himself. Christ is Truth. Consequently, eucharistic truth is fundamentally identical with the truth conveyed in God's word. As Reformed theologian Bavinck puts it: 'They only differ in the external form, in the *manner* in which they offer the *same* Christ to us.'[42] Calvin goes even further by arguing (remarkably!) that the eucharist conveys this truth more ably and better than the word: 'But sacrament bring with them the clearest promises, and, when compared with the word, have this peculiarity, that they represent promises to the life, as if painted in a picture. . . . [the eucharist] testifies his love and kindness to us more expressly than by word.'[43] The eucharist is, in Tim Chester's beautiful phrase, 'truth we can touch'.[44]

---

41. *The Book of Common Prayer* (Glasgow: Collins, 1925), 256.
42. Herman Bavinck, *Reformed Dogmatics, vol. 4, Holy Spirit, Church, and New Creation*, ed. John Bolt, trans. John Vriend (Grand Rapids: Baker, 2008), 479.
43. John Calvin, *Institutes of the Christian Religion*, trans. Henry Beveridge (Peabody: Hendrickson, 2008), 4.14.5–6.
44. Tim Chester, *Truth We Can Touch: How Baptism and Communion Shape Our Lives* (Wheaton: Crossway, 2020), 35.

What, then, is the specific *eschatological* truth of Christ conveyed in and through the eucharist? As has been noted, the past aspect of the eucharist points us to the prophetic ministry of Christ – the reality of our pneumatological participation in Christ's death and resurrection. The present aspect of the eucharist points us to the priestly ministry of Christ – our pneumatological participation in Christ's filial relationship with his Father. And the future or eschatological truth of Christ conveyed through the eucharist is his kingly ministry. Christ is king! Through taking the bread and the cup we pneumatologically celebrate the reality that even as exiled strangers living in a foreign land (Phil. 3.20, 1 Pet. 2.11-12), we are truly subjects of Christ the king, and he is actually the one on the throne. When we take the bread and the wine together, we imagine, experience and practise living out the truth that Jesus truly is our king.

For the first-century Christians who were oppressed and overwhelmed by the cultural, political and economic agenda of their Roman oppressors, the writer of the book of Revelation painted an alternative picture. Caesar is not in charge, for the lamb that was slain has risen again and has been given all authority (Revelation 4–5). Babylon (or Rome) is not the ultimate centre of power. That city is destined for destruction and those who belong to Christ must come out from her and not live according to her demands anymore (Revelation 17–19). It is precisely this alternative, more accurate and more compelling vision of reality that is created and stimulated in our imaginations as we celebrate the eucharist together. The central insight is the reality of resurrection. When we eat and drink, we are simultaneously reminded of both Jesus' death and his genuine presence with us. Such a tangible recognition of Jesus' past and our future resurrection reminds us that death is not the end and reality exists far beyond this world that we can see and this time that we currently experience. Through the eucharist, we view this world and this time through the spectacles of the resurrection, with Christ as progenitor, foretaste and the true and coming king. The clarion call of the eucharist therefore is to stop living according to the rules and regulations of a flawed and failing world order, where death is viewed as final, and to anticipate in our community life the characteristics of a kingdom which extends well beyond such a limited vision.[45]

Resurrection, though, is not merely a past reality for Christ and not merely a future reality for us. As was noted in Section 3.2, because we participate in Christ's life and he participates in ours, our existence is constantly one not only of a past and single birth, or a future death and resurrection, but of all three repeatedly and simultaneously. As Karl Barth (quoting Nietzsche!) famously quipped, 'Only where graves are, is there resurrection.'[46] Because the entirety of Christ's reality in new time is brought to bear on us at the current moment in which we exist in

---

45. Although not directly related to the eucharist, Paul's urgent call to the Corinthian church to not be fooled by the world's apparent wisdom in 1 Corinthians 1–2 provides an excellent example of this clarion call.

46. Karl Barth, *The Epistle to the Romans*, trans. Edwyn C. Hoskyns (London: Oxford University Press, 1933), 416.

new time, we have a fundamentally new way of being where the old rules of before and after do not simplistically apply any more. We are living, moment by moment and day by day, a communal experience of life in death, of joy in suffering, of self-giving love. But as we live in this reality, through the Spirit we are transformed into the image of Christ for whom this cruciform, self-giving way of being is simply the way he was and is. Particularly at the eucharist, this fractal reality of life, death and rebirth is not just cognitively imagined but spiritually experienced front and centre through the tangible presence of Christ in the bread and the cup.

Once again, however, there is continuity and discontinuity to recognize – both being and becoming need to be simultaneously acknowledged. We are true subjects of the king, and death neither is nor will it ever be the final word in our stories, but in many aspects of our current existence we simply do not live this way. Our actions are motivated by the desires of this world and not those of the coming kingdom we are looking forward to. During our celebration of the eucharist, however, as we 'practise' our future participation in the wedding supper of the lamb, the Spirit reveals to us the truth of those areas which are not yet submitted to Christ's kingship. Our practice is not mere pretence, because we are truly part of the kingdom. But in the practising, omissions are revealed that the Spirit can begin to transform.

The fundamental feature of the eucharistic eschatology, and indeed of an eschatological Third Article Ecclesiology overall, therefore, is a call to holiness. As citizens of heaven, we *are* separate from the world and so we need to *intentionally* distinguish ourselves from the world. God has set us apart as a holy people. Through the resurrection life of Christ in us, we are empowered and transformed to live lives that declare the goodness of the one who has formed us into his own community, a people who live in light and not in darkness, a people who truly belong to God (1 Pet 2:9).

5.3.4 Justice and equality

As a set apart, distinctive and holy people, one of the chief ways in which we both are and will be distinguished from the world is that our church communities both are and are becoming places of justice and freedom. In a world that lacks and longs for socio-economic, gender, ethnic and racial equity, the church community should display precisely these features, for within Christian community there is no longer Jew nor Greek, slave nor free, male or female, all are one in Christ (Gal. 3.28). Moreover, we look forward and anticipate a time when people from every nation and tribe and people and language will stand before the throne of God shouting their praise in a great and united roar (Rev. 7.9-10).

It is this imaginative vision of social equality, justice and freedom that fills our hearts and minds as we gather together. And it is precisely this vision that should be practised and particularly evident at the Lord's table. The lack of such equity appears to be the primary cause of Paul's significant angst with the Corinthian church and its celebration of the eucharist. 'For some of you hurry to eat your own meal without sharing with others. As a result, some go hungry while others get drunk' (1 Cor. 11.21 NLT). Acting in such a way during the Lord's supper disgraces God's church and shames the poor (1 Cor. 11.22). According to Paul, the remedy is simple: 'wait for each other' and if you are really hungry, eat at home before you come. For to practise genuinely being part of the kingdom without demonstrating the equity and justice that is one of the kingdom's fundamental features brings judgement (1 Cor. 11.33-34).

The central phrase in Paul's passionate remonstration with the Corinthian church for its evident injustice is verse 26: 'For every time you eat this bread and drink this cup, you are announcing the Lord's death until he comes again.' This 'announcement' can be characterized as referring specifically to the eating and drinking of the bread and the cup. Understood this way, the communion feast is a re-enacted passion play. While such an explanation is perhaps partially true, it is at least equally true that the proclamation is not the eating and drinking in itself but the reality that we eat and drink *together*. In this complementary interpretation, the problem with the Corinthian church and its enactment of the eucharist was that because they were not eating together, they were not announcing the Lord's death. Their performance of the eucharist was therefore a perversion of what it was intended to be. As Leithart puts it:

> The difference between the Lord's Supper and its perversion does not consist in any difference in the ritual actions, the elements used, or the words spoken, but rather lies in the way people behave toward one another. The Lord's death is proclaimed only when the church celebrates rightly, that is, when Christian peace, love and unity are manifested in the meal, and when their conduct at the meal fits the way the community lives together.[47]

This dual interpretation of how the Lord's death is proclaimed is strengthened through Paul's phrase in verse 29, accusing the Corinthians of not honouring *the body*, a description that can simultaneously refer to Christ's physically broken body but equally and perhaps more profoundly to the church community. Paul's response to this flagrant violation of the sacrament was to recommend that the Corinthian church examine themselves (1 Cor. 11.28), so as not to eat and drink judgement upon themselves (1 Cor. 11.30).

So, again in this final aspect of justice and equality there are three intertwining aspects of imagination, experience and practice coming together to enable transformation. In terms of imagination, our minds and hearts are (more than noetically) filled with the vision of a united and egalitarian community. In terms of presence, our ontological existence is changed through Christ's presence where existing gradations and divisions based on gender, race or socio-economic position are intrinsically nullified. And during the eucharist we practise for that future. That practice has two aspects. Positively, as we experience a foretaste of genuine equality, we long more and more for that day. This was referred to

---

47. Leithart, 'The Way Things Really Ought to Be', 173.

above as enhypostatic transformation. Negatively, it isolates for us (as it did for the Corinthians) areas where we are not living as Christ's true community and therefore we are not proclaiming Christ's death as fully and completely as we can and should. This was referred to as anhypostatic transformation. The Spirit is at work in both, and the result is genuine, teleological transformation through time.

There is no suggestion here that love and unity, abundant life and joy, truth and holiness, and justice and equality are the only kingdom aspects towards which our lives are transformed through the eucharist. But as illustrative examples, they demonstrate quite clearly how the Spirit transforms us through the interplay of imagination, experienced presence and empowered practice as we go about participating in regular aspects of church worship. And what we are increasingly transformed into is a holy community. Here, holiness must be understood in dual dimensions. It refers to the fact both that the church is set apart from the world and that the church is a place of growing purity. 'By the Spirit, believers are set apart for (and from) the future, journeying towards the eschaton and uniquely on earth carrying the foretaste of it within them.'[48] Of course it is not only through the eucharist that the Spirit transforms the church. Before turning to an analysis of these other church practices in Chapter 6, however, the following section compares the explanation of pneumatological transformation within the eucharist outlined earlier with the understandings of Barth and Hütter.

5.4 Hütter and Barth on the eucharist

This section explores Hütter and Barth's accounts of the eucharist and argues that for all of their great insights, they do not provide an adequate description and understanding of ecclesial transformation. In Barth's explanation of the eucharist, ecclesial transformation is virtually unachievable; in Hütter's work, it is almost unnecessary. Both understandings can be contrasted with the account of pneumatological transformation outlined earlier, which through recognizing both the eschatological and teleological tensions involved has developed a balanced and concrete understanding of the ecclesial change and growth that occurs within the eucharist.

As noted in Section 2.3, Hütter's understanding is that the church grows and develops through time because the Spirit exists in and works through the church's core practices. Unsurprisingly, for Hütter, the eucharist is a pre-eminent example of such ecclesial practice. It is through the eucharist (together with other activities) that the church both receives her identity and actively experiences the coming kingdom. Regarding the church's identity, Hütter argues that the Spirit's actions (or *poiesis*) determine the church's passively received

---

48. Liston, *The Anointed Church*, 361–2.

identity (*pathos*) as the church performs the eucharist, among other practices. It is through the Spirit that the church is 'hypostatized' to become Christ's body. Regarding the church's relationship with its promised future, Hütter maintains that the church does not just anticipate the kingdom when celebrating the eucharist but actually is the kingdom. He writes that the Lord's supper is 'not the "anticipation" of something yet to come, but the pneumatic manifestation of the eschaton'.[49]

For Hütter, then, there is limited 'imagination' created or developed in the church's practice of the eucharist, because in it the future kingdom is already here. Hütter strongly emphasizes the already over and against the not yet, so the church does not anticipate the coming kingdom but enjoys and experiences it in the eucharist here and now.[50] Positively quoting Zizioulas, he writes: 'By bringing the eschaton into history, the Spirit enables the church through its sacramental structures to lend presence to the eschaton in history, and at the same time to point beyond history'.[51] The challenge with such an understanding is that if the future is already substantially and significantly present, then any 'longing' for the future is minimized. As MacDougall writes, a 'lack of focus on futurity tends to foster imaginative complacence with the status quo, since the salvific purposes of God are thought to have been largely realized'.[52] The church does not look forward to the coming kingdom with hope, for the future is already here. Moreover, Hütter's approach displaces and sidelines the church's missional participation in Christ's redemption of the world.[53] The eucharist, for Hütter, essentially removes the church from the world, rather than moulding it from within the basis of its current location. The desire and need for the transformation of the church, and the desire and need for the church to be transforming the world are both significantly curtailed.[54]

The reverse is equally true. If Hütter's overemphasis on the teleological tension and the coming kingdom's presence within the eucharist leads to a stunted imagination, so too does Barth's excessive focus on the eschatological tension. In the former, transformation is almost unnecessary; in the latter, it is virtually unachievable. As noted in Section 2.2, Barth sees Christ as time and eternity's mediator. The Son anticipates, recapitulates and then fulfils time, enabling eternity to exist within time and time to exist within eternity. Christ is contemporaneous with all times and history, and even more than that, he is actually present at this

---

49. Hütter, *Suffering Divine Things*, 120.
50. See particularly the discussion in Hütter, *Suffering Divine Things*, 121–4.
51. Hütter, *Suffering Divine Things*, 120. Quoting from John Zizioulas, 'Die pneumatologische Diemension der Kirche', *IKZ Communio* 2 (1973): 145.
52. MacDougall, *More Than Communion*, 44.
53. This missional role will be discussed in Chapter 9.
54. For a more detailed explanation and critique of an overly realized eschatology, and its implications for imagination, see particularly MacDougall, *More Than Communion*, 13–61.

moment in fallen time by his Spirit. He cannot be absent, or his presence would require being mediated by the sacraments, and ecclesial role would go beyond witness. This means that for Barth, the sacraments do not and cannot represent a particular point of union between divine action and human response. Indeed, according to Helmich, in Barth's later work, he forges a 'much stronger distinction between God's action than what we see [even] in his earlier theology'.[55] As Barth writes in *The Christian Faith*,

> Baptism and the Lord's Supper are not events, institutions, mediations, or revelations of salvation. They are not representations and actualizations, emanations, repetitions, or extensions, nor indeed guarantees and seals of the work and word of God, nor are they instruments, vehicles, channels or means of God's reconciling grace. They are *not* what they have been called since the second century, namely, mysteries or sacraments.[56]

Turning specifically to the question of the eucharist, the literature on Barth's understanding of the Lord's supper is 'predictably voluminous'[57] even though Barth never completed the promised treatment on the Lord's supper in *CDIV.4* as he did with baptism. Nevertheless, Barth's invitation to deduce from his comments on baptism how the unwritten section on communion would have been played out suggests a significant overlap between the two. The modest aim of this discussion is simply to show that in line with previous claims on Barth's work, his analysis of the eucharistic 'sacrament' does not provide a nuanced understanding of how this church practice leads to ecclesial transformation.

The interaction between presence and practice in Barth's eucharistic understanding, and its implications for ecclesial transformation, will be explored subsequently. At this point it is merely necessary to recognize the more simple and indeed rather obvious point that in terms of imagination, the significant discontinuity between our present existence and the coming kingdom in Barth's understanding has strong implications for his analysis of the eucharist. For Barth, the eucharist is 'a thanksgiving which ... looks forward to the future'[58] merely in symbolic or 'neo-Zwinglian'[59] terms and is not one in which the future is already present to us, even in a partial or incomplete way. Christ is present but the future is not. This is because for him the emphasis is on the eschatological and not the teleological tension. The eucharist, as such, does not even anticipate the coming kingdom, but rather it simply noetically (and prophetically)[60] reminds us of and

---

55. Bo Helmich, *Karl Barth and the Beauty of God* (Duke University, 2017) 176.
56. Karl Barth, *The Christian Life: Church Dogmatics IV,4 Lecture Fragments*, trans. Geoffrey W. Bromiley (London: Eerdmans, 1981), 46.
57. Helmich, *Karl Barth and the Beauty of God*, 145, n. 3.
58. Barth, *Church Dogmatics*, IV.4 ix.
59. Ibid., IV.4 127.
60. Recall the discussion in Section 4.4.

witnesses to what Christ has objectively achieved for us in eternity. Given such a perspective, it is not surprising that the eucharist does not engender longing. Indeed, any subjective response is more or less irrelevant, overwhelmed as it is by the objective reality of Christ's completed work. The church's role in present time is simply to bear witness to Christ. Subjective transformation is entirely secondary and completely subsumed beneath the objective reality to which we witness. Given such a perspective, it is not hard to see why even sympathetic observers of Barth recognize that he could have made more room for 'gradual or cumulative regeneration within the spiritual life of the believer . . . it seems undeniable that in Barth's soteriology this aspect is underdeveloped and excessively diminished'.[61]

It is not merely in terms of imagination that Barth and Hütter's understanding of the eucharist leads to limited notions of pneumatological transformation but also in terms of experienced presence and empowered practice. Both Barth and Hütter strongly emphasize the reality of the experienced presence of Christ in the eucharist as well as the importance of empowered practice. However, by excessively separating or excessively merging presence and practice respectively, both understandings lead to the same end result: a minimalized account of ecclesial transformation.

Hütter excessively merges experienced presence and practice within the eucharist. As noted earlier,[62] he uses the Christological language of *enhypostasis* to describe the relationship between the Spirit's activity and the church's practices. To be fair, Hütter maintains that his proposals recognize a distinction between these two aspects; however, this distinction is sustained only through an entirely asymmetrical relationship between the Spirit's action and the church's identity. The Spirit is always giver; the church is always receiver. So when the church practises the eucharist, the Spirit works in and through those practices so that the church (pathically) receives its identity and is transformed towards its coming *telos*.[63] What is missing from this account is, first, any understanding that the physical actions of church practices could occur without the empowering presence of the Spirit and, second, any recognition that the Spirit could work against or in spite of the church and its practices.[64] While the analogy Hütter utilizes between Christ's divine and human nature on the one hand, and divine and human interactions in church practices on the other, is useful to a degree, it must always be paired with the equally important recognition of the 'fundamental disanalogy'[65] between the

---

61. George Hunsinger, 'The Mediator of Communion: Karl Barth's Doctrine of the Holy Spirit', in *Disruptive Grace: Studies in the Theology of Karl Barth* (Grand Rapids: Eerdmans, 2000), 167-8.
62. See Section 2.3.
63. Hütter, *Suffering Divine Things*, 144.
64. See the more expansive discussion on this point in Mawson, 'The Spirit and the Community', 461-2.
65. McFarland, 'The Body of Christ', 245.

life of Christ and the life of the church. Christ and his life always were, are and will be enhypostatic. The church and its practices *can* be enhypostatic with the work of the Spirit, but at times they are decidedly anhypostatic.[66]

The analysis of this chapter has claimed that the Spirit works in or on the church in both of these situations, and both the church's enhypostatic and anhypostatic practices (or a combination of both) can lead to transformation. For example, when through the power of the Spirit, the church comes together in unity to celebrate the eucharist, it receives a foretaste of the wedding supper of the lamb. Longing for that future day to become more completely a part of our present reality grows and develops within our community as a result of such an enhypostatic and positive experience and practice. However, when the church's practice of the eucharist is (even to a degree) divided or unjust (such as occurred in the Corinthian church) then the Spirit also works among us but not as foretaste but as judge and bringer of conviction. Such negative pneumatological activity also leads to transformation, but it certainly cannot be characterized as enhypostatic. The Spirit works not only in the church's practices but over and against them, convicting the community of their sinfulness. Hütter's account does well at describing the positive and enhypostatic action of the Spirit. Whether it can equally explain the negative and anhypostatic action is questionable.

Barth's analysis of presence and practice is virtually the opposite of Hütter's understanding. Where Hütter essentially confuses and merges presence and practice, Barth excessively separates them. Christ is present. And the eucharist is important. Both are rightly valued and recognized. But in Barth's understanding, there is little correlation or coordination between the presence and the practice. As Bender explains,

> Especially in the final volumes of *Church Dogmatics*, Barth often speaks of a parallelism of action, rather than an embodied action, so that divine and human activity are portrayed as in conjunction, rather than in terms of the divine acting in and through the human, Christ acting in and through the church. The point might be illustrated by asking whether Christ comes to us *through* the proclamation of the church or *alongside* of it.[67]

Using Chalcedonian terminology, the emphasis is on the presence and the practice being unconfused and unmerged, not on them being unseparated. Thus, if Hütter makes the mistake of sacramental Eutychianism, Barth makes

---

66. An excellent example of this is 1 Corinthians 11, where the Corinthian church was critiqued because of the inadequate way it was enacting the Lord's supper, which was denying rather than affirming the reality of Christ and the kingdom among them.

67. Bender, *Karl Barth's Christological Ecclesiology*, 280–1. Note that Bender here is talking generally of Barth's ecclesiology and not specifically about Barth's understanding of the eucharist.

the opposite error of sacramental Nestorianism. For Barth, the eucharist is not Christ's gift to the church or the means by which Christ comes to the church, but rather the response of human beings to Christ's eternal presence and completed work.

In making such a distinction between the presence of Christ and the practice of the eucharist, Barth is no doubt reacting to what he terms the perils of religion, where practice overtakes and overwhelms presence. Barth's concern is that in the sacraments particularly, the church's attention is taken away from Christ as the ultimate and only mediator between God and humanity, and equally from the church's only role as witness to this.[68] As he polemically (and rightly) proclaims: the gospel 'does not say "Go and celebrate services!" . . . "Go and celebrate the Sacraments!"'[69] When the sacraments (or other church practices) trend towards becoming an end in themselves (as Hütter's position, among others, no doubt heads towards with his close identification of kingdom and eucharist) then Barth is quite justified in his forceful and negative reaction.

It is questionable, though, whether in contemporary Protestant churches at least, the practice of taking the Lord's supper is in danger of being excessively confused with Christ's presence and the transformation that it brings. Perhaps Barth's concern could be more justifiably aimed at other aspects of church practice, where the quality of the music, lighting and other aesthetic attributes leading to emotive moments are seen as necessary and human-controlled factors for the Spirit to truly work. Adopting Barth's neo-Zwinglian position certainly rids the church of the possibility of confusing any aspect of church practice with God's presence. Worship, whether in more traditional formats or more modern, is never an end in itself. Form cannot be confused or equated with content. We do not worship the practice of worship.

The question is whether Barth's reaction swings too far in the other direction. Thomas Torrance, for example, argues against an excessive separation between form and content. He writes,

> In the ordinance of Christ, through His command and promise, the outward sign and the inward reality belong together as form and content of the sacramental Communion, although the form is not the content, and the participation of the outward sign is not the Communion, nevertheless it is the form in which the content is communicated to us, so that apart from the specific form commanded and to which the promise has been attached we cannot conceive or receive the

---

68. For a more detailed examination of this point, see Trevor Hart, 'Calvin and Barth on the Lord's Supper', in *Calvin, Barth, and Reformed Theology*, ed. Neil B. MacDonald and Carl Trueman (Milton Keynes: Paternoster Theological Monographs, 2008), 52. Also, Helmich, *Karl Barth and the Beauty of God*, 169–74. Barth's defence of this position with regard to baptism can be seen in Barth, *Church Dogmatics*, IV.4 72.

69. Karl Barth, *Dogmatics in Outline* (New York: Harper and Row, 1959), 147.

reality. Whenever the outward sign or form is neglected or repudiated the inner content inevitably goes with it.[70]

The excessive separation of presence and practice in Barth's understanding stops communion from having any transformative effect. Communion in Barth's understanding is merely a witness to an eternal and objective truth. Ecclesial transformation through genuine response and interaction with the Spirit is simply not considered.

Summarizing, then, this subsection has explored both Hütter and Barth's accounts of the eucharist, demonstrating that while both have positive features, neither provides an adequate description of how the Spirit enables and empowers ecclesial transformation through this church practice. Hütter emphasizes the continuity existing between the eucharist and the coming kingdom to such a degree that transformation is almost unnecessary. Barth, in contrast, emphasizes the discontinuity to such an extent that transformation is virtually unachievable. Genuine transformation, in contrast to both accounts, requires the development of an ecclesial imagination, and as such requires a balanced recognition and experience of both the continuity and the discontinuity between the church and the coming kingdom. It is only through recognizing that the future is not truly and completely present that we can look forward with longing; and it is only through experiencing a pneumatological foretaste of the coming reality that we can recognize what we are missing. Transformation occurs through this pneumatological renewing of our minds. But change, development and growth do not come through ecclesial imagination alone. For genuine and effective transformation, imagination must be complemented by both experienced presence and enacted and empowered practices. Hütter merges presence and practice together (what could be termed 'ecclesial Eutychianism'), while Barth excessively separates them (what could be termed 'ecclesial Nestorianism'). The result is that for both (again) ecclesial transformation is minimized. What is needed, in contrast, is a pneumatologically enabled but Christologically inspired, Chalcedonian-type relationship between divine and human action in the eucharist. Human practice of the eucharist empowered by the Spirit can result in genuine and ongoing transformation 'enhypostatically', as we pneumatologically experience a foretaste of the coming kingdom. But even when our practice of the eucharist is flawed and sinful, the Spirit can transform our communities 'anhypostatically', convicting us of our misdeeds and writing on our hearts a renewed desire and ability for genuine and authentic communion.

It should also be noted that the underlying cause for these imbalances in both Barth and Hütter's eucharistic understandings is pneumatological. Barth underemphasizes the Spirit's ecclesial role in comparison to that of the Son, and this leads directly to his overemphasis on the eschatological tension and an

---

70. Thomas F. Torrance, *Conflict and Agreement in the Church, Vol II: The Ministry and the Sacraments of the Gospel* (Eugene: Wipf & Stock, 1996), 141.

exaggerated discontinuity between the present church and the coming kingdom, as well as his excessive separation of presence and practice. Hütter in contrast overemphasizes the Spirit's ecclesial role at the expense of the Son, which leads to an overemphasis on the teleological tension and an exaggerated continuity between the present church and the coming kingdom, as well as his merging and confusing of presence and practice. As has been consistently maintained during this research, it is clearly evident in this analysis of the eucharist that a nuanced understanding of ecclesiological transformation requires a mutual emphasis on the existentially integrated but logically distinct ecclesial missions of both the Son and the Spirit.

While this chapter has focused in depth on the ecclesial practice of the eucharist as the central enacted aspect of the church's journey through time as a prototypical example, Chapter 6 contains a broader and briefer account of a number of other church practices. It similarly and comparatively outlines how through the same three intertwined realities of imagination, experienced presence and enacted practice, the Spirit uses the full range of the church's activities to set us apart for (and from) the future as the coming kingdom's proleptic anticipation within this world and at this time.

Chapter 6

AN ESCHATOLOGICAL THIRD ARTICLE ECCLESIOLOGY

Through focusing on the eucharist, the previous chapter outlined how the Spirit transforms the church towards its kingdom future through the interplay of imagination, presence and practice. Following that analysis the twofold objective of this chapter is to first broaden that understanding with a briefer account of some other ecclesial practices and then to generalize the perspective gained over the last several chapters into a comprehensive but concise summary of the constituent features of an eschatological Third Article Ecclesiology. The overall intent is to provide a convincing account of the church's journey through time and how the Spirit transforms the church towards its teleological goal. While it would be profitable, a detailed and exhaustive explanation of all the practices the Spirit uses to draw Christ's kingdom future back and transform the present would require a substantial, book-length analysis. The general principles, however, can emerge through a few pertinent examples. Consequently, this chapter chooses just a few practices and examines how the Spirit uses these to transform the church. The aim of the initial sections in this chapter is therefore illustrative rather than exhaustive.

In terms of which examples to choose, the theological dialogue partners already interacted with can provide some helpful direction. Both Hütter and Barth provide reasonably comprehensive lists of 'church practices' or 'forms of ministry' as they respectively term them. Barth grounds his understanding of these in the concrete life of Jesus.[1] As Bender summarizes, for Barth 'the life of the community corresponds to Christ's own life. . . . [he] grounds the practices of the community in the divine authority that has been given to the person of Jesus Christ and thereby to his teaching'.[2] Barth's comprehensive exploration of these practices occurs in the third part-volume of *Church Dogmatics IV*, the section which centres particularly on Christ's prophetic ministry.[3] As was noted in Chapter 4, Barth's focus on Christ's prophetic office in this part-volume corresponds with his insistence that the church's primary and indeed only role is

---

1. See, for example, Barth, *Church Dogmatics*, IV.3.2 860.
2. Bender, *Karl Barth's Christological Ecclesiology*, 255.
3. Barth, *Church Dogmatics*, IV.3.2 859–901.

witness.⁴ So each of the many and varied 'forms of ministry' he describes witness to Christ and his own self-declaration. Barth divides these forms of ministry into two categories, speech and action, where the first category is primary (for the order of speech and action is 'not reversible'), but speech is not therefore of 'higher value' than action.⁵ In terms of speech, the forms of ministry Barth lists are (s1) praise of God, (s2) gospel proclamation (or preaching), (s3) community instruction, (s4) evangelization (to the immediate environs), (s5) missions (to the wider community and world) and (s6) the ministry of theology. There are also six actions explored: (a1) prayer, (a2) cure of souls (in a contemporary idiom this might be termed *pastoral care*), (a3) the production of clear Christian exemplars, (a4) acts of service (both within and particularly beyond the church community), (a5) prophetic action (speaking into current events, relationships and forms) and (a6) establishing fellowship. Notably, baptism and the Lord's supper fit within this final category.⁶

Hütter, writing after Barth, critiques his understanding of ecclesial practice, arguing that even with the detailed examples in Volume IV of *Church Dogmatics* his understanding of church practice 'remains ultimately transcendental'.⁷ He argues that to think (as Barth does) of the church dialectically as a community that mirrors in its existence the inner dialectic of God's election in Christ 'means unavoidably to turn concretely embodied ways of life and belief into abstract principles'.⁸ In contrast, he argues that the church must be seen as 'a way of life, i.e. a distinct set of practices interwoven with normative beliefs, concretely and distinctly embodied'.⁹ In several works, Hütter points to Luther's treatise *On the Councils and the Church*, which lists out a number of practices that Luther (and Hütter following him) proposes as constitutive of the church.¹⁰ Hütter argues, in contrast to Barth, that these 'are the "holy things" (*Heiltümer*) through which the Holy Spirit enacts his regenerating and sanctifying work. Instead of pointing as witnesses to the Holy Spirit's activity these practices rather embody the Holy Spirit's work'.¹¹ There are seven of these constitutive ecclesial practices, namely: (1) proclamation of God's word (including its reception and consequent action), (2) baptism, (3) Lord's supper, (4) the office of the keys (chiefly community

---

4. See the detailed explanation of this correspondence in Section 4.4.
5. See Barth, *Church Dogmatics*, IV.3.2 863.
6. Ibid., IV.3.2 901.
7. Hütter 'Karl Barth's "Dialectical Catholicity": Sic et Non', 149.
8. Ibid.
9. Ibid.
10. Martin Luther, 'On the Councils and the Church', in *Luther's Works (Volume 41)*, ed. Eric W. Gritsch (Philadelphia: Fortress, 1966), 143–66. For Hütter's lists, see Hütter, 'Karl Barth's "Dialectical Catholicity": Sic et Non', 149–50. Also, Reinhard Hütter, 'The Church as Public: Dogma, Practice, and the Holy Spirit', *Pro Ecclesia* 3 (1994): 353–5. And in the greatest detail, Hütter, *Suffering Divine Things*, 128–34.
11. Hütter, 'Karl Barth's "Dialectical Catholicity": Sic et Non', 150.

6. Eschatological Third Article Ecclesiology

Table 1 A Comparison of Barth and Hütter's Lists of Church Practices

Barth's 'forms of ministry'	Hütter's 'ecclesial practices'
Praise of God (s1)	Public praise and thanksgiving (6)
Gospel proclamation (s2)	Proclamation of God's word (1)
Community instruction (s3)	Proclamation of God's word (1)
Evangelization (s4)	
Missions (s5)	
Theology (s6)	The public stance of theology (9)
Prayer (a1)	Public prayer (6)
Cure of souls (a2)	Office of the keys (4)
	Visitations for support and critique (12)
Production of exemplars (a3)	Remembrance and identification of exemplary witness (8)
Acts of service (a4)	Discerning work outside the church (11)
Prophetic action (a5)	Understanding of (and response to) war (10)
Establishing fellowship (a6)	Communities practising life together (13)
	Baptism (2)
	Eucharist (3)
	Obedient Christlike suffering (7)
	Ecumenical fellowship (14)
	Discerning work outside the church (11)
	Offices and ordination (5)

forgiveness), (5) ordination and offices, (6) public prayer, praise and thanksgiving, and (7) obedient Christlike suffering. In 'The Church as Public', Hütter extends this list with an 'outer circle' which includes but is not limited to the following: (8) the remembrance and identification of exemplary Christian witnesses, (9) the public stance of theology as ecclesial discourse-practice, (10) an ecclesial understanding of (and response to) war, (11) a discerning process for work outside the Christian community, (12) the regular process of church visitations for support and critique, (13) the encouragement of communities that practice life together and (14) a movement towards ecumenical fellowship where historical divisions have existed.[12]

A comparison of the two lists is instructive (see Table 1).

There are some differences: Barth includes evangelization, mission and acts of service beyond the community,[13] while Hütter's list includes a focus on ecumenism, church structure and obedient suffering. These differences illustrate a distinction between Barth's understanding of the church as called to witness to the world, compared with Hütter's understanding of the church as called to endure despite the world's pervasive influence on it. Barth is concerned with how the church is self-

---

12. Also, Hütter, 'The Church as Public', 355–7.

13. Evangelization and mission could be included within the practice of the proclamation of God's word (1) within Hütter's list, and it is perhaps questionable whether discernment about the appropriateness of external vocations fits well with Barth's concept of acts of service. Clearly, Barth emphasizes life beyond the community more than Hütter.

identified,[14] while Hütter (and Luther) focuses on how it is 'externally recognized' or distinguished.[15] While these differences are not negligible, the clearest insight from this comparison is that even with these different understandings of the church's nature, there is still a significant overlap between the two lists. As Bender has noted, 'many of the concrete examples given by Luther, along with the supplements by Hütter, can be found or at least roughly correlated with those in Barth's own list of twelve.'[16] Indeed, at least nine of Barth's original list of twelve can be correlated to some degree with the ecclesial practices in Hütter's listing. Even with contrasting ecclesiological approaches, then, there are still significant overlaps between both ecclesiological outworkings, at least in terms of the high-level naming of lived out practices. This makes choosing illustrative examples a relatively straightforward process, with numerous good options available. The practices chosen as examples in this chapter are those that are most central (e.g. focusing on Luther's original list of seven rather than Hütter's outer circle) and also sufficiently diverse (e.g. choosing at least one speech and one action from Barth's list). Beyond this, I have deliberately selected those practices where the correlation between Barth and Hütter's lists was the closest, as these examples illustrate most clearly how these two theologians see the *same* practice as being useful for *different* purposes, both from each other, but also (to a degree) different from the eschatological Third Article Ecclesiology understanding of ecclesial transformation that has been developed in this volume. So, the initial purpose of this chapter is to explore the question of how the Spirit continuously transforms the church towards its kingdom *telos* through (1) prayer and praise, and (2) gospel proclamation. Consequently, the following two sections will explore how through imagination, presence and practice, the Spirit transforms the church as it engages in these practices. It will describe how these practices enable churches to increasingly live out what it means to be an anticipation of the kingdom, a community transformatively experiencing and demonstrating love, life, truth and justice, among other kingdom qualities. Then, having discussed all of these examples (including the discussion of eucharist in the previous chapter), the final portion of the chapter will give a brief but overarching outline of the constituent features of an eschatological Third Article Ecclesiology.

14. See, for example, Bender, *Karl Barth's Christological Ecclesiology*, 256–7.

15. Luther, 'On the Councils and the Church', 164.

16. Bender, *Karl Barth's Christological Ecclesiology*, 275, n. 11. While Bender concludes from Hütter's lack of explicit acknowledgement of this that his analysis of Barth could do with more nuance, I am not as convinced that Hütter has minimized, dismissed or neglected Barth's detailed listing of church practices. I will argue in the examples further that Hütter's arguments against Barth have some validity (in that Barth has to some degree overemphasized witness at the expense of ecclesial transformation, thereby excessively separating presence and practice), but I will also argue Hütter's response swings significantly too far in the opposite direction, excessively combining them. The distinction could be characterized as that I am arguing Barth is guilty of ecclesial Nestorianism and not ecclesial Docetism. In contrast, Hütter is guilty of ecclesial Eutychianism which leads to ecclesial Docetism.

6.1 Ecclesial transformation through prayer and praise

The first example chosen of an ecclesial practice is prayer and praise. Luther (and Hütter following) combines these together as the sixth church practice. 'The holy Christian people are externally recognised by prayer, public praise, and thanksgiving to God.'[17] Barth divides these practices into two forms of ministry – a speech and an action. For Barth, praise of God is the very first form of ministry he mentions, and he places it within his 'speech' grouping. 'To praise God . . . is to affirm, acknowledge, approve, extol, and laud both the being of God as the One who in His external majesty has become man, and the action in which He has taken man, all men, to Himself in His omnipotent mercy.'[18] Prayer, similarly, is the very first 'action' he mentions. Barth writes, 'Prayer involves in inseparable union both thanksgiving and intercession: the one in relation to the past for the free grace of God already received in it; the other related to the future for the same grace which will be needed in it.'[19]

There are some commonalities between Barth and Hütter's understandings. Both of them see prayer and praise as intrinsically communal activities, for example. And both focus on the objective and divine rather than the subjective and human aspect of the activity. Neither see prayer and praise as offering to God our own human-inspired desires and assessments.[20] But while the manner and form of the practices may be similar for both theologians, their purposes are clearly distinct. Indeed, in discussing Barth's and Hütter's analyses of these practices, the approaches taken by each strongly echo the discussion that has already occurred regarding their understanding of the eucharist.[21]

For Barth, both praise and prayer have two interrelated purposes: identity and witness. So the community is identified and defined by its praise: 'the community that does not sing is not the community,'[22] and the purpose of such identity defining activity is precisely so that it can witness to the world. Barth writes, 'when it praises God its particular concern is to set up that banner, to raise a standard, to lift up an escutcheon, in the ministry of its witness.'[23] Similarly, for

---

17. Luther, 'On the Councils and the Church', 164. Luther's full description of this practice within this treatise is contained on this page.

18. Barth, *Church Dogmatics*, IV.3.2 865. For Barth's full description of praise as a form of ministry, see Barth, *Church Dogmatics*, IV.3.2 865–7.

19. Barth, *Church Dogmatics*, IV.3.2 863. For Barth's full description of praise as a form of ministry, see Barth, *Church Dogmatics*, IV.3.2 882–4.

20. For example, Barth writes: 'In prayer . . . we do not have a purely subjective exercise of piety with only subjective significance. Such an exercise might well lead into the void.' Barth, *Church Dogmatics*, IV.3.2 883.

21. See Section 5.4.

22. Barth, *Church Dogmatics*, IV.3.2 867. Barth sees singing as the highest form of human expression and praise.

23. Barth, *Church Dogmatics*, IV.3.2 865.

Barth, prayer serves as an identity marker for the church: 'Where else in the world does it take place that God is thanked for his love . . . Where else . . . does there operate the certainty which enables us to . . . accomplish something in our dealings with him?'[24] And the purpose of this prayer-inspired identity is witness. So Barth writes that the church 'is the community which with its prayer no less than its praise can act representatively for the world, going on before and introducing as a witness this fact, this obvious likeness, of reconciliation, the covenant and fellowship between God and man.'[25] What is missing from Barth's discussion of prayer and praise, however, is any notion that through this activity the church is transformed. The practices of prayer and praise witness to the actions of the Spirit, but any notion that the Spirit acts through our prayer and praise to transform our communities is noticeably absent. Using the terminology of the last chapter, presence and practice are both realities within Barth's understanding of prayer and praise, but they are kept distinct from each other, with the result that transformation is minimized or, at the very least, unacknowledged. In his discussion of these practices, Barth's focus is much more on the eschatological rather than the teleological tension.

For Hütter and Luther, in contrast, the purpose of prayer and praise is almost entirely and only teleological, emphasizing the church's transformation. For example, in Luther's rather brief account of this particular practice,[26] he writes that prayer 'is one of the holy possessions whereby everything is sanctified, as Paul says [1 Tim. 4.5]'.[27] He also critiques what he considers to be a distinctly Roman Catholic approach to prayer and praise specifically because it is not done 'in quest of any reform or sanctification or of the will of God'.[28] What is particularly significant for this discussion, though, is Hütter's innovative explanation of *how* this practice effects transformation.[29] Noting that Luther's descriptive term for this and the other practices is of a 'holy possession', Hütter argues that the transformative effect of these practices is found not in what we do but in what is done or given to us through our actions. While all of the practices (including prayer and praise) intrinsically involve human activity, it is actually not the human but the Spirit that is the active agent. Humans may do the praying and praise (in this example), but

---

24. Ibid., IV.3.2 883.

25. Ibid., IV.3.2 883-4.

26. Luther spends less than a page on the practice of prayer, praise and thanksgiving in 'On the Councils and the Church'.

27. Luther, 'On the Councils and the Church', 164.

28. Ibid.

29. Although it is referenced at times, a detailed assessment of whether Hütter's understanding of how transformation occurs truly matches Luther's will not be addressed in detail within this work. I would argue that Luther's account is more closely aligned with the eschatological Third Article Ecclesiology approach to sanctification that is espoused in this volume than with Hütter's understanding.

the true subject of this practice is the Holy Spirit who offers to the human 'goods inherent in these practices'.[30] Hütter writes,

> The disposition of all seven practices is that in them the human being is always the *recipient*, that is, always remains in the mode of pathos. The human being remains the one who *through* these works of the Holy Spirit is qualified and receives a new 'form,' the one who thus is modelled through the Spirit of Christ, the *forma fidei*.[31]

This understanding, where the human community engaging in the practice is entirely a recipient, accounts for Hütter's initially surprising lack of detail about the form of each of the practices. Even compared to Luther, who spends relatively few words on the practice of prayer and praise,[32] Hütter barely mentions the detailed manner in which any of the practices should occur.[33] The exact manner in which a community prays or praises seems for him rather unimportant, for it is the Spirit who acts in prayer and praise to transform the community. He writes that while 'standards of excellence could doubtless be applied for each' of the seven practices, the '"excellence in question" involves' not the way the practice actually occurs but 'a person's growth in faith, or sanctification'.[34] What is absent from Hütter's account, then, is any acknowledgement that the specific way that a person or community prays contributes or affects in any meaningful way to the Spirit's transformational role. It is simply in the action of prayer and praise, rather than in the particular way they are done, that the Spirit acts and transformation happens.

To be fair to Hütter, there is some recognition that prayer and praise, or other practices, can be done in such a corrupt manner that they cease to be prayer and praise at all. He writes, 'Each of these practices is open to misunderstanding, distortion, and abuse, as Luther is himself quite aware of.'[35] By this, Hütter is no doubt referring (among other practices) to Luther's description and critique

---

30. Hütter, *Suffering Divine Things*, 131–2.
31. Ibid., 132.
32. Many of the other seven practices are treated in significantly greater detail, though.
33. In his essay on 'The Church' in *Knowing the Triune God*, Hütter does briefly reference several subsequent chapters written by other authors that deal in a little more detail with the specific mechanics of prayer within the liturgy. (See, for example, Hütter, 'The Church', 35, n. 40.) Regarding prayer and praise in particular, he references Susan K. Wood, 'Liturgy: Participatory Knowledge of God in the Liturgy', in *Knowing the Triune God: The Work of the Spirit in the Practices of the Church*, ed. James J. Buckley and David S. Yeago (Grand Rapids: William B. Eerdmans, 2001), 95–118. While Wood's article contains a very helpful explanation of how participating in the liturgy can be viewed as tacit knowledge (following Polanyi), it is similarly short on concrete details on how the manner of participating in the acts of praise and prayer effects transformation within the church community.
34. Hütter, *Suffering Divine Things*, 132.
35. Hütter, 'The Church', 35.

of inappropriate prayer and praise: 'We are now speaking of prayers and songs which are intelligible and from which we can learn and by means of which we can mend our ways. The clamor of monks and nuns and priests is not prayer, nor is it praise to God, for they do not understand it, nor do they learn anything from it.'[36] But given the nature of Hütter's characterization of the transformation, which occurs as a pneumatological gift received entirely pathically, there seems to be no space left for nuance or degree in his account. How a church acts in worship either *is* prayer and praise (in which case the Spirit works transformatively and the human community receives this as a gift) or it *is not* prayer and praise (in which case the Spirit does not work). Indeed, as Mawson comments, 'If the church were ever to be sinful in this way, then the Holy Spirit would simply no longer be present, and this community would no longer be a church.'[37] Using the terminology of the last chapter, then, presence and practice are both realities within Hütter's understanding, but they are merged and confused, and in such a way that the Spirit's action overwhelms human action. His ecclesial Eutychianism leads inevitably to ecclesial Docetism. There is no acknowledgement in Hütter's account that a community could pray or praise in such a way that the Spirit is not transforming them through their practice. If this were to happen, the community would no longer be a church at all. Concerningly, this Boolean distinction seems directly in contrast to numerous biblical passages where people and communities are critiqued not merely for their lack of praying but for the inadequate manner in which they prayed (Lk. 18.9-14, Jas 4.3, Jas 5.16, etc.). In short, there is insufficient acknowledgement in Hütter's understanding that the church community could be sinful and yet still be a church.[38] One questions therefore why transformation is even necessary in his account.[39] No doubt God could affect transformation within church communities without our active involvement, but Hütter's account seems totally at odds with the biblical witness where time and again God utilizes human effort (at least participatively) to achieve his divine ends.

As should be evident from the previous discussion, neither of these options is satisfactory. Barth's understanding (at least through omission) neglects or minimizes ecclesial transformation, treating it as virtually unachievable. And it is questionable whether Hütter's approach actually leads to any genuine transformation, given the lack of meaningful human participation in the Spirit's transforming work or whether it is actually necessary, given the inadequacy of his account of the church's present sinfulness. For Barth, practice and presence are excessively distinguished, as the Spirit's role is minimized. For Hütter, practice

---

36. Luther, 'On the Councils and the Church', 164.
37. Mawson, 'The Spirit and the Community', 462.
38. See the discussion of Hütter in Mawson, 'The Spirit and the Community', 459–62.
39. As noted in Section 5.3, Hütter's account sees little distinction between the church and the coming kingdom. This is why the 'imagination' aspect that is being advocated in this account as a core component of ecclesial transformation is severely diminished and unnecessary in his understanding.

and presence are excessively confused, as the Spirit's role is overstated. What is needed for genuine and effectual transformation, then, is a balanced approach: a pneumatologically enabled Chalcedonian relationship between (eschatological) presence and (teleological) practice, both of them being empowered by the Spirit, an understanding which combines the two without confusing or excessively distinguishing them. Further, the account must acknowledge both the present reality of sinfulness that exists within the church and the potential for the ecclesial community to grow in holiness over time. The following discussion briefly explores how an eschatological Third Article Ecclesiology account of prayer and praise enables such transformation.[40]

Within the context of Third Article Theology, the nature of prayer and praise – worship – has already been discussed in the development of a Trinitarian Third Article Ecclesiology.[41] Viewed through the lens of the Spirit, the simple but profound characterization arising from that discussion was that prayer should be seen as believers joining in with the already ongoing dynamic Trinitarian life of worship and adoration. Prayer is

> initiated by the Father, who through the Spirit directs Christ as to how we should pray, and Christ in turn directs us as we are in him (opening our lives up to his reign in us) and in the Spirit (enabled to hear him guiding us). Then, because of our union with Christ, as we obediently follow the guiding of the Spirit, the Father accepts our prayers as if they were from Jesus.[42]

The question that arises in this particular discussion is how does prayer and praise, understood in this way, contribute to human transformation? And the now familiar answer is that such transformation occurs through the interplay of imagination, presence and practice that occurs as we pray.

Beginning with presence, the very nature of prayer as affirmed in the brief outline here is that it centres on genuine participation in the life of God. Prayer and praise at its core involve the presence of God, and if it does not do so then it is not prayer or praise at all but merely human bleating. In the discourse on prayer that occurred in the development of a Trinitarian Third Article Ecclesiology, the strong emphasis was on God as the 'life, source, and object' of prayer.[43] If the Father directs us in and through Christ and the Spirit as to how we should pray, then his guidance will quite naturally lead us towards prayers saturated with features of the coming kingdom. Our prayers and praise will be focused on the themes

---

40. Note that this discussion is not intended to give a detailed account of prayer and praise in all of its various forms and purposes. This would go well beyond the scope of this volume. The only intent is to discuss how the church's prayer and praise contributes to the ongoing transformation of the community.
41. Liston, *The Anointed Church*, 329–33.
42. Ibid., 332.
43. Ibid., 333.

of truth, justice, life and love, for these are the characteristics and heartbeat of God himself. And God does not merely direct us as we pray, he empowers our prayers and praise. One could even say that through his indwelling Spirit, God prays through us.

While the emphasis in *The Anointed Church* and to this point in the discussion of prayer has been strongly on divine agency and presence, human activity cannot therefore be discounted. Indeed, in that original discussion of prayer, human agency was explicitly affirmed, but it was intentionally recognized as a 'participating, corresponding agency'.[44] God is the source and life of prayer, but humans are nevertheless active participants. We do not merely receive from God (contra Hütter), nor are we merely witnesses to God's activity (contra Barth). Rather we are participants in God's ongoing life. As we pray and praise together – as we participate in this Trinitarian life – two simultaneous experiential recognitions occur. The first is that actively enjoying and participating in God's life is the kind of existence and activity for which we were truly intended. Life in communion with God, where he speaks to us and through us, where we delight in him and he delights in our praises, this is true living – human life at its culmination and as it was originally envisioned – zoë life. The second recognition is that in our present condition, we are not yet the kind of people who can or do fully participate in God's life. Sometimes, even though we are a community indwelled by the Spirit, we do not clearly hear Christ's directing of our prayers and praise. And sometimes, although we may hear quite clearly, we wilfully ignore his leading. These two factors (our positive enjoyment of God in prayer and our negative inability or willingness to fully participate in his life of worship) both combine to focus our *imagination* on the time coming when our ears will be fully attuned and our wills will be fully surrendered – a day when we can fully participate as humans in the ongoing life and worship of God. Both our present experience of prayer and the acknowledgement of our present limitations feed this longing to more truly and completely be part of the life of God, so that our participation in his Trinitarian life may be more fruitful, free and instinctively unhindered. This is precisely why we fervently pray together (as we were instructed): 'Your kingdom come. Your will be done, on earth as it is in heaven' (Mt. 6.10, NIV).

The presence of God in our prayers, and our imagination-driven longing for lives that are more truly and completely participating in his life, therefore, motivates and leads us directly to empowered practice. Prayer and praise occur when together we *practise* participating in the life of God – practising his presence. We pray and praise because of both our longing to participate more fully in the life of God and our recognition that our experience of God's life (although at times overwhelming) is neither consistent nor complete. And through God's pneumatological presence, our sanctified imagination and our practise of the practice of prayer and praise, our lives are continuously and gradually transformed

---

44. Ibid.

towards this ultimate goal. As James K. A. Smith says, 'Worship is the arena in which God recalibrates our hearts, reforms our desires, and rehabituates our loves.... Worship is the heart of discipleship because it is the gymnasium in which God retrains our hearts.'[45] As we hear and obey the Spirit's guidance about what to pray for and how to pray, we are reinforced in our obedience by seeing God act in accordance with those prayers, for these prayers are sourced from the Father's heart, spoken in the authority of the Son, and enabled through the power of the Spirit. Prayer and praise thus develop an action/reflection model in which our obedience to the Spirit's guidance is reinforced through seeing God's action both in and beyond the life of our community.[46] As we increasingly follow the Spirit's guidance, our obedience grows to mimic that of Jesus, who only did what he saw his Father doing.

This characterization is not to suggest that the transformation of our community life through prayer and praise is cumulative and smoothly continuous. Rather it is jagged and messy, experiencing multiple births, deaths and resurrections on both individual and community levels, and across various timescales. Such a meandering journey is thoroughly to be expected given the fractal nature of time and our echoing of Christ's master-story within our own life stories.[47] But while the road may be doglegged with both steep inclines and rapid descents, the ultimate destination of the prayers and praise we offer is not in question. It is holiness. Not merely that we are set apart in prayer and praise as God's own people, people participating in his very life. But that we are increasingly transformed to reflect his nature in character, word and deed. Our practise of the practice of prayer and praise transforms our communities to more truly reflect the kingdom we are heading towards. As Luther notes, 'For Christian holiness, or the holiness common to Christendom, is found where the Holy Spirit gives people faith in

---

45. James K. A. Smith, *You Are What You Love: The Spiritual Power of Habit* (Grand Rapids: Brazos, 2016), 77.

46. This action reflection model could be described using the terminology of enhypostasis and anhypostasis, as for the eucharist, although the analogy is less obvious and a little more forced in this situation than it was for the eucharist (see the discussion in Section 5.3). If one were to force the analogy, 'enhypostatic' prayer would be prayer where we hear and act on the words of God guiding us through Christ and the Spirit as we pray, and as a result we see God's action in and beyond our lives as a response. Such prayer, even though it is prayed by flawed and fallen human beings, is effective and transformational (see, for example, Jas 5.16), not in the least because it reinforces for us the value of listening and praying God's prayers after him. 'Anhypostatic' prayer, in contrast, is prayer which does not derive from listening to and active obedience to God's directions of us. The result is ineffective prayer. Even in this situation, though, the Spirit can use our failure to bring us to repentance and enable transformation. Obviously, there is nuance needed here. Most prayer is not entirely 'enhypostatic' or 'anhypostatic' but contains an integrated mixture of both.

47. See the discussion in Section 3.2 on the fractal nature of time and our participation in Christ's master-story.

Christ and thus sanctifies them, Acts 15 [.9], that is, he renews heart, soul, body, work, and conduct, inscribing the commandments of God not on tablets of stone, but in hearts of flesh, II Corinthians 3 [.3].'[48]

Viewed from the perspective of Third Article Theology, then, prayer and praise lead the Christian community on a jagged but sure transformational journey towards holiness. It does this through the interplay of imagination, presence and practice. As we pray and praise together, we participate by the Spirit in the very life of God: enjoying God's presence, longing for a future where our experience of it will be deeper still and practising the practices through which we will become a people who can and do increasingly live out that future kingdom reality in our present experience now.

6.2 Ecclesial transformation through gospel proclamation

The second example of a transformative practice explored in this chapter is gospel proclamation: the 'Word of God'. Hütter, following Luther, notes this as the first 'holy possession' or practice of the church. And Luther in particular places a very high priority on it, writing that 'This is the principal item, and the holiest of holy possessions, by reason of which the Christian people are called holy; for God's word is holy and sanctifies everything it touches'.[49] Note that when Luther and Hütter write of God's word, they do not merely refer to the external, objective manuscript but the comprehensive act through which it is read, preached and received: gospel proclamation. Wolterstorff explains that the churches of the reformation 'were inclined to see the reading of Scripture and the sermonic explication and application thereof as a single liturgical unit'.[50] Or in Luther's words: 'Wherever you see this word preached, believed, professed, and lived, do not doubt that the true *eccleia sancta catholica*, "a Christian holy people" must be there'.[51] Barth has two closely related 'forms of ministry', which are associated with this transformative practice. The first is the 'explicit proclamation of the Gospel in the assembly of the community, in the midst of divine service, where it is also heard directly or indirectly by the world, i.e. in what is denoted by the overburdened but unavoidable term "preaching"'.[52] The second is 'the instruction which is given to the community'.[53] While the two are clearly related, Barth maintains a distinction between them, arguing that 'as preaching should not degenerate into mere instruction . . . so instruction

---

48. Luther, 'On the Councils and the Church', 145.
49. Ibid., 149.
50. Nicholas Wolterstorff, 'The Reformed Liturgy', in *Major Themes in the Reformed Tradition*, ed. Donald K. McKim (Eerdmans, 1992).
51. Luther, 'On the Councils and the Church', 150.
52. Barth, *Church Dogmatics*, IV.3.2 867.
53. Ibid., IV.3.2 870.

... should not degenerate into preaching'.[54] This is particularly because while preaching is primarily declarative (although it is also an action of sorts, as Barth notes),[55] instruction's firm intent is towards action. For instruction, as Barth characterizes it, is 'not merely the speech but the action of the community – an indispensable and unique contribution to the introduction and confirmation of the fact of a people of God capable of bearing witness to the world and actually bearing it by its very existence'.[56]

Once again, there are some significant similarities between Barth's and Luther's/Hütter's understanding of this ecclesial practice. Both characterizations see preaching as much more than simply insightful human musings on the objective, written word. In the preaching act, God himself speaks to the congregation, and the Spirit acts within the gathering. As Barth comments, 'the pulpit has been called the true arena of the kingdom of God'.[57] Similarly, while Barth's emphasis is more on the word being spoken and Luther's more on the acknowledgement of the word within the congregation ('many possess it but do not believe in it or act by it'[58]), both see preaching/teaching as including both of these aspects – gospel proclamation includes *both* the declaration of truth inherent in preaching and instruction *and* the consequent actions and response of the congregations when that truth is heard. But despite these similarities, their understanding of the purpose of this particular ecclesial practice again diverges. The analysis of Barth and Hütter that follows echoes what has already been seen in the previous examples, and so while it could be explored in great detail, the following explanations will be kept relatively brief.

Barth's understanding of the purpose of preaching, like his understanding of prayer and praise, focuses on the church's identity and witness. By the act of preaching, the church's unique identity is confirmed (preaching is 'a pregnant reminder and confirmation of the vocation to which it owes its gathering and upbuilding and indeed its very existence'[59]), and its specific and unique role of witness is reiterated ('What is at issue with preaching? Decisively that the community ... should remind itself or be reminded explicitly of the witness with which it is charged ... that reflected in it Jesus Christ Himself should speak afresh to it'[60]). Indeed, perhaps more clearly in gospel proclamation than in all the other ecclesial practices, these two aspects come together. For from Barth's perspective, the church's identity is precisely and only that of a witnessing community. Once again, though, Barth

---

54. Ibid., IV.3.2 871.
55. 'Preaching as the work of human speech is the human action by which the fact of this divisive but positively significant sign is established.' Barth, *Church Dogmatics*, IV.3.2 870.
56. Barth, *Church Dogmatics*, IV 3.2 871.
57. Ibid., IV.3.2 867.
58. Luther, 'On the Councils and the Church', 149.
59. Barth, *Church Dogmatics*, IV 3.2 867.
60. Ibid., IV.3.2 868.

makes no mention of preaching as a means to congregational transformation, even as merely one of many purposes. Evidenced here again with this practice, therefore, is Barth's common tendency to view the church as something that simply is, not something that, enabled by the Spirit, grows and develops over time. His emphasis is on the eschatological tension rather than the teleological. Presence and practice are both important for Barth, but both are separated, connected only by the witness through which the practice points to the presence. This overarching criticism which has been repeated several times in this volume is closely linked to the fact that Barth primarily utilizes the mostly static image of the church as Christ's body, to the exclusion of many other intrinsically dynamic images contained within the New Testament (e.g. the church as Christ's bride). Bender comments,

> This is a parallel and accompanying difficulty to Barth's overshadowing of the third article with the second, the sign of an underdeveloped, if not neglected, pneumatology. One might argue that such concerns may well have been addressed had Barth completed volume five of the *Church Dogmatics*. Yet such an argument from silence should not be used to stifle legitimate questions based upon Barth's extant ecclesiology.[61]

The lack of acknowledgement of ecclesial transformation in Barth's discussion of church practices is yet another evidential point backing up this conclusion.

Luther and Hütter, again in contrast to Barth, see ecclesial transformation as the primary, if not the sole, purpose of gospel proclamation. Given the close association between theology (which is Hütter's primary topic of focus in his monograph *Suffering Divine Things* as well as in many of his other publications) and gospel proclamation, Hütter is a little more forthcoming on the specifics of this practice compared with the others. (Details on what constitutes exemplary or satisfactory performance of the practice are still largely unaddressed, however.) He notes, for example, that 'the presentation and communication (catechesis) of the gospel in light of its doctrinal specification constitutes . . . [one key] task of theology as ecclesial practice in relationship to doctrine'.[62] And making the distinction between the gospel at its core which is Christ's own presence in his promise (*doctrina evangelii*) and dogma which is what the church teaches (*doctrina definite*) Hütter characterizes his core thesis: 'Knowledge of God is achieved in and through the reception of the gospel proclaimed and taught (*doctrina evangelii*), which takes place via the church's constitutive practices and via doctrine (dogma; *doctrina definita*).'[63] Referring specifically to gospel proclamation or preaching, then, Hütter's argument is simply that the church develops and grows as it gathers to hear and respond to the gospel being proclaimed to it in preaching. Such a proposition may seem initially unobjectionable and indeed almost obvious,

---

61. Bender, *Karl Barth's Christological Ecclesiology*, 224.
62. Hütter, 'The Church', 44.
63. Ibid., 32. For more detail, see the discussion in Section 2.3.

but problems emerge when it is tied together with the entirely pathic nature of pneumatological transformation for which Hütter concurrently argues. Because for Hütter, it is not the content or manner of what is preached that contributes to ecclesial transformation (for these are human actions or 'excellences'), but rather it is in the mere act of preaching and responding through which the Spirit acts. Following Luther, one would suppose that Hütter would classify some preaching as to be so corrupt and sinful as to simply not qualify as gospel proclamation.[64] But apart from that Boolean distinction between true and false teaching, all gospel proclamation that is responded to with any levels of energy or enthusiasm by the hearers enables pneumatological transformation. Once again for this practice of gospel proclamation, human practice and the divine presence are both acknowledged by Hütter, but they are intimately confused and merged to such a degree that human action is essentially overwhelmed by the work of the Spirit. The recognition of shades or degrees of sinfulness that exist in ecclesial preaching, or varying levels of human reception to the spoken word, and the fact that such variations of articulation or response contribute in some meaningful way to the ongoing pneumatological transformation that occurs are simply absent in this system.

What is required, then, in contrast to both Barth's understanding where the effect of gospel proclamation on church transformation is unacknowledged and presence and practice are kept excessively distinct, and Hütter's understanding where the presence and practice are merged and confused to such a degree that the former overshadows the latter, is a perspective on gospel proclamation that maintains a pneumatologically enabled Chalcedonian-like relationship between presence and practice, and an imaginatively inspired eschatological understanding where the future is partly anticipated but not yet completely present. The following discussion briefly outlines how through the appropriate interplay of imagination, presence and practice, a coherent account of what happens in gospel proclamation can illustrate how the Spirit transforms the church community through time. An appropriately construed eschatological Third Article Ecclesiology of preaching will inform how in and through this practice the Spirit draws back future truths to inform and enhance the church community at the present time.

Beginning again with presence, the first point to emphasize is the extraordinary truth that the church hears God's voice through Scripture reading and preaching. The reality that God himself is present in and through gospel proclamation is an almost universally held belief across the diversity of the Christian church. As noted earlier, both Barth and Hütter affirm this understanding. And the Catholic scholars responsible for Vatican II also emphatically agree, writing: 'Christ is always present in his Church, especially in her liturgical celebrations. . . . He is

---

64. See Luther's comments on the preaching of the Roman Catholic Church, for example. He says, 'They themselves confess that it is God's word and Holy Scripture, claiming, however, that one fares better with the fathers and the councils.' Luther, 'On the Councils and the Church', 151.

present in his word, since it is he himself who speaks when the holy scriptures are read in the church. . . . The homily is to be highly esteemed as part of the liturgy itself.'[65] The churches arising from the reformation hold to an even stronger and more extraordinary affirmation, that God is not merely statically present but actually speaks through the preaching of the gospel. For example, Calvin writes that 'it is a singular privilege that he deigns to consecrate to himself the mouths and tongues of men in order that his voice may resound in them'.[66] More recently, Reformed theologian Wolterstorff has affirmed that 'The sermon is sacramental of the speech of God – not of the static presence of God but of God's very speaking'.[67] The situation for Christ's presence within gospel proclamation consequently echoes, to some extent, the preceding discussion about the eucharist. While there is debate regarding the manner of Christ's presence in gospel proclamation (i.e. whether it should be viewed sacramentally or not), it is not really necessary for the purposes of this volume to define with crystal clarity the exact manner of his presence. My understanding matches most closely the Reformed articulation of preaching, but the much more crucial point is that (in whatever manner) Christ himself presences himself among his people and communicates with them in and through gospel proclamation.

Upon the recognition of God's presence within our preaching, the similarities between gospel proclamation and the ecclesial action of prayer and praise that has already been discussed become immediately obvious. If, as explained in the previous section, worship is 'the gift of participating through the Spirit in the Son's communion with the Father',[68] then preaching should similarly be seen as the gift of participating through the Spirit in the Son's declaration of himself to the church and the world to the glory of God the Father. So in preaching, God the Father directs the preacher as to what they should declare of the Son in the power of the Spirit, and the Spirit empowers the congregation who hear these words to respond appropriately to the Father through their ongoing union with Christ. The Spirit is always the means: inspiring the text, anointing the preacher, illuminating the congregation and convicting the world. The Son is always the content. And the Father is always the source and the goal. Just as God is the 'life, source, and object' of prayer and praise, so he is the 'life, source, and object' of gospel proclamation.

Human activity is not therefore discounted, however. As with prayer and praise, human agency must be explicitly affirmed in gospel proclamation, but it must again be recognized as a participating, corresponding agency. In gospel proclamation, we do not merely receive from God (contra Hütter) nor are we merely witnesses to his activity (contra Barth). There are times when God's presence within the act of

---

65. Constitution on the Scared Liturgy, par 7, 33, 52. There are some gradations here. Note that Wolterstorff comments that for the Roman Catholic Church, 'the sermon (homily) is not yet understood "sacramentally"'. Wolterstorff, 'The Reformed Liturgy', 289.

66. Calvin, *Institutes of the Christian Religion*, 4.1.5.

67. Wolterstorff, 'The Reformed Liturgy', 288.

68. Torrance, *Worship, Community and the Triune God of Grace*, 20.

gospel proclamation is experientially undeniable and the resulting transformation is virtually instantaneous. Long lists of examples could be given: Peter's gospel proclamation to a crowd from many nations on the day of Pentecost (Acts 2.14-42) is one such example, another is Wesley and Whitefield's preaching to the poor in the eighteenth century,[69] and yet another is David Wilkerson's gospel proclamation to drug-addicted gang members in New York in 1957.[70] Such biblical, historical and more recent events are particularly notable, though, because they are not consistent, everyday occurrences. While affirming the truth about God's presence in our preaching, preachers and congregations alike readily acknowledge that at this point in our ecclesial journey our experience of God's presence through gospel proclamation is nevertheless limited and inconsistent, and our response is not always characterized by unfettered faith but too often by weak-wills, grudging obedience or even outright resistance. Our positive experiences of those moments when God's presence is clear and undeniable and our responses sure and certain make us long for the day when this will be our constant reality. And our negative experiences of those moments when this is not the case remind us all too clearly that this future hope is not yet entirely our present reality. So both our positive and negative experiences of gospel proclamation (and the nuanced shades between these extremes that characterize most of our present reality) fuel our imagination. There is a day coming when our response to gospel proclamation will be comprehensive and consistent, for then we will truly see and know the Father as Christ knows him, for then God will truly have made his home among us (Rev. 21.3).

God's ongoing presence in our gospel proclamation, and our pneumatologically enabled imagination of the day when our experience of that presence will be full, constant and complete, leads directly to pneumatologically empowered practice. Gospel proclamation occurs when we *practise* speaking the words of God to each other and as we *practise* responding to them with faith and fervent devotion. Characteristically, C. S. Lewis illustrates this transition from presence and imagination through to practice with remarkable lucidity:

> He will set them off with communications of His presence which, though faint, seem great to them, with emotional sweetness, and easy conquest over temptation. But He never allows this state of affairs to last long. Sooner or later He withdraws, if not in fact, at least from their conscious experience, all those supports and incentives. He leaves the creature to stand up on its own legs – to carry out from the will alone duties which have lost all relish. It is during such trough periods, much more than during the peak periods, that it is growing into the sort of creature He wants it to be. . . . He wants them to learn to walk and

---

69. Howard A. Snyder, *The Radical Wesley: The Patterns and Practices of a Movement Maker* (Franklin: Seedbed, 1996), 37–45.
70. David Wilkerson, *The Cross and the Switchblade* (New York Jove Books, 1977).

must therefore take away His hand; and if only the will to walk is really there He is pleased even with their stumbles.[71]

To say explicitly what C. S. Lewis alludes to metaphorically, there will come a day when we shall truly and completely experience the presence of God, a day when we will hear his voice and respond entirely and only with pure love, obedience and devotion. And even now we get echoes and foretastes of that wonderful day when the kingdom will be truly and completely here, and we will be like the king as we see him (1 Jn 3.2). But at present we are not yet prepared and ready for the coming kingdom and so we need to practise for it. We need training to discern God's voice and training to respond appropriately to it. This is what the practice of gospel proclamation does for us. It is the training ground where we learn how to hear and respond to God's voice speaking to us.

It is at this point that the distinction between the eschatological Third Article Ecclesiological understanding developed in this volume and that of Barth and Hütter becomes particularly clear. In Hütter's understanding, God acts and through our ecclesial activities we *receive* his speech and actions. In Barth's understanding, God has acted and through our ecclesial activities we *witness* to his speech and actions. But in the eschatological Third Article Ecclesiological understanding developed in this volume, God acts, and through our ecclesial activities and empowered by the Spirit we *respond* to his speech and actions. Certainly, it is a pneumatologically empowered response, but it is nevertheless an intrinsically human response that we are offering. The implication is that at the centre of what is happening in ecclesial practice is a genuine relationship between God and humanity, where even at this point in our journey, for all of our flaws, failings and ongoing sinfulness, we are nevertheless God's people and he is our God. Certainly, our ability to truly participate in relationship with God is limited at the present time, but that is precisely why we are in the process of being transformed. It is in and through, but primarily *for* this relationship that God through imagination, presence and practice is taking us on a journey towards our common future together, a journey where we will increasingly live out these kingdom characteristics of life, love, justice and unity. As Wolterstorff says, 'The liturgy is a meeting between God and God's people, a meeting in which both parties act, but in which God initiates and we respond.'[72] This is the controlling idea from which transformation occurs, that in ecclesial practices a genuine and real relationship is occurring between God and his people. It is not merely encounter, and it is not merely reception. It is relationship. And it is precisely this ongoing but growing relationship that marks the ecclesial community as holy. By this ecclesial mark it is affirmed not just that the church is developing in purity through our practising of God's presence as we undertake our ecclesial practices, but more importantly that we are set apart as

---

71. C. S. Lewis, *The Screwtape Letters: Letters from a Senior to a Junior Devil* (London: HarperCollins, 2002), 40.

72. Wolterstorff, 'The Reformed Liturgy', 291.

God's holy people. We are the community which belongs to him and to which he has bound himself.

6.3 Constituent features of an eschatological Third Article Ecclesiology

Many more examples of church practices, and how through imagination, presence and practice they contribute to the transformation of the church through time, could be considered. Indeed, the following chapter makes the argument that in 1 Corinthians, Paul specifically uses what I am calling an eschatological Third Article Ecclesiology approach to commend and critique the practices in which the early Corinthian church was engaged. So those specific biblical examples could be added to the list of detailed practices already examined in this volume. But the repeated commonalities evident over the last two chapters suggest that the examples already given of the eucharist, prayer and praise, and gospel proclamation are more than adequate to indicate the emerging pattern.[73] This final section consequently draws on the insights gained to this point in the volume to briefly summarize the core and constituent features of an eschatological Third Article Ecclesiology.

Three key affirmations outline the core thesis of this volume and the constituent features of the eschatological Third Article Ecclesiology that have emerged. First, the church is the proleptic anticipation of the coming kingdom. Second, through enabling Christ's kingly presence, the Spirit draws back to the present church characteristics of the coming kingdom. Third, doing this enriches, influences and transforms the present church towards the coming kingdom.

The first of these affirmations – that the church is the proleptic anticipation of the coming kingdom – can be undergirded with two supporting subpoints. The first is that the anticipatory relationship between church and kingdom is characterized by both continuity and discontinuity. This is true noetically (where we know some but not all of what the coming kingdom will be like), ontically (where our present ecclesial reality is defined in part but not in its entirety by what will be) and also in a telic sense (where our journey towards the kingdom involves both continuous growth and discontinuous change). The second supporting subpoint is that the relationship between the church and the coming kingdom is not merely chronological or timebound. Christ's incarnation involved not merely a hypostatic union between divinity and humanity but also a union between eternity and time. Christ, after his resurrection, exists in 'redeemed' or 'new' time, which must be distinguished from the present 'fallen' or 'old' time that we dwell in,

---

73. While I don't necessarily own all of their theological positions, the works of Abraham Kuyper and Nicholas Wolterstorff give a much broader and more detailed account of church practices and how they contribute to ecclesial transformation. See particularly Abraham Kuyper, *Our Worship*, trans. Harry Boonstra, et al. (Grand Rapids: William B. Eerdmans, 2009).

as well as being distinguished from eternity which is God's time. The implication is that in considering the relationship between the church and the kingdom we need to consider not just the relationship between our present time and eternity (the teleological tension) but also the relationship between our present time and Christ's new time (the eschatological tension).

Terminologically, this understanding of the church as the proleptic anticipation of the coming kingdom was characterized as a *Logos* eschatology. The reason for adopting such nomenclature is because this understanding is the viewpoint gained when the relationship between the church and the kingdom is examined through a specifically Christological lens. While the understanding gained from this perspective was accurate and helpful, it was also argued that it was not complete. Just as a Spirit Christology is required to complement a Logos Christology, so a Spirit eschatology is required to complement a Logos eschatology. This leads to the second affirmation noted earlier: through enabling Christ's kingly presence, the Spirit draws back to the present church characteristics of the coming kingdom.

Once again, though, this broad affirmation is undergirded by several supporting subpoints. The first of these is the foundational role of the Spirit in understanding the relationship between the church and the kingdom. We only know of the kingdom because of the Spirit (noetic); the church only reflects the kingdom's identity because of the Spirit (ontic); and together we are being increasingly transformed towards the kingdom only because of the Spirit's work in us (telic). In short, the pneumatological perspective is vital and without it any understanding of the relationship between the church and the kingdom is inadequate and incomplete. The second supporting subpoint is that viewed through the lens of the Spirit, all of Christ's experience in new time impacts our present reality in old time. This means that the church has a fundamentally new way of being where the old rules of before and after do not simplistically apply. Through the Spirit we participate in Christ's ongoing life in redeemed time (via the eschatological tension) and so our lives repeatedly take on the shape of his entire existence: life, death and resurrection. This union in the eschatological tension in turn feeds our conformation process in the teleological tension, as through these repeating cruciform patterns we are gradually transformed into a more Christlike community. This transformation happens through the same process Christ experienced, that is, through giving up our rights to self-determination and allowing the Spirit to guide us. In other words, transformation occurs through obedient suffering. This overarching concept of Christ's life shaping our own lives is well illustrated through the mathematical concept of a fractal. Individuals and communities echo Christ's cruciform pattern of life, death and resurrection across a variety of timescales. Each cruciform moment and pattern joins together with other moments and patterns to create in the overall journey a growth and development towards a fundamental and final, self-giving, cruciform reality.

The interaction between Christ's new time and old time can be addressed and expanded in more detail by exploring Christ's eschatological offices. This forms the third supporting subpoint of the second affirmation. The church's participation in Christ's past in new time can be appropriated to a sharing in his prophetic eschatological office and leads to an ecclesiology of witness, an understanding that Barth explores. The church's participation in Christ's present in new time can be appropriated to a sharing in his priestly eschatological office and leads to an ecclesiology of communion, an understanding which T. F. Torrance unpacks. The church's participation in Christ's future in new time can be appropriated to a sharing in his kingly office, and this leads to an ecclesiology of transformation. This kingly aspect is rich in terms of implications, but it has not yet been explored as deeply as the other two eschatological offices. The fourth supporting subpoint consequently expands on this kingly eschatological office and its implications. It is because Christ the king is pneumatologically present in the church that the features of the coming kingdom are drawn back to characterize (in part) our present ecclesial existence. The coming kingdom is characterized by traits such as life, love, justice and truth, among others. These characteristics describe the coming kingdom because in that space and time Christ is truly and completely king, so his character is perfectly reflected in his kingdom. Through the Spirit's mediation of Christ's presence to the church at the present time, the characteristics of the coming kingdom also become (in part) features of the present church.

This recognition of Christ's pneumatologically enabled kingly presence within our churches at the present moment we experience in fallen time leads directly to the third affirmation: that in drawing back Christ's kingly presence, the Spirit enriches, influences and transforms the church towards his coming kingdom. It is this third affirmation, then, that directly addresses the question that launched this research: How does God go about transforming the church so that the breath-taking picture of our future reality increasingly becomes a part of our lived experience now? The answer is that the church is transformed through pneumatologically participating in Christ's kingly office. And again, this broad affirmation is undergirded by several supporting subpoints. The first of these is that this transformation specifically occurs through the interplay of imagination, presence and practice, each of which is intrinsically pneumatologically enabled. Presence obviously refers to the genuine reality of Christ among us as king and our consequent ecclesial experience (at least in part) of his kingly reign. Imagination refers to our simultaneous recognition both that the kingdom (and the king) is genuinely present among us through the Spirit and that we are not yet experiencing the full reality of the coming kingdom. This leads to a longing for what will be, a longing that is not merely future based or wishful thinking but is determined and guaranteed by Christ's past life, death and resurrection in his earthly session. Such an imagination (or a 'social imaginary') provides the fundamental understanding through which we make sense of our existence. Practice refers to how we intentionally gather as a church to practise living as a part of this kingdom. One important aspect of the repeated performance of our regular church practices (eucharist, praise and prayer, gospel proclamation, etc.) is that through them we are training to become (and thereby being transformed into) people who more truly belong in the kingdom and are even in this time and space more and more intentionally live out its kingdom reality.

The remaining subpoints undergirding this third affirmation expand on this understanding of practice. So, the next subpoint notes that the relationship between presence and practice can be cautiously characterized in a Chalcedonian manner, particularly using the enhypostasis/anhypostasis couplet. If done in isolation from the pneumatological presence of the king, practising being part of the kingdom through repeated church practices is completely ineffectual in transforming a church community (in analogy with anhypostasis). In contrast, the pneumatological presence of Christ makes the practise of the practices genuinely and effectively transformational (in analogy with enhypostasis). One can characterize ecclesial errors that focus only on presence or practice (ecclesial Docetism or ebionism respectively), or acknowledge both presence and practice, but excessively confuse (ecclesial Eutychianism) or excessively distinguish (ecclesial Nestorianism) between them. None of these are satisfactory. A pneumatologically enabled Chalcedonian connection between presence and practice leads to an understanding where what is occurring in our ecclesial activity is a genuine relationship, where God acts and his church (empowered by the Spirit) appropriately responds. It is only in and through such genuine relationship that effectual transformation occurs. The third subpoint of this transformational affirmation is that there is no expectation that this ecclesial transformation will be smoothly continuous and cumulative. In fact, given the fractal nature of time, and the way our individual narratives echo Christ's overarching narrative of life, death and resurrection, a more jagged path of growth and development is thoroughly to be expected. Genuine relationships are not characterized by artificial smoothness and development. The final subpoint is that both the core and the outcome of this transformational understanding is holiness. In terms of its core, this relational reality marks the church out as holy, intentionally set apart for God, for it is this ongoing relationship which separates us from the world and makes us distinct from it. And the outcome of transformation is holiness, where because of this relationship – through imagination, presence and practice – we become more and more a people who are defined by the characteristics of the kingdom and its king.

Chapter 7

READING 1 CORINTHIANS AS AN ESCHATOLOGICAL THIRD ARTICLE ECCLESIOLOGY

To this point, the aim of this volume has been to construct an eschatological Third Article Ecclesiology – an understanding of the church when viewed from the vantage point of eschatology through the lens of the Spirit. Using Wolterstorffian terminology, eschatology has been the control belief, ecclesiology the data belief and everything else (such as Scripture and the Creeds) has been viewed as background beliefs. This analysis has led to a coherent and compelling (but not complete) view of the church, an understanding that has been outlined in detail in the previous chapters. In brief, viewed from an eschatological vantage point through the lens of the Spirit, the church is the proleptic anticipation of the coming kingdom. Through enabling Christ's kingly presence, the Spirit draws back to the present church characteristics of the coming kingdom. Doing this enriches, influences and transforms the present church towards the coming kingdom.

In this chapter, however, the control and data beliefs will be altered. The pneumato-ecclesiological understanding that has been developed from the vantage point of eschatology will now be utilized as a control belief to examine the Scriptures and in particular 1 Corinthians. There are two reasons for altering the control and data beliefs at this point. The first is simply to explore a Scriptural text from the vantage point of an eschatological Third Article Ecclesiology. What insights arise when 1 Corinthians is viewed through this particular lens? What features of the epistle stand out most clearly? The second reason is a corollary of the first: How can the text of 1 Corinthians inform and confirm our understanding of an eschatological Third Article Ecclesiology? Will tensions arise between the text of 1 Corinthians and the ecclesiological understanding developed, or will they complement and mutually inform each other?[1] This chapter argues that because the text and the ecclesiological understanding do complement and mutually inform one another, this supports the conclusion that the eschatological vantage point developed in past chapters and utilized in this chapter is valid, ordered,

---

1. See the similar set of questions explored in Richard Hays, 'Spirit, Church, Resurrection: The Third Article of the Creed as Hermeneutical Lens for Reading Romans', *Journal of Theological Interpretation* 5, no. 1 (2011): 37.

coherent and viable. In other words, because an eschatological Third Article Ecclesiology provides a clear and compelling perspective on 1 Corinthians, this provides confidence that the ecclesiological understanding being constructed in this volume is itself sensible and systematic.

Using recent nomenclature, then, this chapter utilizes the practice of theological exegesis or undertakes a theological interpretation of Scripture. As such, it finds 'hermeneutical aid (not hindrance) in the church's doctrinal traditions' while simultaneously going 'beyond repeating traditional interpretations' to provide 'fresh readings, new performances of Scripture's sense that encounter the texts anew with eyes of faith'. To do this, 'Spirit-led imagination, an imagination converted by the word, is an essential faculty'.[2] Specifically, what is being argued in this chapter is that Paul's addressing of the various issues facing the Corinthian church can be insightfully viewed from the perspective of an eschatological Third Article Ecclesiology. Exploring the letter in this way assists in making sense of the manner in which Paul frames the discussion, the topics he addresses, the recommendations he makes, the veracity with which he writes and particularly the letter's overall thematic unity.

Two related questions need to be briefly addressed before such a broad theological exegesis can be undertaken. The first is to what extent a theological exegesis (or theological interpretation of Scripture) of 1 Corinthians is compatible with or overrides the more common approach of historical critical analysis, with its strongly contextual focus. The second is why 1 Corinthians should be chosen as the specific epistle to examine from the perspective of an eschatological Third Article Ecclesiology. Regarding the first question, several scholars have noted that among the many Pauline epistles in the New Testament, 1 Corinthians is the most evidently occasional, with a clear focus and heavy emphasis on the specific social practices and arrangements in which the Corinthian church was engaged at that particular time.[3] The letter provides genuine insight into lived Christian reality, with Paul addressing the most pressing community issues experienced by first-century Corinthian believers. As a result of this emphasis, some have concluded that the epistle has little to add to our understanding of Paul's theology or his perception of the gospel. Indeed, Bauer claims that 1 Corinthians is 'that unit among the major Pauline letters which yields the very least for our understanding of the Pauline faith'.[4] Such a conclusion, however, involves a misunderstanding of how

---

2. Richard B. Hays, 'Reading the Bible with Eyes of Faith: The Practice of Theological Exegesis', *Journal of Theological Interpretation* 1, no. 1 (2007): 15.

3. See, for example, David Ian Starling, '"Nothing Beyond What Is Written"?: 1 Corinthians and the Hermeneutics of Early Christian Theologia', *Journal of Theological Interpretation* 8, no. 1 (2014): 47–8.

4. Walter Bauer, *Orthodoxy and Heresy in Earliest Christianity*, trans. Robert A. Kraft and Gerhard Krodel (Philadelphia: Fortress, 1971). This understanding is noted and critiqued in Hans Conzelman, *1 Corinthians: A Commentary on the First Epistle to the Corinthians*, trans. James W. Leitch (Philadelphia: Fortress, 1976), 9.

Paul's letters should be read, where there is both the 'possibility and the necessity of combining rigorous historical investigation and engagement with Paul's letter as a theological text'.[5] Just as for any other Pauline (indeed for any pseudo-Pauline or general NT) epistle, the contextual situation and the theological understanding of the epistle mutually inform each other. Despite its clearly occasional nature, 1 Corinthians is no exception to this rule.[6]

Nevertheless, the focus on everyday church life in the letter makes it of particular value for this examination; indeed it is for this reason that 1 Corinthians has been specifically chosen as the focus of the theological exegesis in this chapter. In this epistle, Paul is practising an integrated and applied theology, 'theology is here translated into an illumination of the existence of the church, and of the individual Christian in it . . . he can therefore spotlight the church and the individual in the concrete position of the moment'.[7] It is precisely because of this 'integrated and applied theology' focus and its emphasis on the 'concrete position of the moment' that 1 Corinthians gives the clearest possible glimpse into how Paul sees ongoing transformation occurring within ordinary church life, why such ongoing transformation matters and the theological basis undergirding that transformation. As Fee remarks, 'Even though Paul is clearly after behavioural change, his greater concern is with the theological distortions that have allowed, or perhaps even promoted, their behaviour. This alone accounts for the unusual nature of the argumentation.'[8] Perhaps more than any other epistle, 1 Corinthians reveals how Paul thought the church should be practically living out the journey it was called to, how it was being transformed in and through its day-to-day practices and why such transformation and the altered behaviour it led to were of such importance. Indeed, the broad question Paul was addressing with the Corinthian church is strikingly similar to the overall question being addressed in this volume: How does God go about transforming the church so that the breath-taking picture of our future reality increasingly becomes a part of our lived experience now?

A core contention of this volume has been that ecclesial transformation is most clearly viewed as intrinsically eschatological and pneumatological. In other words,

---

5. Gregory M. Barnhill, 'The Paradox of Ecclesiology: A Theological Reading of 1 Corinthians 5', *Journal of Theological Interpretation* 12, no. 2 (2018): 243, n. 2.

6. It should be noted that in the following, I assume a contextual understanding similar to that outlined by Fee, Furnish, Johnson and others. The letter is one of a series between Paul and this church, with the key point of tension between them being that the practice of *glossolalia* among some of the Corinthian believers has led to them believing that they are already experiencing a higher level of Spiritual experience, one that requires no future resurrection and one that distinguishes them from other believers. See, for example, the succinct summary in Gordon Fee, 'Toward a Theology of 1 Corinthians', in *Pauline Theology Volume II: 1 & 2 Corinthians*, ed. David M. Hay (Minneapolis: Fortress Press, 1993), 37–8. Or for more detail, see Fee, *The First Epistle to the Corinthians*, 4–15.

7. Conzelman, *1 Corinthians*, 9.

8. Fee, 'Toward a Theology of 1 Corinthians', 38–9.

what is being argued is that an *eschatological* Third Article Ecclesiology gives a clear insight into the ongoing transformation of the church in time. The argument of this chapter is that Paul viewed the Corinthian church in this way and responded to their challenges and questions from precisely this vantage point. This chapter therefore endeavours to demonstrate that it was from a primarily eschatological perspective and through a pneumatological framework that Paul based both his reactions to the occurrences in and questions from Corinth and determined his recommendations regarding appropriate responses. Again, using the terminology developed in this book, what is being argued in this chapter is that Paul essentially saw the church of Corinth from the control belief of an eschatological Third Article Ecclesiology and that he evaluated and reacted to them on this basis.[9]

7.1 1 Corinthians 15: Pneumatologically enabled transformation

While eschatological factors are common throughout 1 Corinthians, the most explicit and lengthy eschatological discussion occurs near the conclusion of the letter in chapter 15. It is here that Paul addresses the coming resurrection of believers. While there are dissenting voices,[10] many biblical scholars echo Barth's assertion that this chapter 'forms not only the close and crown of the whole epistle, but also provides the key to its meaning from which light is shed onto the whole,

---

9. Given the breadth of the engagement, which explores the overall argument and themes of 1 Corinthians, it is not possible or beneficial in this chapter to drive down into the depth of detail that is often engaged by biblical scholars. Rather, the following analysis tends to utilize and draw on the findings of biblical scholars and show the overlap between their understanding of Paul's approach and that of an eschatological Third Article Ecclesiology. Not surprisingly, the pneumato-eschatological focus of 1 Corinthians is not a completely novel insight. Indeed, if these themes had not been previously noted it would call the premise of this chapter into question. The work of Gordon Fee and Luke Johnson has been particularly helpful in illuminating these aspects in detail. See particularly Fee, *The First Epistle to the Corinthians*. Also, Luke Timothy Johnson, *Contested Issues in Christian Origins and the New Testament: Collected Essays* (Leiden: Brill, 2013). Several other helpful references from these authors are noted in the following references.

10. For example, Conzelman considers this chapter as a 'self-contained treatise on the resurrection'. Conzelman, *1 Corinthians*, 249. Others who argue that this section was not a part of the original epistle include Jewett, Weiss, Schimithals, Hering, Dinkler, Goguel, Walker and Sellin. Arguing for the integrity of the epistle are Mitchell, Fee, Allo and Barret. For an overview, Anthony C. Thiselton, *The First Epistle to the Corinthians* (Grand Rapids: Eerdmans, 2000), 1171–2. Also, 36–41. See particularly the detailed and convincing arguments for the integrity of the epistle in Margaret Mary Mitchell, *Paul and the Rhetoric of Reconciliation: An Exegetical Investigation of the Language and Composition of 1 Corinthians* (Louisville: Westminster/John Knox Press, 1993).

and it becomes intelligible, not outwardly, but inwardly, as a unity.'[11] Thiselton maintains that seventy-five years of research has 'provided no convincing reason for disputing' Barth's conclusion and notes supporting theological voices such as Luther, Calvin and Moltmann, together with more modern biblical exegetes such as R. A. Harrisville, M. C. De Boer and H. Moxnes.[12] Justification for the claim that 1 Corinthians 15 with its pneumatological and eschatological focus provides the key to understanding Paul's approach to the entire epistle is detailed within the content of this chapter. The intent of this introductory section, however, is simply to note the key aspects of 1 Corinthians 15 and particularly the significant overlap these themes have with those of an eschatological Third Article Ecclesiology.

1 Corinthians 15 is primarily an eschatological treatise. Directly addressing that segment of the Corinthian church who doubt the reality of their coming resurrection, Paul points in response first to the resurrection of Jesus (15.1-11), but then even more fully to the nature and implications of the Corinthian believers' coming resurrection (15.12-58). Paul's overarching point is that their resurrection, like Jesus' resurrection, involves a fundamentally ontological transformation. As Johnson summarizes, 'Full participation in God's rule is not available to "flesh and blood," that is, ordinary human existence, much less such an existence defined precisely by "flesh." The corruptible – that is the mortal – cannot without change inherit immortality (15.50).'[13] Three points about this ontological transformation, all of which align closely with the core themes of an eschatological Third Article Ecclesiology, are particularly clearly emphasized within Paul's treatise: its intrinsically pneumatological nature, its already present and ongoing reality within the life of the community, and its clear moral implications for the entire ecclesial community.

Paul characterizes the ontological change occurring in the resurrection through pneumatological language. Immediate evidence for this can be seen from the fact that Jesus (following his resurrection) is referred to as the 'life giving Spirit' (15.45) and believers' post-resurrection existence is repeatedly described through the terminology of 'Spiritual bodies' (e.g. 15.44). Paul in this chapter sets up a clear contrast between our present earthly bodies and these future 'Spiritual' bodies. The former are mortal, corruptible, broken, weak, earthly and destined for death, while the latter are immortal, incorruptible, raised in glory, strong, heavenly and will last forever. The prototypical example of each is Adam, who was given life, and Christ, who is the giver of life. While the distinction between the two states of existence is marked, a continuity also exists in that both are 'bodies' – indeed the latter 'Spiritual' body grows out of, builds on or is derived from the

---

11. Karl Barth, *The Resurrection of the Dead*, trans. H. J. Stenning (London: Hodder & Stoughton, 1933), 5.

12. Thiselton, *The First Epistle to the Corinthians*, 1169. For the discussion, see 1169–72.

13. Luke Timothy Johnson, 'Life-Giving Spirit: The Ontological Implications of Resurrection in 1 Corinthians', in *Contested Issues in Christian Origins and the New Testament: Collected Essays* (Leiden: Brill, 2013), 286.

former.[14] What, then, are we to make of Paul's descriptive use of the term *Spiritual* (or 'spiritual') to characterize our future resurrected bodies: *soma pneumatika*? Viewed simplistically, the combination of 'spiritual' and 'body' is oxymoronic, pushing language well beyond its normal and expected meaning. Identifying Paul's use of 'spiritual' as a synonym for incorporeal is completely unsatisfactory, as this would negate the bodily continuity already noted, as well as Jesus' ongoing corporeal existence following his resurrection. So while Paul during 1 Corinthians does at times use the term *pneuma* in reference to the incorporeal dimension of present human psychology (5.5, 7.34, 16.18, etc.),[15] this identification is completely insufficient for its many references in 1 Corinthians 15. The only possible conclusion to be drawn from the list of qualities associated with our resurrection bodies noted earlier is that 'spiritual' inherently refers to something intrinsically divine. Consequently, when Paul speaks of the 'spiritual' bodies we will have, he can only be referring specifically and clearly of our receptiveness to, awareness of and interaction with the Holy Spirit.[16] Both Jesus' resurrection and our coming resurrections are empowered by the Spirit. And the primary ontological difference between this life and the life to come centres on the way our future bodies can and will interact with the Holy Spirit. In short, the Spirit in 1 Corinthians 15 (and also, as will be seen further, in the earlier chapters of the epistle) can be identified very closely with the transforming power of God enabling our (ongoing) resurrection. As Fee comments, 'In Paul, the terms "Spirit" and "Power" are at times nearly interchangeable. . . . To speak of the Spirit is automatically to speak of power.'[17]

But for Paul, this resurrection transformation is not merely something to look forward to but something that the Spirit is already empowering and effecting in the present life of the Corinthian believers. 'The process of this ontological change through the [Spirit], however, begins already in this mortal, empirical existence that humans share.'[18] This is the second key recognition arising from Paul's eschatological treatise in 1 Corinthians 15. He identifies the Corinthian believers with *both* Adam and Christ, *both* the earthly and the heavenly, *both* the weak and the strong. While the former aspect may be more obvious and prevalent than the latter at this point in their journey, the two exist simultaneously. In his most extended analogy, for example, Paul describes how the present body relates to the future body as a seed relates to the plant that emerges from it (15.35-44). It is not only through our future and final death and resurrection, then, but through our

---

14. This recognition is discussed further in the following paragraph.

15. Johnson, 'Life-Giving Spirit', 288.

16. It may be that the 'Spiritual' refers also to our human spirit's increased receptiveness to the Holy Spirit, but if so, then it is the latter aspect that is by far the most significantly emphasized.

17. 'In Paul, the terms "Spirit" and "Power" are at times nearly interchangeable. . . . To speak of the Spirit is automatically to speak of power.' Fee, *The First Epistle to the Corinthians*, 97.

18. Johnson, 'Life-Giving Spirit', 287.

present and ongoing deaths and resurrections (our cruciform lives) that we are transformed. As Johnson comments,

> It is entirely legitimate to read in this connection a passage from Paul's second letter to the Corinthians, which serves as a virtual commentary on the argument Paul makes in 1 Corinthians 15 . . . (2 Cor. 3.17-18). Reading the passages from the two Corinthian letters side by side, it seems evident that Paul sees the process of ontological transformation as already at work through the resurrection Spirit.[19]

So the ontological transformation of resurrection life, characterized as it is by an increased awareness of and interaction with the Holy Spirit, is not something that we just look forward to but something that through our cruciform lives we are presently experiencing and being transformed towards. It should also be emphasized here that this transformation is ecclesial and not merely individualistic. Just as we are 'all' resurrected together, so we are transformed together.[20] Paul's understanding of eschatology and the resurrection is fundamentally ecclesiologically focused.

It might be expected that Paul would end his discussion of resurrection with an exclamation of praise and hope, but it concludes instead with a moral exhortation (15.58). The importance of such moral implications arising from Paul's understanding of the resurrection is the third recognition arising from Paul's eschatological treatise in 1 Corinthians 15. And it is not merely at the end of the chapter that the Corinthians' attention is drawn to the moral implications of their eschatological hope (see, for example, 15.34). Insistence on moral change is a regular theme not only through this chapter but also throughout the entire epistle. In concluding his eschatological treatise in this way, however, Paul provides an overarching and theological reason for why the moral changes he has insisted upon earlier in the epistle are so pivotal. '1 Corinthians 15 provides the eschatological-ontological assumptions underlying Paul's moral exhortations, and makes of them something much more than mere moralism.'[21] This is where the maturity that Paul is demanding of the Corinthians, and chiding them for lacking, both stems from and leads. Using the language of an eschatological Third Article Ecclesiology, this is where our 'imagination' about what is coming impacts our present ecclesial practice. The Corinthian church is to 'come to a sober and right mind, and sin no more' (15.34), they are to be 'always excelling in the work of the Lord' (15.58), because the Spirit is already beginning a process of transformation among them that is leading to their resurrection 'Eschatological salvation, the great concern of the epistle, includes proper behaviour or it simply is not the gospel Paul preaches.'[22]

---

19. Ibid.
20. Note the prevalent use of 'all' and the use of the first-person plural throughout the passage. For example, 15:51. See also the discussion of body and bodies in Section 7.4.
21. Johnson, 'Life-Giving Spirit', 287.
22. Fee, 'Toward a Theology of 1 Corinthians', 58.

It is because the Corinthian believers have been marked out by the Spirit as fundamentally different from those around them, because they are set apart for a future that is distinct, that they can no longer live according to the standards of the world. 'This hope invests the believer's life with a moral seriousness it would not otherwise have; it makes the distinction between good and bad important.'[23] The Spirit-filled, Spirit-led, resurrection-bound life that Paul talks of is consequently an expression of both gift and demand. For Paul, ethics is a theological issue. And the theological truth of their coming resurrection has marked ethical implications for how the Corinthian church was to behave.

Fee's definition of Paul's understanding of the gospel in Corinthians (which he argues is Paul's prime motivation throughout this letter) provides an excellent summary of the key themes outlined earlier. He characterizes it as follows: 'God's eschatological salvation, effected through the death and resurrection of Christ, and resulting in an eschatological community who by the power of the Spirit live out the life of the future in the present age as they await the consummation.'[24] The resonances between Fee's characterization of Paul's gospel understanding as expressed within 1 Corinthians and the key themes of an eschatological Third Article Ecclesiology as developed in this volume are very clearly evident. The priority of eschatology, the empowering role of the Spirit, the ongoing experience of transformation, the immediate and present implications for morality and holiness, the present experience of crucifixion and resurrection as the means of effecting our transformation – all of these feature heavily both in 1 Corinthians 15 and in the development of an eschatological Third Article Ecclesiology as it has been outlined in this volume.

The following subsections work sequentially through the earlier chapters of the epistle, demonstrating that as Paul addresses the day-to-day issues that have arisen in the Corinthian church, he does it through applying the key themes noted here – the themes of an eschatological Third Article Ecclesiology. In each, the present implications of the ontological resurrection transformation – its intrinsically pneumatological nature, its already present and ongoing reality, and its clear moral implications – form the core of the argument that Paul makes in advising the Corinthian church on how they should go about living their ecclesial lives.

7.2 1 Corinthians 1–2: Pneumatologically enabled imagination

The core of Paul's discourse in Corinthians starts in earnest at 1.10, but even in his prior introductory remarks, he foreshadows the key themes to which he will repeatedly return. Note, for example, the emphasis on holiness in his description of the Corinthian church (1.2) and on Christ's coming return and the need for

---

23. Victor Paul Furnish, 'Theology in 1 Corinthians', in *Pauline Theology Volume II: 1 & 2 Corinthians*, ed. David M. Hay (Minneapolis: Fortress Press, 1993), 78.

24. Fee, 'Toward a Theology of 1 Corinthians', 38.

endurance in his expressions of thankfulness for them (1.7-9). Repeatedly during these brief remarks, Paul notes that the Corinthians are defined by their relationship with Jesus – they belong to him (1:4), they are in partnership with him (1.9) – Jesus (the crucified and risen one) distinguishes the Corinthian believers as holy and separate from the world. Even at this very early stage, then, the eschatological vantage point through which Paul is observing and responding to the Corinthian church and its moral implications for them is very evidently foreshadowed.

Following these opening salutations, Paul's introductory exhortation to unity in 1.10-17 is recapitulated and extended in chapters 3–4, so the themes introduced in this brief introductory paragraph will be addressed in the next subsection (7.3). The purpose of this prior subsection (7.2), though, is to examine Paul's argument in 1.18–2.16 and to demonstrate that Paul's approach in this discussion can be understood and illuminated from the perspective of an eschatological Third Article Ecclesiology framework. Recalling the comments in Chapter 5 of this volume that ecclesial transformation occurs through the interplay of imagination, presence and practice, this section demonstrates that Paul's primary purpose in these early paragraphs is to address and radically alter the Corinthians' imagination. Paul wants the Corinthians to see the world in a whole new way. As Cousar argues, this passage presents

> a new epistemology commensurate with the message of the cross, appropriate to the eschatological times. In the long run, behaviour can only be superficially changed unless imaginations are changed, unless angles of vision are renewed. Thus the text confronts the readers with an alternative perspective, albeit a radical one, to their way of understanding God and their life in community.[25]

Consider the logic of Paul's argument. Broadly, the passage can be divided into two sections. In the first section (1.18–2 5), Paul talks of the 'foolishness' of God's plans. That which the world admires (signs from heaven for Jews or human wisdom for gentiles) is not that which should be truly valued. To see and judge the world this way is to see and judge wrongly! God's wisdom and actions may seem weak and foolish from the world's perspective, but they are (being from God) where true strength and wisdom lie. Strength comes through weakness; wisdom comes through foolishness; in short, life comes through death. The central, primary and defining exemplar of this is Christ's crucifixion (1.18-25), but the general principle also applies to the experience of the Corinthian believers (1.26-31) and to Paul's preaching when he first came to Corinth (2.1-5). In the second section (2.6-16), Paul talks of the 'hiddenness' of God's plans. God's wisdom is so antithetical to the world's perspective that humanity could never have discovered or determined it alone. The Corinthians know of God's wisdom only because of the Spirit, who has revealed both it and God's secret plan to Paul, and (in turn) to the Corinthian

---

25. Charles B. Cousar, 'The Theological Task of 1 Corinthians', in *Pauline Theology Volume II: 1 & 2 Corinthians*, ed. David M. Hay (Minneapolis: Fortress Press, 1993), 97.

believers. Through the Spirit they can see and understand the world in a brand new way, discerning not just the way the world is but the very mind of God.

The overarching purpose of this part of the letter, then, is to fundamentally change the way that the Corinthians conceive of and understand the world, and their place in it. Paul wants his Corinthian readers to stop thinking and seeing like people who are restricted to a vision of just this world, and to start thinking and seeing in a completely new way, a way that reaches well beyond their current horizon. Three aspects of this new 'social imaginary' are pertinent. First, it is fundamentally eschatological, it transcends the time and space of this world, looking well beyond them. Second, this new 'imaginary' applies to the Corinthians because of their current and ongoing ontological union with Christ – it is because 'life through death' is Christ's way of being that it is now their way of being (and thinking and seeing) as well. Third, this new 'imaginary' is pneumatologically enabled. The only possibility of thinking about and seeing reality in this new way is through the Spirit. Each of these points is briefly expanded in the following paragraphs.

First, the new 'social imaginary' that Paul is commending to the Corinthians is intrinsically eschatological – it transcends the time and space of this world. 'God's power and wisdom are presented not merely as superior to the world's but belonging to an entirely different order.'[26] This eschatological focus is perhaps not superficially obvious from a first reading of the passage, but there are several suggestive indications. Primarily these include the repeated references to God's immeasurable power (1.18, 24, 2.5) and impenetrable wisdom (1.21, 24-25, 2.6-7, 9, 16), which are categorized as not only distinct from but infinitely superior to the strength and wisdom of the world. The primary reason given for this superiority is the fact that God and his wisdom and power is not of 'this age' (2.6). God is utterly unlike the rulers of this age who are 'doomed to perish' (2.6). In addition (and related) to these points, the constant and repeated references to 'Christ crucified' also implicitly point the Corinthian readers beyond this world's schema, where death is the ultimate end. Importantly, these references do not merely look backwards at Jesus' past act of being crucified. (Note, for example, the use of present tense to describe the crucified Christ in 1.23 and 2.2). Nor is there any mention of Jesus' death atoning for our sins, despite this important explanatory point occurring later in the epistle.[27] Rather, the emphasis in this section is on the fact that Jesus, who continues to be the crucified one – the one who died but did not remain dead – the crucified Jesus' ongoing existence even after his death demonstrates both the nature and the superiority of God's wisdom and power over that of the world. The point Paul is making in repeatedly referring to the 'crucified Christ' in this passage is therefore epistemological rather than purely soteriological. Jesus clearly shows that this world's wisdom is not as wise as it claims to be and that the world's power is not as strong as it appears to be. Christ the ongoing crucified

---

26. Furnish, 'Theology in 1 Corinthians', 67.
27. See 1 Corinthians 8.11, 11.24, 15.3 for example.

one uncovers the fundamentally eschatological nature of God's power and wisdom. So the imagination that Paul is calling the Corinthians to in this passage, precisely like that described in the development of the eschatological Third Article Ecclesiology, can be best characterized as Christo/eschato-logical.[28] It is forward looking and filled with longing, but this hope engendered is based securely on the knowledge of Jesus' earthly session and particularly his resurrection, which is the one defining event where the coming kingdom has most obviously broken into our present timeline.

The question that deserves to be addressed is why Paul is not more explicit about the clearly eschatological underpinning of his argument in this discussion? Why, for example, is there no explicit mention of Jesus' resurrection, and why is it that 'explicit language of the new age does not appear in 1.18–2.16'?[29] This question aligns with another about why Paul leaves his detailed discussion of resurrection until 1 Corinthians 15? Why is resurrection the last substantial topic addressed in the epistle, when it forms the hub of the argument around which the rest of the epistle converges? The most convincing explanation is contextual. Paul's major theological difference with the Corinthian church centred on their understanding of the nature of their coming resurrection. The Corinthian's experience of *glossolalia* meant that some in the church thought themselves to already be experiencing a 'higher or fully spiritualized existence, even to the point where no future resurrection was necessary.[30] Because this is the point of his greatest theological disagreement with the Corinthians, Paul wisely chooses not to explicitly address the issue of resurrection early on, until he has 'subdued their pride and made them willing to receive his teaching'.[31] Paul needs to convince the Corinthian believers that they are not as mature and 'Spiritual' as they think they are, before they can hear his recasting of their understanding of the resurrection. While this is a convincing reason for Paul's reticence to directly mention the resurrection and the new age in the very early discourses in the letter, it should also be noted that his readers do not have to wait long for the eschatological underpinning of Paul's argument to become explicit (see 3.12-15, for example). And even in this section the (implicitly eschatological) wisdom Paul presents is directly and explicitly contrasted with the wisdom of the rulers *of this age* (2.6). Such a reference foreshadows the direction Paul's ongoing argument will take, providing 'an insight critical for the rest of this letter . . . where this new way of knowing is given an eschatological cast'.[32]

---

28. See the discussion in Section 5.2.1.

29. Cousar, 'The Theological Task of 1 Corinthians', 96.

30. See the succinct and helpful summary of the Corinthian context in Fee, 'Toward a Theology of 1 Corinthians', 37–8.

31. John Calvin, *The First Epistle of Paul to the Corinthians*, trans. John W. Fraser (Edinburgh: Oliver and Boyd, 1960), 312. See the more detailed discussion in Thiselton, *The First Epistle to the Corinthians*, 1170–1.

32. Cousar, 'The Theological Task of 1 Corinthians', 96.

The second key characteristic of this new 'social imaginary', an understanding of reality where strength comes through weakness and wisdom through foolishness, is that it is not merely God's way of being and working, but that it applies particularly to the Corinthian believers in their present situation as present participants in the new age. 'The marks of the new age are at present hidden *in* the old age. At the juncture of the ages, the marks of resurrection are hidden and revealed in the cross of the disciple's daily death, and *only* there.'[33] So the Corinthian believers can and should see the world differently from others because, in contrast to others, they are those 'who are being saved' (1.18), they are the 'called' ones (1.24, 26-28). More specifically, God has become the source of their life in Christ Jesus (1.30), so Christ's wisdom has become their wisdom, and Christ's strength has become their strength. In Christ, the eternal wisdom and saving power of God have entered history. What is being argued in this Pauline passage, therefore, is not just that Christ is the Corinthian believers' pattern and example, but because they have been united with Christ, his cruciform way of being has become their new way of being. The point is ontological and only as a consequence of that epistemological. The Corinthian believers' new way of seeing follows from their new way of being. As Furnish comments, 'It is on behalf of this believing community that Paul affirms, "We have the mind of Christ" . . . , meaning that the lives of believers are both *formed* and *informed* by the wisdom of the cross.'[34]

If Christ is the essence of the Corinthians' newly derived status and sight, the Spirit is the means by which this newly derived condition and perspective occurs. This pneumatological enabling is the third key characteristic of the 'social imaginary' that Paul commends to the Corinthian church. Indeed, Paul's logical argument here is an excellent example of applying a Third Article Theology approach to epistemology! Having focused on the distinction between God and the world's ways in the first half of the passage, Paul focuses particularly on the crucial enlightening role of the Spirit in the latter section of 1 Corinthians 2. From Paul's perspective, the Corinthians' ability to perceive the world from the vantage point of 'Christ and him crucified' comes not merely from the fact that they have been united with Christ and therefore have their being defined by his but also from the gift they have received of God's Spirit. This gift enables them to see and understand things that those who only have the world's spirit simply cannot see or understand. In the latter half of 1 Corinthians 2, Paul strongly contrasts God's Spirit and the spirit of the world, maintaining that it is only through the former that we can participate in and understand God's truth and reality. For Paul, then, 'the Spirit is the key to everything. For him the Spirit is an eschatological reality, marking

---

33. J. Louis Martyn, 'Epistemology at the Turn of the Ages: 2 Corinthians 5:16', in *Christian History and Interpretation: Studies Presented to John Knox*, ed. W. R. Farmer, et al. (Cambridge: Cambridge University Press, 1967), 286. While derived from another text, Martyn's comments are equally applicable here.

34. Furnish, 'Theology in 1 Corinthians', 69 (italics added).

the turning of the ages.'[35] Every Corinthian believer can and should see the world through an intrinsically pneumatological lens. In fact, it is only pneumatologically that they *can* see the world in this new and Godly way.

Having explored Paul's argument in this passage– its overarching Christo/ eschato-logical framework, its cruciform vantage point and its pneumatological enabling – the overlaps between these themes and those developed in the earlier construction of the eschatological Third Article Ecclesiology as outlined earlier in the volume are very apparent. The most significant and overarching overlap, however, is the way Paul is attempting to transform the Corinthians' imaginations. Chapter 5 argued that ecclesial transformation occurred through the interplay of three pneumatologically enabled aspects: imagination, presence and practice. Imagination was described as that which provides the fundamental understanding of who we are as a community, how we relate to one another and what our common life should be like. Our ecclesial imagination provided the framework through which we make sense of our existence and actions. It was noted that for the Christian community, this imagination centres on the cross and resurrection of Jesus, which is the defining story of both Jesus' and our existence. But it was also noted that this master-story of birth, death and resurrection is not just the overarching story of divinity and humanity seen through the broad expanse of time, but it gets lived and repeated over and over again, at successively smaller scales. 'The past "work" of God's Son, embodied on the cross, has become the present work of the Spirit of God's Son, embodied in the believer and in the community.'[36]

Viewed from the perspective of an eschatological Third Article Ecclesiology, then, Paul's primary purpose in 1 Cor. 1.18–2.16 is to fundamentally alter the imaginations of the Corinthian readers, so that they can understand and view their current situation from a new perspective. The kind of social imaginary that Paul commends to them is intrinsically eschatological – it looks beyond the confines of this world. It is intrinsically cruciform – it defines their position in and interaction with the world through the master-story of Jesus' crucifixion and resurrection.[37] And it is pneumatologically enabled – the only way the Corinthians can see reality this way is through the lens of the Spirit. The problem is that even though the Corinthian church exists in this new pneumatologically enabled and Christologically defined paradigm, they are not actually seeing the world this way (as Paul has explained in chapters 1 and 2) or living in light of it (as Paul goes on to explore in chapters 3 and 4 of Corinthians). The implication is that not just their imaginations but also their ecclesial practice and their experience of Christ's presence are fundamentally distorted.

---

35. Fee, *The First Epistle to the Corinthians*, 100.
36. Gorman, *Cruciformity*, 58.
37. Although the resurrection is only implied and not directly mentioned, as noted earlier.

7.3 1 Corinthians 3–4: Pneumatologically enabled unity

In 1 Corinthians 1–2, Paul was emphatic that the Corinthian believers' existence is defined by Christ and enabled by the Spirit. In chapters 3–4, which continues Paul's argument, he expresses deep concern that he cannot speak to them as people who are defined and enabled this way, because they are currently behaving as if their ontological reality had not in fact been so drastically altered. His focus thus moves from Christo/eschato-logical imagination to their experienced presence and empowered practice, and particularly its transformative moral implications. This is precisely the kind of logical move we would expect to see from Paul if he were applying an eschatological Third Article Ecclesiology approach to the present situation of the Corinthian church. These latter two chapters (3–4) bring to a close the initial discourse that Paul began in 1.10. The presenting issue was the Corinthian believers' factions and quarrelling (1.10-17). The underlying issue was their inadequate grasp of God's Christologically centred, pneumatologically enabled and eschatologically directed wisdom and power (1.18–2.16). But the crux of the issue for Paul is 'their radically misguided perception of the nature of the church and its leadership'[38] (3.1–4.21). It is in these chapters, therefore, that Paul's Third Article Epistemology in the earlier two chapters becomes an explicitly eschatological Third Article Ecclesiology.

In chapters 3 and 4, the eschatological presuppositions which were latent in 1.18–2.16 become explicit. 'What Paul is trying to do above all else is to get the Corinthians to enter his orbit, to see things from his eschatological perspective.'[39] Consider the logical flow of Paul's argument in these chapters. After reminding the Corinthian believers of the immaturity of their present factionalism (3.1-4), Paul goes on to classify leaders as servants (3.5-9), whose role is to see the church growing and being built up over time (3.10-15), so that it can both be and become all that it is intended for it: a united people in whom the Spirit dwells (3.16-23). Chapter 4 recapitulates much of this material but applies it specifically to Paul's relationship with the Corinthian church. Paul and Apollos are servants and so their work for the church will be judged by the Lord, not by the Corinthian believers (4.1-7). But the kingdom growth and development they are working towards do not occur through ever-increasing strength and honour but through Christlike obedient suffering (4.8-13). Paul ends his entire argument where it began, with a strong and fatherly plea for unity, but this time particularly for a united relationship between the Corinthian believers and himself (4.14-21).

As Paul turns his attention in these chapters towards ecclesiology and ecclesial practice, two key features become apparent. The first is Paul's description of the church's ongoing growth and development towards its eschatological destination. The second and related emphasis is the moral imperative for present unity and maturity that arises out of that eschatological journey, a journey enabled through

---

38. Fee, *The First Epistle to the Corinthians*, 128.
39. Ibid., 157.

practice and presence. Once again, there are quite obviously significant overlaps here between the themes of an eschatological Third Article Ecclesiology and Paul's approach to the challenges facing the Corinthian church. These will be explored in the following paragraphs.

Consider first Paul's exploration of the church's ongoing journey towards its ultimate destination. There are two aspects to consider here: the church's ongoing journey and the journey's eschatological end point. Regarding the first, Paul uses two images in 1 Corinthians 3 to illustrate the church's present growth and development. The first is a botanical image (3.5-9). Leaders plant and water but God makes the ecclesial plant grow. The second is an image of construction (3.10-15). The church's foundation is Jesus, but leaders build on that foundation with materials of greater or lesser worth. The overall picture that Paul is painting is one where the church changes over time, but that not all change or development is of ultimate value. This is the importance of the second aspect: the journey's end point. Paul notes that growth and development can occur in ways that are either continuous or discontinuous with the church's ultimate eschatological destination. At that end point, what has been grown or built will be tested by fire (3.13) and will either remain or not. Leaders who invested in the church's growth and development will be judged on what remains *after* the eschatological judgement (3.14-15), not on what is there *midway* through the journey (4.1-5).

The questions that immediately arise from this picture are: What are the lasting characteristics of the community that will survive the eschatological purge?[40] And how can a leader instil these qualities into a congregation? Paul's argument points towards answers to each of these questions, answers which align directly with the earlier analysis of an eschatological Third Article Ecclesiology. The first is that the ecclesial developments that will survive the eschatological judgement are precisely those which characterize the coming kingdom. As was noted in chapter 4, this includes but is not limited to community characteristics such as love and unity, abundant life and joy, truth and holiness, justice and equality. A leader who is investing in developing these qualities in their congregation is building something of eternal and lasting value. Paul's clear focus in these chapters is the first of these kingdom qualities: love and unity. The answer to the second question emerges from examining the contrast Paul develops in 4.8-13 between the leadership provided by himself and the other apostles, and that provided by those who are presently influencing the Corinthian believers. The contrast is between leaders who are dying daily, who are seen as fools, weak, in disrepute, hungry, thirsty, poorly clothed, homeless, weary and who return evil with good, as compared with those who are already rich, already kings,[41] wise, strong and already held in high

---

40. Or, in Pauline language: What do these metaphorical valuable materials – gold, silver, precious gems – actually refer to in lived practice?

41. The 'already' qualification is important here. The believers' *telos* includes roles as kings and judges, but it is something to anticipate, not something already being enjoyed and experienced.

honour. The former leads to ecclesial developments that endure; the latter does not. Summarized in a single phrase, the type of leadership that builds something of eternal value is obedient suffering.[42] Consequently, from these chapters there emerges two features of a Pauline ecclesiology, which can be labelled as vision and approach, respectively. The vision of a Pauline church is that it should reflect to as great a degree as possible the coming kingdom. The approach (through which the vision is gradually attained) is that the Spirit transforms the church through (particularly its leaders') obedient suffering.

Paul's clear goal in these chapters is to transform the Corinthian church towards precisely this kind of ecclesiological vision and approach. And he does so not just through correcting their Christo/eschato-logical imagination but also through encouraging them to alter both their enacted practice and their understanding and experience of Christ's presence among them. Regarding enacted practice, given such an eschato-ecclesial perspective, Paul's passionate rebuke of the Corinthian church's leader-based factions is unsurprising and in fact entirely warranted. That there should be quarrels among the believers is bad enough, but that they should be quarrelling about leaders' whom they either align with or reject (3.4-5), when the very purpose of leadership is to promote kingdom growth that is the exact opposite of such partisanship, is an even more profound error. Not only are they promoting disunity (the exact opposite of a kingdom trait that will last beyond the eschatological judgement), but they are doing it in a way that endorses the exact opposite of Godly leadership (partisan honouring and factionalism). In short, they are promoting personal, human power and wisdom over and against the unseen, true and greater power and wisdom of God's Spirit. Such behaviour is evidence not just of a lack of maturity (3.1-3) but of missing the point of their new pneumato-eschatological status altogether. And so Paul points them in these chapters not merely towards improved practice but also towards a renewed experience and appreciation of Christ's pneumatological presence among them. 'For when you say ... are you not merely human?' (3.4). 'Do you not know that you are God's temple, and that God's Spirit dwells in you?' (3.16). The point Paul makes is that the experience of Christ through God's Spirit is intrinsically communal and through their factionalism they are neglecting and minimalizing their experience of Christ's pneumatological presence among them. A similar argument can be made about the description of the apostles' behaviour in chapter 4. 'The application of this new perspective to the apostolic ministries underscores that the way of knowing being advocated is not merely a new logic, a new cognitive enterprise, but includes living as well as thinking.'[43]

The key points here are thus both moral and communal. The pneumato-eschatological perspective with which Paul is approaching the Corinthian church's situation has clear moral implications. It is completely unacceptable that Corinthian believers should be 'set apart' for the kingdom and yet not be living

---

42. See the discussion about obedient suffering in Section 3.2.
43. Cousar, 'The Theological Task of 1 Corinthians', 97.

in a way that anticipates that future reality. But these moral implications are not aimed at each person individually but rather towards the entire church body as a unit. Christ's presence dwells in all of the believers together through the Spirit. So independent of which leader they are supporting, the believers together bear the brunt of the apostle's wrath. All of them are evidencing a lack of maturity and consequently harming the church's ongoing growth and development. Unity, perhaps more obviously than the others but in a similar manner to all kingdom traits, is intrinsically communal and not individualistic.

Paul's final comments in this chapter sum up the argument, and they are (as could be expected) explicitly eschatological. 'For the kingdom of God depends not on talk but on power' (4.20). This statement draws together the existential dimensions of what Paul affirms in these chapters about the coming kingdom and clearly references the conversation on resurrection in 1 Corinthians 15 he is leading towards. Paul's unease is not just with the quarrelling. It is not just a forlorn wish that everyone could get along together. 'His primary concern is with the Corinthians' radical misunderstanding of the gospel (1.18–2.16), and of the church (3.5-17) and apostleship (4.1-13) which their sloganeering in the name of wisdom represents.'[44] Carr summarizes the implications well:

> In Paul's portrayal, God's kingdom consists of power. But by exploring the motif of power in 1 Corinthians, and by placing it in conversation with 15:24-28, one can begin to fill out this kingdom reference. By identifying the kingdom with *dunamis*, Paul evokes a cluster of associations related to the Spirit as the mediator of Christ's presence in the Corinthian community. These associations include the reality of Christ's necessary, *present* reign (15:25a), which involves the resurrected Lord as a power sphere that grounds the Corinthians' current existence, energizes their practices and moral transformation, and will ultimately empower their life from the dead. To seek status by other means is to derive their being from a different power sphere and therefore, to align with powers that are being put under Christ's feet. (15:25b)[45]

Looking at the argument overall, what Paul is presenting through the interplay of pneumatologically enabled imagination, practice and presence is that the aspects of the future kingdom (with an emphasis here on unity) should be developed and grown in the Corinthian community through the practice of obedient suffering, where the life of Christ and him crucified becomes definitive and exemplary for the life of the church. It is hard to conceive of an example of practical theological reasoning that is more aligned to the application of an eschatological Third Article Ecclesiology.

---

44. Fee, 'Toward a Theology of 1 Corinthians', 39.
45. Frederick David Carr, 'Beginning at the End: The Kingdom of God in 1 Corinthians', *Catholic Biblical Quarterly* 81, no. 3 (2019): 459.

7.4 1 Corinthians 5–10: Pneumatologically enabled community

In the next chapters, Paul deals with several practical issues in quick succession: a congregation member involved in an incestuous relationship (5.1-13), lawsuits between believers (6.1-11), relationships with prostitutes (6.12-20), sexual instructions for those who are married (7.1-16), contentedness with your present situation (7.17-24), sexual instructions for those who are not married (7.25-40) and finally food offered to idols (8.1-13), which is then extended into a much longer discourse on rights and freedoms (9.1–11.1). While the topics are varied, the common theme running through all of these issues is the relationship between individuals (and their bodily appetites) and the overall Christian community.

Separate and detailed theological exegeses of each of these individual passages from the perspective of an eschatological Third Article Ecclesiology would be of great value,[46] but the primary point being argued in this chapter can be equally convincingly made through examining in broad strokes the commonalities that exist between each of them. For these commonalities clearly demonstrate the underlying logic that Paul brings to each of these situations, and, further, it shows that his logic matches closely with that of an eschatological Third Article Ecclesiology. This logic can be summarized as follows. First, the strong emphasis in each passage is on the church community, rather than the individual. The bodies and appetites of the Corinthian believers matter precisely because they are members of the collective community. What they do with their individual bodies affects the overall church and does so in important and non-trivial ways. Paul's focus in these passages is thus clearly ecclesiological; it centres on how what individuals do affects and is reacted to by the community as a whole. In other words, his focus is on empowered ecclesial practice. Second, the reason the collective community is primary is precisely because it is the bodily expression of the risen Jesus. 'There cannot be any doubt . . . that Paul regards the Corinthian community as the bodily expression of the resurrected one, living through the Spirit that comes from him.'[47] Paul's logic in these passages is thus not just ecclesiologically focused but also Christologically situated and pneumatologically enabled. For Paul, the Spirit makes the church the body of the resurrected Christ on earth. This logical step is Paul utilizing the aspect of pneumatologically enabled presence. The final aspect of Paul's logic is to outline how the church as Christ's body on earth is both set apart and in the process of being transformed together into a community of authority, beauty and power. This is the final aspect of eschatological imagination, which for Paul leads directly into the community's ongoing moral transformation. Resurrection is communal; it happens (and is happening) to us collectively. The church together inherits the kingdom. So, our communal and individual actions

---

46. Although it is not an eschatological Third Article Ecclesiology, see, for example, the helpful theological exegesis of the first of these in Barnhill, 'The Paradox of Ecclesiology', 242–63.

47. Johnson, 'The Body in Question', 303.

should reflect this inheritance into which we are growing. Consequently, for Paul, morality and eschatology are intrinsically intertwined. Paul's logic in these passages is consequently not just ecclesiologically focused, Christologically situated and pneumatologically enabled but also intrinsically morally and eschatologically directed. The following paragraphs reflect on this logic that Paul uses in addressing these diverse situations

The first point to note about Paul's logic is that he emphatically focuses on communal or ecclesiological aspects of the Corinthian believers' lives. This emphasis is clearly and explicitly evident within these chapters. In Paul's response to the congregation member's sexual immorality (5.1-13), for example, it is quite remarkable that of the thirteen verses which Paul spends addressing the issue, twelve of them admonish and correct the congregation, and only one addresses the issue itself.[48] The immorality for Paul is only tangentially about the wrongdoer but much more significantly about the congregation and what it reflects about them as a community. And the major feature that Paul discerns and critiques from their actions in this regard is the congregation's self-sufficient arrogance (5.2), which is the very opposite of the new ontological status they have been *gifted* in Christ through the Spirit. The same ecclesiological emphasis can be seen in Paul's discussion of food offered to idols (8.1-13). The apostle's initial comments make it clear that idols are powerless and that God alone is sovereign (8.1-6). One would expect that he would follow this by siding with those believers who exercise their freedom by eating food offered to idols. But the primary issue for Paul is not the individual freedom that following Christ enables but rather the growth and edification of the community. Ecclesiology trumps individual liberty. 'At issue is the nature of community. Is it a community where those with a correct theology can ignore others who have an aversion to eating idol-consecrated food?'[49] The apostles' abdication of their rights reflects a similar communal prioritization (9.12-23), as does Paul's discussion about sexual practice for both those who are married and unmarried. On the latter, over and above the note of spouses' bodies 'belonging' to their partners (7.4), consider the apostle's extraordinary claim that an unbeliever can be made holy through the faith of their believing spouse (7.14). Paul's thinking here is drastically different from our own Western approach. 'Pervasive individualism – evident above all in contemporary American culture – makes talk about a "social body" seem secondary and derivative, at best a metaphor.'[50] For Paul, though, it is not an exaggeration to say that our bodies matter primarily because they are a part of Christ's body, the church. Ecclesial practice is clearly a primary concern of the apostle.

---

48. Perhaps even more apposite is the clarity with which Paul in this passage distinguishes between those in and those out of the community, and how each should be treated differently. For more details on this facet, see Barnhill, 'The Paradox of Ecclesiology', 252–3.

49. Cousar, 'The Theological Task of 1 Corinthians', 99.

50. Johnson, 'The Body in Question', 296.

Why is ecclesiology primary? Why does Paul's focus emphasize community practice over and above the individual? The underlying reason is his close identification between practice and presence, between the church and the risen Christ, which forms the second aspect of Paul's logic. This is ecclesial presence: through the Spirit, the church is identified as Christ's risen body on earth. Obviously, Paul makes this point explicitly later in the epistle (12.12-13), but this experiential and identification aspect of his logic is repeatedly utilized in these earlier chapters. Consider, for example, eating food offered to idols. Why is it that exercising such freedom is unacceptable? Because causing others to stumble is a 'sin against members of your own family' (8.12) and *therefore* a 'sin against Christ' (8.13).[51] In his extended discussion on this issue, Paul makes the point even more explicit – in and through the eucharist we identify ourselves with Christ himself (10.16-17). Indeed, Paul's 'concern through the letter is the social implications of Christ becoming "life-giving" Spirit'.[52] In the example of the incestuous relationship, Paul asserts the Corinthian church should cast the wrongdoer out of the fellowship 'in the power of the Lord Jesus' (5.4). Why can they do this? For together, Paul and the community speak with the risen Christ's authority. Perhaps the clearest instance of experienced presence, however, is in Paul's exhortations regarding prostitutes. Why is such fornication unacceptable? Because 'your bodies are members of Christ' (6.15) and 'anyone united to the Lord becomes one spirit with him' (6.17). Or, even more specifically, in words that refer back to Paul's comments in 1 Cor. 3.16, 'your body is a temple of the Holy Spirit within you' (6.19). Having sex with a prostitute is wrong precisely because through the Spirit the Corinthian believers' bodies form Christ's body on earth. Johnson's comments here are pertinent:

> Paul reminds them of what they should already know: their (plural) body (singular) is the sanctuary of the Holy Spirit which they (plural) have from God that is 'among/with them' (plural). And they do not, therefore, belong to themselves. They have been bought for a price, and should therefore glorify God in their (plural) body (singular). By 'glorifying God,' Paul means that they must recognize and live by the recognition that God is indeed present among them, both individually and corporately. Only such a strong ontological sense between the spirit of the resurrected one and the community can make intelligible Paul's command.[53]

---

51. 'The phrase "sinning against Christ" assumes the strongest sort of connection between each member of the community (or the community as a whole) and the resurrected Lord.' Johnson, 'The Body in Question', 304.

52. Johnson, 'The Body in Question', 300.

53. Ibid., 309-10. Johnson's explanation of 6.18 is relevant here too. He notes that the only way to make sense of this verse is if the second reference to 'body' refers directly to the community. So a person who sins does not sin against their physical body so much as the body of Christ, which is the community of the church. 'By implicating body and spirit

So Paul's logic in these chapters is ecclesiologically focused, Christologically situated and pneumatologically enabled – practice and presence are directly addressed – but where does that lead? How does one determine the implications of this theological understanding? For Paul, it is precisely because of the Corinthian church's identification with and experience of the body of the risen Christ on earth that they are both set apart from the rest of the world in terms of its destiny and in the process of being morally transformed into a community of authority, beauty and power. This is where all three aspects of eschatological imagination, presence and practice come together to enable moral transformation. This intertwining of moral and eschatological understanding is the final aspect of Paul's logical approach to the disturbing reports he has heard and challenging questions he has been asked. The Corinthian church's future destiny and their present and ongoing morality are intrinsically combined. So, it is because of their future roles as judges that they need to disassociate with the incestuous evildoer (5.12), so that he too may be saved when the day comes (6.5). It is because the believers will judge the world that they should not be handing jurisdiction over their disagreements to unbelieving outsiders (6.3-4). Believers should remain in their present situation, says Paul, because (it is implied) their current condition is but temporary. Greater things are coming. Therefore, focus on the transformative essentials (obedient suffering) (7.19) and do not excessively concern yourselves with things that are transient (7.17-24). The present form of this world is passing away (7.31), so deliberately place yourself in situations (e.g. marriage, celibacy) that will enable you to endure and to serve the Lord as best you can, situations that will enable you to be and remain holy and chaste (7.32-35). There is a prize awaiting the church, so let that coming prize direct the way that you are running the race and living your life now (9.24-27). Examples such as these show clearly how for Paul, eschatological destiny and present moral transformation are strongly intertwined.

The thematic overlap between Paul's logic as utilized in 1 Corinthians 5–10 as noted earlier, its foreshadowing of the resurrection eschatology that concludes the letter in 1 Corinthians 15 (with its pneumatological, eschatological and moral foci) and the overarching connection of both with an eschatological Third Article Ecclesiology is thus very clear indeed. Perhaps the most obvious and explicit connection between the explicitly eschatological focus of the latter pair and 1 Corinthians 5–10 occurs in 1 Cor. 6.14: 'And God raised the Lord and will also raise us by his power.' As Johnson comments, 'The implications Paul draws from his statement . . . indicate that, for him, the reality of the resurrection is not merely either past or future; it is above all a present reality. The power of the Lord is already present and active in the somatic existence of the all-too-empirical Corinthians to whom Paul writes.'[54] For Paul, and for an eschatological Third Article Ecclesiology, all three aspects – ontological, communal and moral change – are

---

sexually with the body and spirit of a prostitute, Paul thinks harm is done to the body of Christ and the Holy Spirit in a distinctive fashion.' Johnson, 'The Body in Question', 310.

54. Johnson, 'The Body in Question', 308–9.

linked together, and all three are intrinsically pneumatologically enabled. Through the Spirit we are identified with Christ. His death and resurrection are ours, and because we participate in him, we have a whole new way of being. This identification is not ours alone as individuals, though, but something we share in with others in our Christian community. Our bodies matter because together we form Christ's resurrected body on earth. And precisely because we do form Christ's earthly body, what we do with our bodies matters. Our ongoing deaths and resurrections, our obedient suffering, are preparing us for our kingdom *telos*. To turn Paul's negative warning of 6.19 into a positive affirmation, those who do right – those who anticipate the features of the kingdom in their present earthly lives – will surely inherit the kingdom.

7.5 1 Corinthians 11–14: Pneumatologically enabled worship

As Paul turns in these latter chapters to specifically address the gathered worship of the Corinthian congregation in 1 Corinthians 11–14, he deals with three issues: a brief discussion of head coverings (11.2-16), a slightly longer examination of the eucharist (11.17-33) and a much more extended discussion about the use of Spiritual gifts (12–14). This section will contain some brief comments about the first two issues, before exploring the latter in more depth.

Regarding the discussion of head coverings (11.2-16), Paul does not argue in this small section with the same passion that he has customarily used to this point in the letter and that he continues to use after completing this discussion. Fee comments that 'the differences are as night and day'.[55] The other clear point in 1 Corinthians where Paul's argumentation is less than strident is in 7.1-40, where he is addressing issues that (like this passage) are transitory, predominantly pertaining only to this world. These changes in Paul's rhetorical approach point towards a revealing insight. For issues which impact how the Corinthian community reflect the coming kingdom, Paul is adamant and clear. For issues which are temporary and related only to this world and its customs, Paul still provides theological guidance but does so with much less zeal and implied authority. This lack of veracity reinforces that the argument being made in this chapter that Paul's focus in 1 Corinthians is derived from an intrinsically pneumato-eschatological outlook.

As expected, given its eschatological orientation, Paul's urgency and rhetorical authority return in force as he addresses the topic of the eucharist (11.17-33). An eschatological Third Article Ecclesiology of the eucharist has already been addressed in great detail in Chapter 5, and in that analysis 1 Corinthians 11 was utilized at some length.[56] It suffices here simply to note the increasingly obvious points of overlap between Paul's argument and an eschatological Third Article Ecclesiology. First, Paul critiques two clear deficiencies in the Corinthian believers'

---

55. Fee, *The First Epistle to the Corinthians*, 491.
56. See particularly Sections 5.2 and 5.3.

eucharistic behaviour: their lack of unity (as evidenced in their eating separately (11.18)) and their lack of justice (as evidenced in some gorging themselves while others go hungry (11.21)). Both of these facets are clearly evident features of the coming kingdom which the Spirit draws back to be a part of our present ecclesial life. Second, Paul's remedy for the Corinthian behaviour involves an appropriately interactive combination of both enabled presence and empowered practice. Christ is pneumatologically present in the loaf and the cup, and so it is beholden on the Corinthian believers to recognize and acknowledge this presence in their practice of eating and drinking. To not do so is to eat and drink judgement on themselves. Paul's eucharistic examination in 1 Corinthians 11 provides another compelling, if brief, example of how the interplay of eschatological imagination, empowered presence and enabled practice transforms the church as it journeys through time.

Turning finally to Paul's more detailed treatise on Spiritual gifts in 1 Corinthians 12–14, this extended discussion provides the strongest argument yet for Paul's intrinsically pneumato-eschatological approach to ecclesiology. Indeed, as Paul approaches 1 Corinthians 15 and his explicit discussion of our coming resurrection, the influence of these themes on Paul's argument becomes quite explicit and his utilization of an eschatological Third Article Ecclesiology understanding becomes even more compellingly obvious. Consider the broad logic of these chapters. The centre and high point of the argument lies in Paul's famed discourse on love in 1 Corinthians 13.[57] And the central point of that chapter is love's eschatological endurance: love never ends (13.8). Paul leads up to this in 1 Corinthians 12 with a general discussion about Spiritual gifts within the church and how they are designed to draw the church together and make its members fundamentally interdependent. And he leads out from it with an application of how the Spiritual gifts of prophecy and tongues can be used to build the congregation together into such interdependence, if they are used 'decently and in order' (14.40). The following paragraphs will argue that precisely the same themes that characterize 1 Corinthians 15, and that characterize an eschatological Third Article Ecclesiology, also characterize Paul's discussion in these chapters. Namely, Paul's discussion of Spiritual gifts is intrinsically eschatological: value is ascribed to that which lasts. It is intrinsically moral and transformational: the purpose of the gifts is to see development and growth in the body. It is intrinsically ecclesiological: this desired transformation occurs particularly within the believing community. And it is intrinsically pneumatological: the Spirit is the means through which the ecclesiological transformation towards the desired eschatological goals occurs.

Beginning with the last of these aspects, Paul's exploration of Spiritual gifts is clearly pneumatologically determined. If the descriptor 'Spiritual' in the title of the topic was not indication enough, even a cursory reading of 1 Corinthians 12 (and

---

57. Many scholars also recognise that the discourse in 1 Corinthians 13 should be seen as an integral part of the discussion of spiritual gifts. See, for example, Raymond F. Collins, *First Corinthians* (Collegeville: The Liturgical Press, 1999), 441–3.

particularly the opening eleven verses) reveals an overwhelming preponderance of pneumatological language. The Spirit enables believers to declare their allegiance to Christ (12.3); the Spirit is the source and allocator of the 'Spiritual' gifts (12.4-11); the Spirit forms believers together as Christ's body (12.12-13). Just as 1 Corinthians 2 ascribed all epistemological understanding to the Spirit alone, so 1 Corinthians 12 ascribes all of our functional activity within the believing community to the same Spirit. A defining feature of Third Article Theology is that it 'starts with the Spirit', and Paul in this argument clearly and explicitly begins his argument pneumatologically. And his key pneumatological point is that because there is only one Spirit, then even though there are diverse gifts that the Spirit gives to each individual believer, there is only one community to which all believers belong (which is Christ's body) and only one purpose for these diverse gifts (the edification of this body). 'The Spirit is instrumental in establishing the wholeness as well as the holiness of the believing community.'[58] The clear implication drawn is that every believer in the community is 'Spiritual'. In contrast to the Corinthians who are making a distinction between those who are truly 'Spiritual' and those who are not, Paul is arguing here that 'every Christian is indeed a spiritual person'.[59] There can be no distinction within the community between those who have the Spirit to a greater or lesser degree, 'everyone within the believing community has received the Spirit and is "spiritual"'.[60]

If the lens through which Paul begins his examination is the Spirit, then the focus of his pneumatologically enabled gaze is the believing community. Individuals find their purpose not just *through* the Spirit but *in* the body. True and genuine Christian living is not just pneumatologically empowered, it is fundamentally and exclusively ecclesiologically located. Paul's ecclesiological focus in these texts is common and clear. Consider his detailed defence of believers' interdependence (12.16-31), and his strong preference for gifts that build up the community over those that are merely individualistic experience (14.1-25). In terms of communal focus, the importance of baptism as an initiatory ritual should also be noted (12.13), together with the irrelevance of a believer's previous ethnic or social standing (12.13). Indeed, Paul's comments point to the sheer theological impossibility of division or even gradations within the body.[61] Paul's overall purpose in this extended passage is thus indisputably ecclesiological: 'He is seeking to bring the disorderly and self-centred worship practices of the Corinthians under control, so that the church as a whole may be built up.'[62] 1 Corinthians 12–14 is consequently

---

58. Victor Paul Furnish, *The Theology of the First Letter to the Corinthians* (Cambridge: Cambridge University Press, 1999), 95.

59. M. M. Mitchell, *Paul and the Rhetoric of Reconciliation* (Tubingen: Mohr and Louisville, 1992), 267.

60. Furnish, 'Theology in 1 Corinthians', 70.

61. See Rosato, 'The Mission of the Spirit within and beyond the Church', 391.

62. Richard B. Hays, *First Corinthians* (Louisville: John Knox Press, 1989), 206.

not just an example of Third Article Theology in general but an example of a Third Article *Ecclesiology*.

Using the Spirit as an enabling lens to focus on the Corinthians' ecclesiology, the vantage point from which Paul looks is eschatological. This perspective becomes particularly clear in Paul's magnificent rhapsody on love in 1 Corinthians 13, which serves as the centre of the discourse in these chapters. Love's pre-eminence is that which 1 Corinthians 12 leads towards and that from which 1 Corinthians 14 follows. And the clearest contrast between the gifts (particularly the gift of tongues) that the Corinthians so esteem and the love that Paul points them to as a 'more excellent way' (12.31) is that love lasts (13.7). Love is a defining feature of the kingdom that is coming and as such it will never end (13.8), in contrast to tongues that will cease (13.8). According to Paul, then, the purpose of the gifts is the fruit. The gifts of the Spirit, temporary and partial though they may be, enable the body to experience the fruit of the Spirit, which is neither transient nor incomplete and within which love is primary above all. 'Precisely because the gifts have an end point, which love does not, they are of a different order altogether.... Good as spiritual gifts are, they are only for the present; Christian love... belongs to eternity as well as to the present.'[63] So here at the centre of his argument, Paul is utilizing an *eschatological* Third Article Ecclesiology.

And the purpose and outcome of utilizing this eschatological Third Article Ecclesiology are to effect moral transformation within the Corinthian community as they journey through time. His pneumato-eschatological approach to the Corinthian church has present moral and ethical implications for this community. Because love is an enduring feature of the coming kingdom, through the Spirit, the community of believers need to deliberately and intentionally set themselves the task of growing in love as a complete and united community. The development of such an interdependent, other-focused, loving fellowship is precisely what it means for the Corinthian church to no longer be childish (13.11-12, 14.20) and to grow into maturity. According to the apostle Paul, emphasis should be placed on those gifts and those uses of the gifts that enable the congregation to grow in such love. In this way, the Corinthians are bringing the future reality back to (in part) be a characteristic of their present existence. Such an interpretation of 1 Corinthians 12-14 is not half-hidden but a plain and straightforward first reading. It is not difficult, as Fee comments, 'to emphasize the eschatological dimension of the paragraph, that our present existence, for all its blessings, is but a foretaste of the future.'[64] For Paul, the point is not just that love is emphasized and pre-eminent but that the Spirit gives gifts precisely so that love can grow within the congregation, so that they can anticipate more and more within their community the features of the coming kingdom.

---

63. Fee, *The First Epistle to the Corinthians*, 649. See also the discussion in Furnish, *The Theology of the First Letter to the Corinthians*, 72.

64. Fee, *The First Epistle to the Corinthians*, 651.

As Paul approaches the end of his letter, then, and as he deals with the most contentious, central and important of issues that he must address with the Corinthians, his utilization of the approach of an eschatological Third Article Ecclesiology becomes even more clear and evident. Paul starts with the Spirit and from the perspective of an eschatological vantage point he examines the ecclesiological practice of the Corinthian church. Using a kingdom vantage point and a pneumatological lens, the inadequacy of the present ecclesial practice of the Corinthians, and their understanding of Christ's presence within them, is demonstrated with particular clarity, as is the appropriate course of action required to enable them to mature in such a way that will enable them to reflect and anticipate the kingdom more fully. While no suggestion is being made here that the entirety of Paul's argument in 1 Corinthians 12–14 without remainder can be construed as an eschatological Third Article Ecclesiology, it is being argued that this theological approach comprises the core of Paul's argumentative basis.

7.6 Conclusion

This chapter has argued that throughout Paul's first epistle to the Corinthians and in a way that becomes increasingly evident as the readers worked their way through the letter, the apostle utilized the approach of an eschatological Third Article Ecclesiology to address and respond to the situations the Corinthian church was facing. Indeed, by the time the apostle reaches the central reasons for his theological conflict with the Corinthian believers (resurrection in 1 Corinthians 15) and the use of Spiritual gifts (particularly *glossolalia*) in 1 Corinthians 12–14, the eschatological vantage point, pneumatological lens and moral and ecclesiological outworking he is utilizing are very clear and obvious. The key themes that have been noted in the development of an eschatological Third Article Ecclesiology – the empowering role of the Spirit, the ongoing experience of transformation, the illuminating vantage point of eschatology, the immediate implications for morality and holiness, the present experience of crucifixion and resurrection as the means of effecting our transformation, the interplay of practice, presence and imagination as the practical way that present transformation occurs – all of these feature heavily not just in these final chapters of 1 Corinthians but throughout the epistle.

The conclusions to be drawn from this exercise can be divided into two broad categories. First, there are a set of conclusions that can be drawn about 1 Corinthians itself. What has been demonstrated in this chapter is that when Paul thinks of the Corinthian church's day-to-day life, when he reflects on the issues they are facing and determines how to react and respond, he does so primarily on the basis of an eschatological Third Article Ecclesiology. This points towards the overall unity and coherence of the letter as a single entity. Second, there are a set of conclusions that can be drawn about the theological vantage point of an eschatological Third Article Ecclesiology. Given that this perspective has provided a coherent lens on the epistle, one that clearly informs the arguments that Paul is making throughout, this provides confidence that the ecclesiological understanding constructed in this volume is itself sensible and systematic. The implication of both sets of conclusions is that for contemporary theologians and leaders, an eschatological Third Article Ecclesiology is an indispensable foundation from which to examine, positively influence and morally transform those congregations with which we are involved.

Chapter 8

TOWARDS A THIRD ARTICLE THEOLOGY OF ECCLESIAL MISSION

Jesus' incarnate action of breathing the Spirit on the church was accompanied by an explicit missional call for the church to enter the world as his witnesses (Jn 20.21-22, Acts 1.8). Consequently, it is appropriate that as the discipline of Third Article Theology continues to develop, the pivotal loci of missiology receives detailed attention and analysis. This chapter consequently undertakes another Wolterstorffian exercise, one that pushes the exploration of Third Article Theology into new territory. In the preceding chapters, all the exploration has been specifically focused on the church and its inner transformation. The important question of the relationship between the church and the world has been put to one side. This chapter outlines a way that this question can be addressed. Taking all the ecclesiological perspectives gained from the vantage points of Christology, the Trinity and eschatology, it explores what happens when these three understandings are used as control beliefs to examine the data belief of missiology. This approach contrasts with and complements the more common approach where missiology is seen as determinative of ecclesiology. Initially arguing that ecclesiology and missiology are mutually informing doctrines, this chapter develops a dialogical and pneumatological approach for viewing missiology from the vantage point of ecclesiology. The final and major section of this chapter sketches out the panoramic vision of the church's mission that arises when it is viewed from each of these vantage points, particularly when the Spirit's role is seen as primary and constitutive.

8.1 The relationship between ecclesiology and missiology

There is a continuum of opinions about the relationship between the church and mission. Some argue that mission is primarily God's job and the church's active missional role is minimal.[1] Others see mission as foundationally core to the

---

1. An example of this position is the hyper-Calvinistic position taken by English Baptists in the late eighteenth century, illustrated most graphically in John Collett Ryland Sr's

church's being, even to the point of defining the church entirely by mission.² The divergence is partly due to contrasting definitions. Those who define mission very broadly instinctively view mission as foundational for the church. If mission is everything and everything is mission,³ then it inevitably follows that the church's very being is missional. The point is tautological. Alternatively, a narrow definition of mission (such as merely the winning of converts) clearly omits important ecclesial aspects. If the church is just about recruiting others who are recruiters in turn, ultimately what is all this recruiting for? 'Recruited to what?' as McClendon rightly questions.⁴ Consequently, those who define mission narrowly often view mission as important but not necessarily foundational.⁵

Such terminology-induced diversity means that clear definitions must precede detailed analysis. This chapter adopts a broad but not all-encompassing definition of ecclesial mission as what the church is and does for the world. Or to say the same thing in different words, ecclesial mission is the intentionally outward, world-facing part of the church. Defined in this way, what is the appropriate

---

supposed response to William Carey: 'Young man, sit down; when God pleases to convert the heathen, he will do it without your aid or mine.' See Timothy George, *Faithful Witness: The Life and Mission of William Carey* (Birmingham: New Hope, 1991), 53–5. There is some dispute about whether or not this interpretation of Ryland's words is accurate. See Lon Graham, 'A Showdown or a Put Down? Rethinking an Incident from Early Baptist Mission History', *Journal of European Baptist Studies* 18, no. 2 (2018): 7–18. More recently, extreme advocates of the *missio Dei* have similarly argued that God's mission occurs independently of the church's involvement. See, for example, P. G. Aring, *Kirche als Ereignis: Ein Beitrag zur Neuorientierung der Missions-theologie* (Neukirchen-Vluyn: Neikirchener Verlag, 1971). Also, see the discussion in David J. Bosch, *Transforming Mission: Paradigm Shifts in Theology of Mission* (New York: Orbis Books, 1995), 392.

2. For example, Guder writes that 'The center core of the *missio Dei* is evangelization'. D. L. Guder, *The Continuing Conversion of the Church* (Grand Rapids: Eerdmans, 2000), 49. Similarly, Brunner's often-quoted comment that 'the church exists by mission, just as a fire exists by burning'. Emil Brunner, *The Word and the World* (London: SCM Press, 1931), 11.

3. Some descriptions certainly lean in this direction. For example, Chris Wright argues that 'Mission is not just one of a list of things that the Bible happens to talk about, only a bit more urgently than some. Mission is, in that much-abused phrase, "what it's all about."' Christopher J. H. Wright, *The Mission of God: Unlocking the Bible's Grand Narrative* (Downers Grove: IVP Academic, 2006), 22.

4. 'If the goal is to win others who will win others who will win others, an infinite regress of mere recruitment has taken the place of any real (or realistic) understanding of the point of evangelism. Recruited to what?' J. W. McClendon, *Systematic Theology: Doctrine* (Abingdon Press, 1994), 439.

5. See, for example, Mark Galli, *The Church Does Not Exist for the Sake of the World* [cited 22 November 2019], available from https://www.christianitytoday.com/ct/2019/june-web-only/church-does-not-exist-for-sake-of-world.html?fbclid=IwAR3H7LImTwKuD16vM2jL7qxnsua06LzDbXP6AHSgLxmLAH9YdtBE1nYG7D0.

relationship between the church and mission?[6] How do these two doctrinal realities indwell, inform and improve each other? There are five clear options. The first is that church and mission are distinct, with the two intersecting minimally, merely resourcing and supporting the other. The second and opposite option is that church and mission are identical, so that the church is exactly equated with its outward-focused missional activity, without any remainder.[7] The third option is that the church's ontological nature determines the church's missional activity and the fourth that mission determines the church's ontological reality. So, in the latter case, for example, it is only once an understanding of mission is determined that the question of how to act as church can be explored. In the former, it is only once the intrinsic nature of the church is determined that the church's missionary activity can be considered. The final option is that church and mission mutually inform each other. This first section of this chapter argues that this final option provides the most compelling understanding of the relationship between ecclesiology and missiology.

The first two options outlined earlier are clearly inadequate. Option one is the approach taken by the overseas missionary movement from the late eighteenth century. Recognizing the lack of, and even opposition to, missionary endeavour in many European Protestant churches of that time, those eager to fulfil the great commission formed separate missionary bodies, thus distinguishing between church and mission. As Newbigin writes, 'The correction of a deformity in the Church was itself deformed by its opposition to that which it sought to correct. The New Testament knows of only one missionary society – the Church.'[8] Newbigin justifiably labels this separation of church and mission as one of the 'calamities of missionary history'.[9] Equally mistaken is the second option of equating the church with or subsuming it within mission, as if the church is entirely defined by its outward, world-facing aspect. While an unhelpfully broad understanding of mission can perhaps accommodate such an understanding,[10] the church's primary relationship is with God and not with the world. All ecclesial mission is worship, for missionary activity occurs for God's glory and through his power. But not

---

6. Note that the term 'mission' as utilized here should be seen as broader than ecclesial mission. If ecclesial mission is concerned with the church's actions in the world, then mission overall is concerned with all of God's workings in the world.

7. In this option, ecclesiology can also be seen as an entirely enveloped subset of mission.

8. Lesslie Newbigin, *The Reunion of the Church: A Defence of the South India Scheme* (London: SCM Press, 1960), 11.

9. Lesslie Newbigin, *One Body, One Gospel, One World: The Christian Mission Today* (London: Wm. Carling & Co., 1958), 26. See also Michael W. Goheen, '"As the Father Has Sent Me, I am Sending You": Lesslie Newbigin's Missionary Ecclesiology', *International Review of Mission* 91, no. 362 (2002): 366.

10. Such a broad view would suggest that the church's worship of God is a part of its mission. Using such broad terminology unfortunately gives little insight into appropriate ecclesial actions.

all worship is mission, for there are aspects of worship that are not intentionally world-facing. For example, J. B. Torrance's profound definition of worship as 'participating through the Spirit in the incarnate Son's communion with the Father . . . and in his mission from the Father to the World'[11] has two clear components and only the latter is concerned with what the church is and does for the world.

Given that the absolutist options of complete separation or complete identity are inadequate, church and mission must be considered as partially overlapping realities. Illustrated as a Venn diagram, mission and church are overlapping sets, with ecclesial mission as the area of intersection between the two. The full breadth of the church is larger than just its missionary activity (as the church is more than just world-facing), and mission extends beyond ecclesial activity (for the Spirit is at work within, through *and beyond* the church).[12] This partially intersecting reality means that both missiology and ecclesiology can (at least logically) be divided into two aspects. Missiology includes both ecclesial mission and God's missionary activity beyond the church.[13] And ecclesiology includes both the church's gathered, worshipping community and its missionary activity.

Authors have utilized various nomenclature to express these dual aspects of ecclesiology. Two helpful examples come from Catholic scholars de Lubac and Dadosky. The French priest Henri de Lubac distinguishes between the active and passive aspects of the word *church*, describing the church as simultaneously the 'community of the called together' and the 'community called together'.[14] The first term refers to what we are and the second to what we do. The Canadian scholar John Dadosky expresses the same idea in a different way, arguing that a distinction should be made between 'the nature and the mission of the church – where the nature pertains to the people gathered, and its mission is to gather others'.[15]

Adopting Dadosky's terminology, the question becomes how the nature and mission of the church relate to each other. Does the nature of the church entirely determine its mission (option three), or does the church's mission determine its nature (option four)? Many missional church authors argue for this latter option. For example, Frost and Hirsch argue that ecclesiology is determined by mission.[16]

---

11. Torrance, *Worship, Community and the Triune God of Grace*, 20–1.

12. See, for example, Rosato, 'The Mission of the Spirit within and beyond the Church', 388–97.

13. The phrase 'activity beyond the church' does not refer to anything so simplistic as activity beyond the walls of the church building or activity not formally associated with the church. Rather, it refers to the Spirit's work in people outside of the church community.

14. Henri de Lubac, *The Splendour of the Church*, trans. Michael Mason (London: Sheed and Ward, 1956), 69–86. See particularly 69–73.

15. John Dadosky, '*Ecclesia de Trinitate*: Ecclesial Foundations from Above', *New Blackfriars* 94, no. 1049 (2013): 65.

16. Michael Frost and Alan Hirsch, *The Shaping of Things to Come: Innovation and Mission for the 21st-Century Church* (Peabody: Hendrickson, 2003), 201–23. More specifically, Hirsch comments that 'Christology determines missiology, and missiology

For them, structure follows strategy, or more accurately, identity follows function. Frost and Hirsch suggest the church should adopt a chameleon-like identity depending on how it can best fulfil its mission in the world. 'Our Christology informs our missiology, which then in turn determines our ecclesiology.'[17] Guder comments similarly that 'the witness to which we are called is an all-encompassing definition of Christian existence.'[18] Recognizing that comments like these from missional authors are often made more in a pragmatic than a purely theological sense,[19] the approach is nevertheless unsatisfactory. The end result of determining ecclesiology entirely from mission is an emaciated understanding of both the church and her mission. As Clark comments, 'This completely separates the person of Christ from the body of Christ in mission and relegates the church to a completely instrumentalised tool for individuals.'[20] Such an approach places the value of the individual over and above the community. Further, it 'reduces the church to a project, a means to a functional end'.[21] The biblical vision of ecclesiology is much richer than sheer functionality and goes well beyond collectivized individualism. Indeed, Fitch argues that making mission constitutive of ecclesiology is individualistic not just soteriologically but also epistemologically.[22] He points out the modernist assumptions underpinning the approach, noting that mission only makes sense within the framework of a community that embodies the gospel narrative towards which we witness. Fitch concludes that 'putting missiology before ecclesiology [will] eventually lead to the contextualising of the church into oblivion'.[23] Put simply, the primary underlying reason that missiology cannot determine ecclesiology is that the church extends

---

determines ecclesiology'. Alan Hirsch, *The Forgotten Ways* (Grand Rapids: BrazosPress, 2006), 142.

17. Frost and Hirsch, *The Shaping of Things to Come*, 209.

18. Darrell L. Guder, *Be My Witnesses* (Grand Rapids: Eerdmans, 1985), 233.

19. See, for example, Frost's response to those who question this priority as noted in Michael Frost, *Your Fixed Idea of Church Is Turning You into a Marketer, Not a Missionary* [cited 21 November 2019], available from https://mikefrost.net/fixed-idea-church-turning-marketer-not-missionary/. In making these comments, Frost, Hirsch and Guder's primary concern is those who have not just a previously decided ecclesiology but also a previously decided outworking of that ecclesiology. But like others before them, their justified correction of a deformity in the church is itself deformed by its opposition to that which it seeks to correct. (Note Newbigin's comment earlier.)

20. Jason Swan Clark, 'Just Go to Church' (paper presented at the Society of Vineyard Scholars Conference, London, 2019), n. 15.

21. Patrick S. Franklin, 'The God Who Sends Is the God Who Loves: Mission as Participating in the Ecstatic Love of the Triune God', *Didaskalia* 28 (2017): 77.

22. David Fitch, *Missiology Precedes Ecclesiology: The Epistemological Problem* [cited 22 November 2019], available from https://www.missioalliance.org/missiology-precedes-ecclesiology-the-epistemological-problem/.

23. Ibid.

beyond its world-facing mission. Of course, to say that mission doesn't *determine* ecclesiology doesn't imply that mission doesn't *inform* ecclesiology, but rather that its foundational essence is not intrinsically determined only by its outward-facing purpose.

The same point, but in reverse, is also the reason that the third option of ecclesiology entirely determining missiology is also unsatisfactory – for mission extends beyond the actions of the church. Indeed, mission is ultimately an attribute of God, and the church is only missional to the extent that it participates in God's mission. This understanding, captured most succinctly in the now commonly utilized phrase *missio Dei*, is one of the key missiological insights of the twentieth century. Finding its origin (some say)[24] in the work of Karl Barth[25] and Karl Hartenstein,[26] the idea (although not the terminology) emerged most clearly at the Willingen Conference of the IMC in 1952 and has since become a '*terminus technicus*'[27] in missiological discussion. Anderson summarizes the position reached at Willingen: 'the missionary enterprise . . . is trinitarian in character. . . . The triune God himself is the sole source of every missionary enterprise.'[28] And Bosch comments on its significance: 'The recognition that mission is God's mission represents a crucial breakthrough in respect of the preceding centuries. . . . It is inconceivable that we could again revert to a narrow, ecclesiocentric view of mission.'[29] It is important to be clear about what can and cannot be affirmed in this renewed understanding, however. If the point is overly emphasized, it quickly descends to the position of option four that has already been considered and rejected, an option where missiology becomes entirely determinative of ecclesiology. In some extreme cases the language of *missio Dei* is so drastically overemphasized it leads to an understanding where God almost entirely bypasses

---

24. See, for example, Bosch, *Transforming Mission*, 389–93. Also Johannes Aagaard, 'Trends in Missiological Thinking during the Sixties', *International Review of Mission* 62, no. 245 (1973): 11–12. Alternatively, see the discussion in John Flett, *The Witness of God: The Trinity, Missio Dei, Karl Barth and the Nature of Christian Community* (Grand Rapids: Eerdmans, 2010), 123–33.

25. Karl Barth, 'Die Theologie und die Mission in der Gegenwart', in *Theologische Fragen und Antworten vol 3.* (Zollikon-Zürich: Evangelischer Verlag, 1957), 100–26. See also Bosch, *Transforming Mission*, 389–90.

26. Karl Hartenstein, *Die Mission als theologisches Problem: Bieträge zum grandsätzlichen Verstandnis der Mission* (Berlin: Furche Verlag, 1932). See also Bosch, *Transforming Mission*, 389–90. And Flett, *The Witness of God*, 127–33.

27. Aagaard, 'Trends in Missiological Thinking during the Sixties', 11.

28. Willhelm Anderson, *Towards a Theology of Mission: A Study of the Encounter between the Missionary Enterprise and the Church and Its Theology* (London: SCM Press, 1955), 47.

29. Bosch, *Transforming Mission*, 393.

the church in his missional endeavour.³⁰ Certainly, missiology is Trinitarian and rooted in the very nature of God, but ecclesiology is equally rooted in God's Trinitarian nature. If we affirm the *missio Dei*, we must also affirm *ecclesia Dei*. Ecclesiology does not solely determine mission – this is an error that Bosch rightly insists we avoid – but ecclesiology should inform missiology, just as missiology informs ecclesiology.

Consequently, and in contrast to the previous four options, the only plausible alternative is that missiology and ecclesiology mutually inform each other. The question naturally arises from this, how do they inform each other? How can the insights from missiology be applied to ecclesiology, and how can the insights from ecclesiology be applied to missiology? This question is addressed in the next section.

8.2 A pneumatological and dialogical relationship

If the first major premise of this chapter is that missiology and ecclesiology mutually inform each other, the second major premise is that examining the correspondence between the two doctrines requires giving the Spirit prominence. There are two key reasons justifying this premise. The first is that ecclesiology and missiology themselves cannot be understood without introducing the category of the Spirit at a fundamental level. While the pneumatological foundation of both doctrines has perhaps been overlooked in the past,³¹ the last decade has seen significant development of and justification for the necessity of understanding both missiology and ecclesiology in explicitly pneumatological terms.³² The second reason is that pneumatology not only informs the doctrines

---

30. For example, Aring argues that 'In the final analysis, "missio Dei" means that God articulates himself, without any need of assisting him through our missionary efforts in this respect'. Aring, *Kirche als Ereignis*, 8f. As translated in Bosch, *Transforming Mission*, 392.

31. Regarding missiology, for example, Kärkkäinen writes, 'Given the . . . renaissance of pneumatology, one is also struck by the omission of a distinctive pneumatological outlook in modern missiology.' Kärkkäinen, *Toward a Pneumatological Theology*, 218–19. Regarding ecclesiology, Volf and Lee write that 'the pervasive association between "Spirit" and "church" notwithstanding, theologians have reflected relatively little on precisely *how* the two are related'. Miroslav Volf and Maurice Lee, 'The Spirit and the Church', in *Advents of the Spirit: An Introduction to the Current Study of Pneumatology*, ed. Bradford E. Hinze and D. Lyle Dabney (Milwaukee: Marquette University Press, 2003), 382. See also William R. Barr and Rena M. Yocum, 'Introduction', in *The Church in the Movement of the Spirit*, ed. William R. Barr and Rena M. Yocum (Grand Rapids: Eerdmans, 1994), 1–2.

32. For missiology, see, for example, Kärkkäinen, *Toward a Pneumatological Theology*, 217–27. And more recently, Amos Yong, *Mission after Pentecost: The Witness of the Spirit from Genesis to Revelation* (Grand Rapids: BakerAcademic, 2019). For ecclesiology, see Liston, *The Anointed Church*. Also, Peterson, *Who Is the Church?*.

of ecclesiology and missiology, it *enables* the interaction between them as well. It is by the Spirit that the church participates in God's mission. In John's gospel, for example, Jesus' breathing the Spirit on the church is immediately followed by his missional commissioning of the community (see Jn 20.21-22). The church's missionary mandate in Acts contains a similarly strong connection between the empowering of the Spirit and the church's call to be witnesses (see Acts 1.8). It is not at all surprising that the relationship between ecclesiology and missiology is pneumatologically enabled, as the relationships between all doctrine can and perhaps should be viewed in this way. As Bobrinskoy writes, 'Pneumatology is not so much one specific chapter of Christian theology as an essential dimension of every theological view of the Church and of its spirituality and liturgical and sacramental life.'[33] It is one of the fundamental convictions of Third Article Theology that all theological loci pneumatologically interconnect and mutually inform each other. Simultaneously considering all theological loci, how they pneumatologically impact ecclesiology and missiology, while also considering how ecclesiology and missiology pneumatologically interconnect and inform each other, is a rather insurmountable challenge, however.[34] How can we systematically proceed? The dialogical approach outlined by Nicholas Wolterstorff in *Reason within the Bounds of Religion* introduced in Section 1.2 and used repeatedly throughout this volume again provides a coherent way forward.[35]

Rejecting the enlightenment assumption that there exists an indubitable point of human knowledge which can be utilized as an ultimate foundation, Wolterstorff argues that a coherent understanding of reality can nevertheless be approached through the analysis and interchange of background beliefs, data

---

33. Bobrinskoy, 'Holy Spirit', 470. Heribert Mühlen writes similarly that 'The doctrine and person of the Holy Spirit is not one doctrine among others, but a fundamental doctrine and reality in the church'. Heribert Mühlen, *Una Mystica Persona. Die Kirche als das Mysterium der heilsgeschichtlichen Identität des Heiligen Geistes in Christus und den Christen: Eine Person in vielen Personen* (Paderborn: Ferdinand Schöningh, 1967), 5. As quoted in and translated by Wolfgang Vondey, *Heribert Mühlen: His Theology and Praxis* (Dallas: University Press of America, 2004), xv.

34. For example Franklin writes, 'My own view is that ecclesiology flows from a dialogical and holistic (even systematic) interaction between theological anthropology, soteriology, and missiology, each of which is grounded ultimately in a relational and participatory trinitarian theological framework'. Franklin, 'The God Who Sends Is the God Who Loves', 78. While I acknowledge Franklin's overarching point, addressing all these loci and their implications on ecclesiology simultaneously would be a very challenging theological exercise. The immediate question raised is where should one begin?

35. See Wolterstorff, *Reason within the Bounds of Religion*. Note that although this understanding was introduced in Section 1.2, it is briefly recapitulated here to show its particular applicability to the question of missiology's relationship to ecclesiology and so the argument in this chapter is self-contained (to some approximation).

beliefs and control beliefs.[36] In order to approach such a coherent understanding, he argues that theologians should initially choose one doctrine as a control belief and examine another doctrine from that vantage point. All other loci are classified as background beliefs and not considered in detail at this initial stage. Once the implications and connections from this examination are determined, the doctrines which are control beliefs, data beliefs and background beliefs are swapped around, so that a different doctrine can be analysed from the basis of yet another doctrine. This analysis will lead to an adjustment in our understanding of the data belief. The process continues, and at each step adjustment and refinement of the various data beliefs (doctrinal loci) occur. Utilizing this approach, a coherent and integrated understanding of all the doctrines can be approached, without any one of them considered as indubitably foundational. Wolterstorff's approach here integrates well with a Third Article Theology understanding, if one additional point is recognized – the means through which we examine a data belief from the basis of a control belief is intrinsically pneumatological. Essentially, all of the doctrinal loci should be considered as vantage points from which, through the lens of pneumatology, we can examine other doctrinal loci.

Applied to the ecclesio-missiological situation considered here, there are various initial choices for control and data beliefs that could be considered. The doctrines of the Trinity, Christology and eschatology could be utilized as control beliefs to examine the data belief of missiology, for example. With regard to the Trinity, this is precisely the approach taken in significant discussions about the *missio Dei* that occurred in the mid-twentieth century.[37] Similarly, the insights gained about missiology from this exploration could then be used as a control belief to examine ecclesiology. Again, this is often the approach taken by many recent missional church authors.[38] Such a strategy is entirely valid. Utilizing Wolterstorff's understanding, the only problem occurs when such an approach is considered as exhaustive and intrinsically determinative. An equally valid alternative approach would be to use the doctrines of Trinity, Christology and eschatology as control beliefs to examine the loci of ecclesiology, and then to use the refined doctrine of ecclesiology to examine the loci of missiology. This latter approach is precisely the strategy outlined in the third section of this chapter. No argument is made for this strategy being primary or preferred to the previous alternative where missiology is used as a control belief to examine ecclesiology. Rather, following Wolterstorff's dialogical understanding, it is maintained that for a coherent and complete apprehension of all of these theological doctrines, each loci needs to be considered as both a control belief and a data belief. This alternative strategy which uses

---

36. For a more detailed description of the application of Wolterstorff's approach to Third Article Theology, see Liston, *The Anointed Church*, 71–7.

37. From the perspective of Third Article Theology, however, one could critique these discussions as not giving sufficient attention to pneumatology.

38. Again, while there is significant value in these explorations, a Third Article Theology perspective would critique them as not sufficiently prioritizing pneumatology.

ecclesiology as a vantage point to examine missiology provides a complementary, confirming and correcting influence to the more common 'missional' route that works in the reverse order.

8.3 Towards an ecclesiologically informed missiology

Having established that ecclesiology can pneumatologically inform missiology, the objective of this final section is to take some initial steps in this direction, to determine a broad overview of a Third Article Theology of missiology when viewed from the vantage point of a pneumato-ecclesiology. Examining missiology in this way involves two clear steps. The first is to develop a coherent understanding of a pneumato-ecclesiology. The second is to use that understanding to pneumatologically inform missiology. So in the first step, ecclesiology is utilized as a data belief, while the doctrines of Christology, Trinity and eschatology are used as control beliefs. In the second step, ecclesiology is used as a control belief, while missiology (and particularly ecclesial mission) is used as a data belief.

The first step of pneumatologically exploring the church from the perspective of other doctrines is one that a Third Article Theology of ecclesiology both directly addresses and where significant progress has already been made.[39] So Third Article Theology argues that the constituent features of a pneumato-ecclesiology can be determined by examining the church through the lens of the Spirit from the vantage point of other theological loci. For example, viewing ecclesiology from the vantage point of Christology illuminates the reality that it is the Spirit that forms the church as the body of Christ (1 Cor. 12.13). Viewing ecclesiology from the vantage point of the Trinity emphasizes that it is by the Spirit that we join in the Son's communion with the Father.[40] Finally, viewing ecclesiology from the vantage point of eschatology enables the understanding that it is the Spirit that makes the church the proleptic anticipation of the coming kingdom. All these vantage points provide insight into the constituent features of the church's nature. The rationale behind developing a Third Article Theology of mission is to take these insights and extend them into the church's world-facing missional activity. This final section provides a programmatic overview of such a Third Article Theology of mission, briefly outworking these three connections between ecclesiology and missiology. It takes pneumatological insights about the church derived from the Christological, Trinitarian and eschatological vantage points and applies them to ecclesial mission. Combining the insights derived from all three connections provides a broad overview of the contours of a Third Article Theology of missiology, when seen from the vantage point of a pneumato-ecclesiology. The following examinations

---

39. For example, Cheryl Peterson argues that 'the real crisis facing the churches is one of identity' and 'to discover who the church is ... we ought to "start with the Spirit"'. See Cheryl M. Peterson, 'Who Is the Church?', *Dialog* 51, no. 1 (2012): 24, 28.

40. See, for example, Torrance, *Worship, Community and the Triune God of Grace*, 31.

of these three connections are indicative and not exhaustive, intending to describe merely the broad contours of a missiological landscape which is pneumatologically illuminated.

8.3.1 The Christological connection

Regarding the first Christological connection, the initial pneumatological insight is that the Spirit forms the church as the body of Christ.[41] Viewed through the lens of the Spirit, the church is intimately connected to Christ and reflects him as the incarnation's sequel. The terminology here is indicative.[42] Just as sequels have a continuous, discontinuous and asymmetrical relationship with their original, so too is the church related to Christ. Continuity arises from the church being Christ's body, his physical presence on earth. But the church is not a mere repetition or extension of the incarnation. The discontinuity between the two means that rather than adding to or replicating Christ's completed work, the church is called primarily to witness to and enjoy him. And the relationship is intrinsically asymmetrical. Christ is the source and life of the church, but he exists independently of it. Applying this insight to missiology begins with recognizing how Christ was empowered and guided by the Spirit both to reveal God to the world and to draw the world to God through his obedient suffering. The church in its continuity as the body of Christ, anointed and empowered by the Spirit, has an analogous role. In other words, it is as the church obediently suffers that she both reveals Christ to the world and draws the world to Christ.

In terms of the revealing, Torrance explains it like this: 'wherever the Church shows forth His death until He comes and presents its body a living sacrifice, there the image of Christ is to be seen and His Body is to be discerned in the Church.'[43] Eugene Peterson illustrates this concept using the word *inscape*.[44] He notes how some painters or photographers merely capture the reality in front of them (landscapes). Others, however, convey the inner truth of what is really going on (inscape). Applying this to theology, there are some who looked at Jesus, for example, and seeing only a human, decided there was nothing there worth noticing.[45] But there were a small number who saw through the human component (inscape!) and recognized something of immeasurable worth, God himself. In a similar manner, the church is intrinsically human. Some who look at the church see only the human side and conclude that there is nothing there of importance But that is merely the external, landscape point of view. There are those who see through the human

---

41. For a brief overview, see Section 1.2.1, or for a full analysis, see Liston, *The Anointed Church*, 85–179.
    42. For a detailed explanation, see Liston, *The Anointed Church*, 85–9.
    43. Torrance, 'Atonement and the Oneness of the Church', 259.
    44. Eugene Peterson, *Practise Resurrection* (London: Hodder & Stoughton, 2010), 141, 42, 46.
    45. See Isa. 53.2 for example.

component (inscape!) and so recognize something in the church of immeasurable worth. The church through her obedient suffering reveals Christ to the world.

But the church doesn't just *reveal* Christ in and through her obedient suffering, she *draws* the world to Christ through her suffering as well. Certainly, it is true that Christians suffer and that we should expect to.[46] And certainly, it is true that Christ suffered for us and suffers with us. But the biblical witness goes well beyond this. Because of the Spirit's presence, our suffering is not the end. The theology of the cross means our story extends beyond suffering and death. And as we endure suffering while living in the light of that bigger story, it witnesses to Christ and draws people to him. As people see us suffer and remain obedient in suffering, they realize the extent of the story we are participating in. As Persaud says, 'The thrust of the theology of the cross is missional.'[47] Perhaps the most obvious example of this is the suffering of the martyrs. Holwerda argues that 'Martyrdom is not what it appears to be. It appears to be the cruel cessation of witness, but actually it is its empowerment because martyrdom is the example par excellence of how God's kingdom of peace overcomes the violence of empires and ideologies opposed to Christ.'[48] The disciples recognized Jesus through his scars, and the world will recognize Jesus in us in the same way.

Viewed through the lens of the Spirit, there are important continuities between Christ and the church's respective missional roles. But there is a necessary discontinuity and asymmetry as well. The church reveals and draws people to Christ, only because Christ does so. The church's pneumatologically enabled missional role in the world asymmetrically parallels the missional role of Christ.

8.3.2 *The Trinitarian connection*

Regarding the second Trinitarian connection, the key pneumatological insight here is that it is by the Spirit that the church joins the Son's communion with the Father.[49] Through the Spirit, the church participates in the Trinitarian life. Extending this insight to missiology involves exploring how what the Spirit does in eternity is repeated in time, in the church and in us as individuals, and particularly in our missionary activity.[50] The picture is seen most clearly by starting with the Trinitarian union and then working outwards.

---

46. See 1 Pet. 4.1-2 for example.

47. Winston D. Persaud, 'The Theology of the Cross as Christian Witness: A Theological Essay', *Currents in Theology and Mission* 41, no. 1 (2014): 15.

48. David E. Holwerda, 'Suffering Witnesses – To What End?: A Sermon on Revelation 11:1-14', *Calvin Theological Journal* 41, no. 1 (2006): 131–2.

49. For a brief overview, see Section 1.2.2, or for a full analysis, see Liston, *The Anointed Church*, 181–333.

50. This repeated activity of the Spirit is explained in detail in Liston, *The Anointed Church*, 273–301. The objective of this section is to extend the logic of this understanding to the missional activity of the church.

The Trinitarian union is not lifeless or static. In the Trinity there is an ever-present dynamism. But this life or dance is not random. It has an inherent pattern to it – a pattern of breathing in and breathing out. The Father breathes out the word by the Spirit of love and then through this Spirit given to him, the Son returns love to the Father. And that breathing out and breathing in is ongoing constantly. The Father constantly breathes out the Son by the Spirit and then love is returned from the Son through the Spirit of love and Sonship given to him.[51]

But this pattern occurs not just in eternity but also in time. The same pattern of breathing out and breathing in gets repeated on a new stage. The Father incarnates the Son in time as the human Jesus Christ by the Spirit, and then, by the Spirit the human Jesus returns love to the Father, a human love which the Father gratefully receives. This is the hypostatic union.

The pattern repeats again, not just in eternity or in time but in human community – in the church. God the Father breathes the Spirit on the church through the Son and as he does that Christ is formed in our communities. And then, through this Spirit which has been given to us, together, we breathe out our love to the Father. As Calvin says, 'We are the sons of God because we have received the same Spirit as his only Son.'[52] Through this Spirit of Sonship, we pray, worship and give everything back to the Father. And this giving and receiving, this breathing in and breathing out, is constantly going on. The Son is embodied in the church through the Spirit. This is the mystical union.

Not just in eternity, in time and in the church but in each of us individually, the pattern repeats. As we each participate in Christ's life, we reach out with love to others in the church community through the Spirit of love given to us from the Father. And other believers, by this very same Spirit, respond to us in love. It is through this offering and receiving of love, through bearing one another's burdens, through learning to live with each other's differences, that we are grown and shaped into who Christ made us to be, people who reflect Christ himself. The Father directs us to love others within the church (breathing out) but others accept that love and return it (breathing in), and it is through this breathing out and breathing in that Christ is formed in us, both individually and as a community. The church of God exists exactly and only 'where the love of Christ is found'.[53] This is the ecclesial union.

Working through the spheres of eternity, time, the church and individual believers leads finally to the aspect of mission. The key recognition here is that the same pattern occurs. The same breathing in and breathing out reality that

---

51. Note that this is a particular understanding of the Trinitarian relations as suggested in Weinandy, *The Father's Spirit of Sonship*.

52. John Calvin, *Calvin's Commentaries*, trans. John Pringle, 22 vols. (Grand Rapids: BakerBooks, 2009), Gal 4:6, 23:120.

53. Gregory J. Liston, 'Where the Love of Christ Is Found: Toward a Third Article Ecclesiology', in *Third Article Theology: A Pneumatological Dogmatics*, ed. Myk Habets (Minneapolis: Fortress Press, 2016), 321.

was seen in ecclesial community happens in ecclesial mission. Because God, of course, directs the church not just to love others within the church but to love others beyond it. Just as the church exists exactly and only where, by the Spirit, the love of Christ is offered and returned, mission occurs wherever by the Spirit the love of Christ is offered and salvation comes wherever that love is returned. So there are two aspects to our missional activity. We breath out by showing love to the world and those around us, but then we breathe in by gathering again, centering ourselves and allowing Christ to be formed in us and in our community. And this breathing out and breathing in, going out and coming in, it doesn't just happen once, it happens constantly, again and again, over and over.

While this Trinitarian connection between ecclesiology and missiology is very rich indeed, this overview is restricted to mentioning just two insights. First, as has been previously noted, many missional church authors present the church as being all about what happens out there in the world. Certainly, this is important, but as this analysis points to, it is like constantly breathing out. People and churches cannot last when breath is only being expelled. In contrast, the opposite error is a church that is primarily inwardly focused.[54] But constant intake of breath is just as hazardous. What is required are churches and individuals who reach out and reach in, who breathe out and breathe in. Achieving a balance between these two is not just about creating an approach to mission that is sustainable, although it does have that outcome. More importantly, this approach to mission is about pneumatologically participating in the life of God who in his very Trinitarian nature breathes in and breathes out, and continually does both.

8.3.3 The eschatological connection

Having addressed the pneumatological insights into ecclesiology when it is viewed from the vantage points of Christology and the Trinity, and the missiological implications that emerge from both, the third and final connection to explore is eschatological. Viewed from an eschatological vantage point through the lens of the Spirit, the church is illuminated as the proleptic anticipation of the coming kingdom.[55] Moreover, this viewpoint provides a nuanced picture of how the Spirit is transforming the church through time. Using this understanding as a control belief to examine the data belief of mission leads to not just exploring the Spirit's intra-ecclesial transformative work but also illuminating how the Spirit wields the church as a transforming institution, creating systemic change in the communities and environments that it engages.

---

54. Newbigin's characterization here is apt, saying that such a 'Church becomes an introverted body, concerned with its own welfare rather than with the Kingdom of God, and – even if successful missionary work is carried on by others – the Church will be no fit home for those who are gathered in'. Newbigin, *One Body, One Gospel, One World*, 26.

55. For a brief overview of this understanding, see Section 6.3. For a full analysis, see Chapters 2–7.

Like the other connections, the analysis begins with the development of a pneumato-ecclesiology. Looking at the church through the lens of the Spirit from the vantage point of eschatology reveals how the Spirit draws back features of the coming kingdom to be a part of what we experience now. It is through bringing the future back to the present that the Spirit transforms the church. As discussed in Section 4.6, four key aspects are illustrative. So the coming kingdom is first a place where truth reigns. For in the coming kingdom Christ is king, and Christ is the truth. The Spirit, in part, brings that kingdom reality back to become a part of our present ecclesial existence now. He is the Spirit of truth, leading the church into all truth (Jn 16.13). Second, the kingdom is a place of justice – no more poverty, no more inequality, no more oppression. And the Spirit, in part, brings that kingdom reality back to our reality. He is the Spirit of liberty, leading the church towards freedom, to an existence where righteousness and justice flourish (2 Cor. 3.17). And the kingdom is a place of love, no more divisions, all are one in Christ. The Spirit, in part, brings that kingdom reality back to our current ecclesial existence. He is the Spirit of unity, transforming us from a divided people into a single, united, loving community (Eph. 3.17-18). And finally, the kingdom is a place of eternal life, where there is no more death or disease or suffering. And the Spirit, in part, makes that kingdom reality part of our present reality. He is the Spirit of life, the Lord and giver of life, leading the church towards a fulfilled existence and a renewed creation (Jn 6.63). Truth, freedom, unity, life – each of these is indicative of how the Spirit is transforming the church.

Utilizing this eschatologically inspired understanding of ecclesiology as a control belief from which to examine the data belief of missiology, and particularly ecclesial mission, the initial affirmation is that a core part of the church's mission is simply to live this reality in the world. In other words, a core aspect of the church's mission is to be a sign of the kingdom,[56] showing by its very existence and the way it goes about living in the world the journey the Spirit is taking the church on towards truth, freedom, unity and life.[57] The implications for missiology go beyond this initial affirmation, though. If ecclesiology informs missiology, then the church cannot restrict itself to simply being an institution that is 'being transformed' by the Spirit, it has to be a 'transforming' institution. The Spirit works in the world through the church. What is it that the Spirit does for the world through the church? The Spirit continues to be the Spirit of truth, freedom, unity and life. The Spirit brings all these gifts to the world, and he does it, at least in part, through the church. So it is an aspect of the church's mission to speak public truth. It is an aspect of the church's mission to liberate those who are oppressed. It is an aspect of the church's mission to unite people and draw them together. And it is an aspect of the church's mission to preserve life and bring healing to humanity and to all of

---

56. See, for example, Stanley J. Grenz, *Theology for the Community of God* (Grand Rapids: Eerdmans, 1994), 472-9.

57. As Hauerwas maintains, 'The first social ethical task of the church is to be the church'. Stanley Hauerwas, *The Peaceable Kingdom* (Notre Dame: SCM Press, 1983), 99.

creation. These are essential parts of the church's mission because our ecclesiology informs our mission. The church must act in the world in a way that is consistent with the reality of who the church is.

8.4 Conclusion

The purpose of this chapter has been to outline the development of a Third Article Theology of mission. In the initial sections, two key premises were developed and justified. The first was that missiology and ecclesiology mutually inform each other. This contrasts with the more common understanding that missiology determines ecclesiology. The second was that examining the correspondence between the two doctrines requires giving the Spirit prominence. Wolterstorff's epistemological framework of control beliefs, data beliefs and background beliefs provided a helpful system for exploring how one doctrine informs the other. Utilizing Wolterstorff's framework, the common approach where the doctrines of the Trinity, Christology and eschatology are utilized as control beliefs to inform missiology, which in turn is used as a control belief to determine ecclesiology, needs to be complemented by an alternative strategy. This alternative approach utilizes the doctrines of Trinity, Christology and eschatology as control beliefs to inform ecclesiology, which in turn is used as a control belief to inform missiology.

The final section took some initial steps towards the development of a Third Article Theology of mission using this alternative approach. Three connections to ecclesiology were examined. First, the Christological connection revealed how the church's mission has both a revealing and a drawing aspect to it. Guided by the Spirit in its obedient suffering, the church both reveals God to the world and draws the world to God. Second, the Trinitarian connection revealed that the church's mission reflects God's existence in having a breathing in and breathing out rhythm to it. We breath out, directed by the Father to love the world through his Spirit, and then we breathe in, gathering to allow Christ to be pneumatologically formed in us. And finally, the eschatological connection revealed that the church's mission is not just about being a sign of the kingdom but also about being its purveyor. The Spirit wields the church in order to transform the world, bringing to it truth, freedom, unity and life. Engaging with all three of these connections results in a broad, grounded and balanced understanding of the church's mission. It is as the church lives out the breadth and depth of this mission that the world sees the church for what it truly is, much more than a mere human institution but a group of people defined and enlivened by Christ's pneumatologically enabled presence.

Chapter 9

CONCLUSION

The overall thesis underlying this research is that exploring the relationship between church and kingdom through the lens of the Spirit enables the construction of a nuanced account of the church's ongoing transformation, an *eschatological* Third Article Ecclesiology. The church, as pictured in this volume, is the proleptic anticipation of the coming kingdom. Through enabling Christ's kingly presence, the Spirit draws back to the present church characteristics of the coming kingdom. This enriches, influences and transforms the present church towards its intended *telos*. This understanding was summarized at the end of Chapter 6, and that outline will not be repeated in this conclusion. Rather, this final chapter has three key purposes. First, based on the combined insights from the previous volume on a Christological and a Trinitarian Third Article Ecclesiology,[1] the development of an eschatological Third Article Ecclesiology in this volume and the pointers towards a missiological Third Article Ecclesiology provided in the previous chapter, it will outline the coherence and consistency not just of an eschatological Third Article Ecclesiology but of an overall Third Article Ecclesiology. Second, one of the arguments made repeatedly in this volume is that an eschatological Third Article Ecclesiology is practical. Just as Paul's viewing of the Corinthian situation from the perspective of an eschatological Third Article Ecclesiology led to concrete insight and advice for that first-century church, so viewing more contemporary ecclesial challenges through this lens will provide practical insight into how they should be addressed. The second section of this chapter puts this claim to the test by (quite briefly) applying this approach to the contemporary question of race relations within churches. Third, this chapter will conclude by exploring some future directions the study of Third Article Ecclesiology and Third Article Theology could profitably take.

---

1. See Section 1.2 for a more detailed summary of the material contained in the previous volume: Liston, *The Anointed Church*.

9.1 A coherent Third Article Ecclesiology

This volume (together with the previous volume that it follows[2]) has utilized a Wolterstorffian approach to develop the constituent features of a Third Article Ecclesiology. Just as an astronomer triangulates the position of a star by measuring its position from various vantage points, or a surveyor examines a mountain from various perspectives to gain a full three-dimensional appreciation of its grandeur, this approach argues that a broad and full understanding of ecclesiology is gained by examining it, through the lens of the Spirit, from various theological perspectives. The previous volume examined ecclesiology from the perspectives of both Christology and the Trinity. This volume used the vantage point of eschatology. And Chapter 8 initiated an exploration of ecclesiology through its interaction with missiology and God's overarching work in the world. What is important to note in this concluding chapter is that although each of these perspectives gained of ecclesiology is distinct, they nevertheless helpfully integrate with and complement each other to provide a coherent and complete picture.[3]

To illustrate, consider first the marks of the church: one, catholic, holy, apostolic. Each of the different vantage points most clearly and insightfully illuminates a particular one of these ecclesial marks.[4] The Christological vantage point illuminates the ecclesial mark of oneness: the church is one because by one Spirit believers participate in Christ's one relationship of Sonship with his one Father. This leads to the immediate implication of the church's unique context: having a relationship with Jesus and being a part of the church cannot be distinguished. A Trinitarian vantage point complemented the Christological perspective in that it particularly illuminates the ecclesial mark of catholicity: believers are personed not just through Christ alone but through others, as by the Spirit they offer Christ's love to each other and so share in his ecclesial consciousness. This catholicity is secure and unchangeable, rooted in the church's pneumatological union with Christ, but it also has to be increasingly realized for the mind of Christ to be fully formed in us. As this volume has demonstrated, eschatology illuminates the ecclesial mark of holiness: we are set apart for and from the future. This eschatological orientation distinguishes us from the world, but it also transforms us so that the characteristics of the kingdom increasingly define the kind of people we are. We are holy, but also being gradually transformed towards becoming people who truly belong in the coming kingdom. Finally, the vantage point of

---

2. See Liston, *The Anointed Church*.

3. The way these complementary understandings are derived from each of the viewpoints was briefly alluded to in the concluding paragraphs of *The Anointed Church*. See Liston, *The Anointed Church*, 361–3. And significant detail on how the Christological and Trinitarian vantage points point to their respective marks and sacraments is contained earlier in that volume.

4. This is not to say that two or three marks cannot be seen from each perspective but that the view of one mark is clearest from each vantage point.

missiology illuminates the ecclesial mark of apostolicity, although Third Article Theology requires a refined understanding of this ecclesial mark.[5] The church is not only apostolic in the sense that it is built on the *teaching* of the apostles (the Scriptures that we take to be our primary sources of revelation (e.g. Eph. 2.20)) or on the *line* of the apostles (the historical continuity through the passing on of faith from generation to generation), but the particular facet of apostolicity illustrated through the development of a Third Article Ecclesiology is that it is also built on the *example* of the apostles. To say the church is apostolic is to recognize that it 'must be understood in the original New Testament sense of being sent out to bear witness to the eschatological future that has broken forth in the life, death and resurrection of Jesus Christ'.[6]

A similar kind of observation can be made regarding the sacraments, although here the word *sacrament* must be understood broadly as any human activity through which Christ is particularly present to the church. The Christological perspective points particularly to the sacrament of baptism, through which believers are pneumatologically united with both Christ and other believers. A Third Article Theology approach illuminated the complementarity between water baptism and Spirit baptism, which are connected through the pneumatologically enabled Chalcedonian relationship of unity, distinction and asymmetry. Through this lens, water baptism became the analogy of Spirit baptism, the human counterpart of a divine action. The Trinitarian perspective provided insight into the sacrament of fellowship. Christ is particularly present with us in our gathering (Mt. 18.20). A Trinitarian Third Article Ecclesiology argues that our means of approaching the Father is not merely through Christ but through each other as well. It is through pneumatologically enabled fellowship that the mind of Christ is formed in each believer. As this volume has demonstrated, the eschatological perspective particularly illuminates the sacrament of the eucharist, for it is this sacrament that is the central and defining aspect of the *ongoing* life and worship of the church. Through this (and other ongoing ecclesial practices), the Spirit draws back features of the coming kingdom, enriching and transforming our current existence through the interplay of experienced presence, enabled imagination and empowered practice. Finally, the vantage point of missiology points to mission itself as a sacrament.[7] Matthew 18:19-20, for example, suggests a very close relationship between the presence of Jesus with us and our mandate to make disciples. And even our preliminary discussion of the pneumatologically enabled relationship between ecclesiology and missiology in Chapter 8 concluded that it is as the church lives out mission's breadth and depth that the world sees the church for what it truly is, much more than a mere human institution but a group

---

5. This refined understanding of apostolicity is one area that would benefit from further research. See the discussion in Section 9.3.
6. Peterson, *Who Is the Church?*, 133.
7. Again, further investigation into this area is warranted.

of people defined and enlivened by Christ's pneumatologically enabled presence. Christ is particularly present to us when we intentionally act as his witnesses.[8]

The overall theological programme of developing a Third Article Ecclesiology is still continuing, but it is an encouraging sign that as new vantage points are utilized, their insights complement the previous ones developed and also combine to create a systematic, coherent and more nearly complete understanding of the church's constituent features. The sections that follow attempt to demonstrate that the Third Article Ecclesiology being developed is not merely systematic but also concrete and practical (being applicable to real-life situations in the contemporary church), and rich and fertile (suggestive of several other aspects of ecclesiological and theological research that have yet to be explored in detail).

9.2 Applying an eschatological Third Article Ecclesiology

One of the recurring themes of this research has been the concrete and practical nature of eschatological Third Article Ecclesiology. Specific examples of this have included the application of this approach to the practice of the eucharist and the way Paul utilized it to practically address the situation of the church in Corinth. The purpose of this section is to demonstrate that an eschatological Third Article Ecclesiology approach provides concrete and practical assistance to address the most pressing issues facing the contemporary church at a local level. The ability to make this case convincingly is hindered to some extent by the generality and brevity any treatment is restricted to within a volume such as this. Any issue that is significant enough to be broadly applicable is complex enough to require a book-length treatment, while the analysis given here can at best be indicative. Further, there are always local factors to consider which have a substantive impact on how the application is outworked. Nevertheless, even a cursory and generalized treatment such as provided here gives an indication of the profitability of addressing specific contemporary issues through an eschatological Third Article Ecclesiology approach.

The contemporary issue chosen for examination here is racial reconciliation and integration within the church. While this is just one of many issues that could be chosen, its contemporary applicability and broad resonance make it a suitable example. To what extent should a church community be working towards growing

---

8. It is interesting that in the recently released first instalment of his trilogy *Dogmatic Ecclesiology*, Tom Greggs makes a division and attribution that overlaps significantly with what has been outlined in this section. He associates priestly catholicity with participation, prophetic apostolicity with encounter and kingly holiness with transformation. The third set of associations made (his third promised volume) aligns particularly closely with the eschatological affirmations and emphases contained within this volume. See Tom Greggs, *Dogmatic Ecclesiology: The Priestly Catholicity of the Church* (Grand Rapids: BakerAcademic, 2019), xxi.

a genuinely multicultural community, with real and substantive interactions across cultural borders? And in what ways can genuine transformation in this area be achieved? This is increasingly becoming a global challenge and opportunity for the church. Whether it be the relationship between European immigrants and local indigenous populations, or the more recent growth in global immigration, the question of racial integration and reconciliation is something the church urgently needs to address within its own communities, and not merely as a global or national participant. The following discussion works through each of the affirmations made about an eschatological Third Article Ecclesiology in the summary at the end of Chapter 6 and then applies them to the issue of racial reconciliation and integration within the church.[9]

The first affirmation of an eschatological Third Article Ecclesiology is that the church is the proleptic anticipation of the coming kingdom. This speaks to the issue of priority and intent. Given that one of the most prominent constituent features of the coming kingdom is that it is a place of racial harmony, equality and integration, a place where people from every nation and tribe and people and language are joined together in their worship of one God (Rev. 7.9), then each of our local churches should intentionally be anticipating this future in our present practice. As was noted in the analysis of 1 Corinthians, there are some issues for which Paul was adamant and clear in his writing and other areas where he was much more relaxed and lenient.[10] The issues he was most concerned about were those where the church was (or was not) reflecting the coming kingdom. Given the significant emphasis on the coming kingdom as a place of racial equality and harmony, there can be little doubt that contemporary churches should also be deeply adamant and clear about the need to intentionally prioritize reflecting their local community's ethnic and racial make-up, not just in attendance but in genuine fellowship and interaction. Reconciliation and integration across cultural and ethnic boundaries within our church communities should be one of our foremost priorities. Moreover, we should be deeply remorseful when this is evidently not the case. In my own country of New Zealand, for example, which has an extremely ethnically diverse urban population, Sunday morning is the most racially segregated time of the week. On any given weekday, Māori, Chinese, European and Pasifika people attend school or their places of employment together, forced by economic imperative to integrate and comingle, while on Sunday, freed from such economic necessity, they worship separately in their own implicitly (and often explicitly) segregated churches. The fact that we have created church communities that, by either design or accident, do not welcome those who do not look and act

---

9. Note that the focus of this section is on racial reconciliation and integration within the church. The issue of how this impacts wider society will be (partly) addressed in the next subsection.

10. See the discussion in Section 7.4.

like us is a key point of challenge and growth for the churches in this country and in much of the Western world.[11]

As subpoints of this first affirmation, two supporting statements were made. First, that the relationship between the church and the kingdom is characterized by both discontinuity and continuity. Two related recognitions arise from this first subpoint that are of importance for racial reconciliation within churches. The discontinuous aspect informs us there are facets of relationships between cultures that will never be resolved on this side of the eschaton; the continuous aspect emboldens us to be eagerly searching for the next steps we can take in making our church communities places where all races and ethnicities genuinely belong, however small those steps may be. The result of both recognitions is a cautious optimism about ecclesial development in this area, where each small improvement can be celebrated without an idealistic utopia becoming an unrealistic burden. The second subpoint was that the relationship between the church and kingdom is not merely chronological or timebound. This provides the substantive grounds for our cautious optimism about development and growth in this area. Because we are connected with the coming kingdom not merely teleologically but eschatologically – because, in other words, the kingdom is not just something we look forward to but something that already exists among us – the journey we are making towards racial reconciliation and community within our churches is not one we take alone but one that is aided and empowered through Christ's kingly presence among us. This Christological grounding is the ultimate source of our confidence in making progress within this challenging area.

If the first affirmation had implications for the intent and grounding of racial reconciliation, the second has implications about the means through which it will occur. This second affirmation of an eschatological Third Article Ecclesiology was that through enabling Christ's kingly presence, the Spirit brings back to the present church characteristics of the coming kingdom. The immediate implication is that the anointing of the Spirit and racial reconciliation intrinsically and inseparably belong together. To expand upon the same point (but in a negative sense), attempts at racial reconciliation outside of the Spirit's empowering are ultimately doomed to failure, as are attempts to utilize the Spirit's empowering to create and sustain a monocultural congregation. These theological insights are matched by our experience. Many of us know people who at some point in their lives were passionate about racial equality and integration both within and externally to church contexts, but they neglected the Spiritual disciplines: prayer, community, gathering, worship – those practices that connect us with the Spirit. The end result

---

11. It would be a significant exaggeration to paint the existence of culturally focused churches as an unalloyed negative. Unity in diversity should exist both within and across congregations. In particular, the need for people to be able to worship and be taught in their own language is both important and necessary. It is unfortunate and all too common, however, that these practical and justifiable reasons for (limited) exclusion often lead to an excessively divided ecclesial reality that is much less theologically and pragmatically defensible.

was that their passion gradually burned up and was replaced by a dry cynicism. On the other hand, there are also many who crave the Spirit's anointing in their lives but keep it for themselves or use the gifts he gives only for others who are like them. To act in such a way is to bring judgement upon ourselves (e.g. 1 Cor. 11.29). Monolithic, monocultural, megachurches are monstrosities. The anointing of the Spirit and intentionally building a community of others who are unlike us go together, and when we implicitly or explicitly exclude others because of their cultural differences, to some degree we lose the anointing of the Spirit. As Mike Riddell pithily but accurately remarks, 'There is nothing miraculous about a group of people who are all the same as each other hanging out together.'[12]

Several subpoints undergirded this broad affirmation. The first was that it was through the Spirit that the noetic, ontic and telic connection between the church and the kingdom was maintained. From a racial reconciliation and integration perspective, this insight informs us of concrete areas in which growth can be seen. Through the Spirit's empowering we can seek to understand each other's differing cultural perspectives at a deeper level (noetic), we can increasingly relate to each other as the brothers and sisters in Christ that we truly are (ontic) and we can intentionally and practically work together towards a future where we are increasingly growing into one united family (telic).[13] The second supporting subpoint was that given the interaction of Christ's entire redeemed time with our present moment in fallen time, our lives at the present moment take the shape of his entire existence: life, death, resurrection. Consequently, the transformational journey we take as churches towards racial reconciliation is unsurprisingly jagged and twisted, with progress followed by apparent backtracks and success followed by seeming failure, on both short and long time scales, within individual lives and broadly across communities. The practical point to be recognized here is that it is precisely through this jagged and staggered journey that we 'give up our rights to self-determination' and allow the Spirit to guide us into a greater appreciation of and unity with those who are different from us. This cruciform concept of giving up of our rights, and of deliberately and intentionally choosing a path that includes our own mini-deaths with hope for a coming resurrection, is especially pertinent to the issue of race relations, particularly in terms of the attitude that the majority culture adopts to minorities. Moreover, this recognition gives us both the opportunity and the necessity to explore those aspects of our Christian history which are less than optimal. If it is true that there is only resurrection where there are graves, then the 'death' that comes from recognizing, owning and apologizing for the significant errors of the past is intrinsically connected with moving forward

---

12. This often-quoted statement originates from Riddell's speaking and not his writing. For an example of Riddell's provocative and often insightful writing, see Mike Riddell, *Godzone: A Guide to the Travels of the Soul* (London: SPCK, 2011).

13. These points will be expanded further when the three aspects of imagination (noetic), presence (ontic) and practice (telic) are discussed in detail with regard to the issue of racial reconciliation and integration.

in a genuinely integrative manner. In terms of racial relations, churches taking seriously their culpability for past atrocities and negligence is a necessary 'death' for the resurrection of reconciliation and integration to occur.

The third and fourth subpoints expand on this understanding, dividing Christ's eschatological interaction with the contemporary church into three categories: prophetic (leading to an ecclesiology of witness), priestly (leading to an ecclesiology of communion) and kingly (leading to an ecclesiology of transformation). The kingly aspect, which has been less developed than the other two, explores how through the Spirit mediating Christ's kingly presence, characteristics that describe the coming kingdom become (in part) features of the present church. With regard to race relations, the kingdom characteristics of unity and justice discussed in Sections 4.6 and 5.3 are particularly pertinent. For the Spirit is the Spirit of unity, and it is through this Spirit that our hearts are filled with love for each other, even and especially those who are significantly different from us. Moreover, it is through this Spirit that our love grows ever more perfect as we lose our fear of judgement and look forward to the coming kingdom with longing. And the Spirit is the Spirit of justice, leading the church towards freedom, to an existence where righteousness flourishes, one which increasingly reflects the character of our king. It is one of the signs of the Spirit within a community that they increasingly embrace the neglected and disenfranchised within society, including those who are culturally marginalized. What is important to recognize is that these kingdom aspects which are so necessary for racial reconciliation and integration are not intrinsically developed and grown through our own efforts, absent or separated from the Spirit's work. Rather, they are gifts to us through the Spirit from the future. We do not transform ourselves. Rather we are transformed through the work of the Spirit. And it is only as gifts from the Spirit that the church then has something to offer the world.

So, if the first affirmation spoke to the intent and grounding of racial reconciliation and integration within the church, and the second affirmation spoke to the pneumatological means through which this can occur, the third affirmation speaks to the practical mechanisms by which transformation towards these kingdom features become increasingly evident in the church. This third affirmation notes that in drawing back Christ's kingly presence, the Spirit enriches, influences and transforms the church towards his coming kingdom. Again, this affirmation is undergirded by several supporting subpoints. The first is that transformation occurs through the interplay of presence, imagination and practice. The implications of this for racial reconciliation and integration are significant. For it is particularly when we gather that we are being transformed together by the Spirit in preparation for the kingdom that is coming. First and foremost, we gather to enjoy God's presence. When we sing, God inhabits our praises (Ps. 22.3). When we listen to a sermon, it is God who speaks. When we take communion together, Christ is in the bread and the cup. And most pertinently here, even in the act of gathering itself, Christ is with us, as Jesus said explicitly (Mt. 18.20). Sometimes the experiencing of God's presence together immediately leads to transformation, so that simply by coming together racial integration occurs, and we join together as brothers and sisters despite our differing backgrounds, revelling in and enjoying our differences. But such instantaneous transformation does not always occur. Both positive and negative encounters fuel our imagination, though, making us long for a day when awkwardness and misunderstandings will be replaced by insight and acceptance. And this longing itself fuels our practice. Given the kingdom will gather people from every tribe and tongue and nation, our church gatherings should become places where we intentionally practice for this coming eventuality.

The second undergirding subpoint notes the Chalcedonian relationship between presence and practice that is required for transformation to occur. Four errors were noted, each of which are applicable to this situation of racial reconciliation. First, the error of ecclesial Docetism is the assumption that God will transform us without any corresponding human action. Clear examples include those churches who profess a divinely inspired love for others who differ from their own majority culture but nevertheless have little or nothing to do with people who are different from them. The second error is ecclesial ebionism, which is to work towards racial reconciliation without any acknowledgement of the crucial role the Spirit has in uniting us – without practising the Spiritual disciplines and practices. This error ignores the fact that racial integration is a gift of God from the future and not something that emerges through our own effort. The third and fourth errors are more subtle. Ecclesial Nestorianism would maintain that our efforts to create racial integration and the work of the Spirit are intrinsically linked, that the Spirit is bound in some way to our gathering and cannot work outside of or against it. This view would maintain that simply because of our ecclesial efforts to cross cultural borders the Spirit is bound to work. Ecclesial Eutychianism, alternatively, would maintain that ecclesial gatherings across races are necessary and important, and would also maintain that transformation towards unity is a miraculous gift of the Spirit, but it maintains an unhealthy distinction between these two aspects, not acknowledging that the human action complements the divine. What is needed, in contrast to each of these errors, is a Chalcedonian connection between presence and practice, which emerges from an understanding that genuine transformation emerges from genuine relationship both with God and with each other. Our love for each other as people of different cultural backgrounds corresponds, reflects and derives from God's love for us. It emerges from this love. Reconciliation with each other thus follows from our mutual recognition of the primary reconciliation we have with and in Christ.

The third undergirding subpoint is that there is no expectation that ecclesial transformation towards racial reconciliation and integration will be smooth, continuous and cumulative. This arises from the fractal nature of time that has already been discussed. This jagged journey should be recognized not only over historical timescales (as noted earlier) but also in the day-to-day life of the congregation and the individuals that comprise it. As we interact more with others, it is understandable and expected that we will learn things about them that both delight and repulse us. No doubt, others will have similarly polarized reactions as they learn more about us. Having said that, seeing exactly what is wrong (and right) with the people closest to you and choosing to walk beside them anyway – recognizing they are doing the same with you – are as close to a working definition of love as can be imagined this side of eternity. Some of the things we abhor (or cling to) may be merely cultural difference, while others may be genuine aspects of our reality which need to be transformed through Christ's kingly presence empowered by the Spirit.

This leads to the final undergirding subpoint which is that the core outcome of this ongoing transformation is holiness. Transformation emerges from our unique relationship, both with the triune God as his chosen people and with each other. Through interacting with those who are different from us, and intentionally moving towards life together with them, we are both made aware of our weaknesses (and those of others) and learn to humbly appreciate our strengths (and others' strengths as well). As we learn to look through others' eyes, we will see in ourselves both the things they love and the things they abhor. This occurs not just on an individual but more importantly on a community level. It is precisely because of our genuine interactions and relationship with God and with each other, therefore, that we are gradually transformed into kingdom people – people who are holy not just because we are set apart for the kingdom and its awesome king but also because through our transformed character we increasingly and truly belong and fit in that coming kingdom.

A specific example of this transformation process in a local church may be helpful as a crystallizing conclusion. Mount Albert Baptist Church is a predominantly middle-class church congregation located in a wealthy area of the multicultural city of Auckland, New Zealand. While to a great degree, the church reflects the multicultural nature of its immediate vicinity, there are relatively few indigenous Māori attenders. Through his reading and research, the pastor of this church became aware of the story of Parihaka – a Christian, pacifist, Māori community that was forcefully ejected from their tribal land in 1881 by the governing authorities. It is a powerful story taught to young Indian children because of its influence on Gandhi – a story which directly affected his adoption of non-violent resistance as a political strategy. Unfortunately, though, it is also a story that is rarely discussed in New Zealand. Convicted by the power of the story, its important message of grace and the fact that most New Zealand Europeans (commonly termed *Pākehā*) were largely unaware of it, this pastor was moved to write and stage a high-quality musical about these events. This vision was birthed and catalysed by a song performed at Mount Albert Baptist Church by a gifted Māori family who had only recently discovered their Parihaka heritage. The song and the vision it inspired led to the formation of a long-lasting collaboration between this Māori family and the pastor. As a relatively small church, the production of a high-quality musical was an oversized vision, requiring resources going well beyond those to which it had access. It was, however, a vision that the pastor, his leadership team and the new collaboration that was forming between him and the Māori family believed through prayer and conviction was divinely inspired.

The journey to the production of the musical was fraught with many seemingly insurmountable challenges. At a writing and directing level, there was a necessity to forge strong relationships between Pākehā and Māori so that the story would be authentically and appropriately told. The people of Parihaka were initially hesitant to having someone else (a collaboration including a white European male) tell their story. However, through a clear movement of the Spirit and gradually growing relationships minds were changed, and written permission was given. Both the growing collaboration at the writing and directing level, and the permission given by the people of Parihaka speak to a development of trust and a partial reconciliation and integration between the Parihaka Māori and the collaboration of storytellers involved. In the telling of the Parihaka story, there was a necessity first for the writing and directing team, and then the cast and crew to inhabit and own the story of their past. This involved significant emotional angst, both for the Māori cast, as they relived and revived the memories of hurt at the hands of racist attitudes and actions suffered by both their ancestors and themselves, and for the Pākehā cast, as they appreciated and then owned their culpability for the way their ancestors had so unfairly acted. On a more practical level, rehearsals and performances had to be regularly cancelled and rescheduled due to the continual lockdowns required because of Covid-19 From these deaths, however, resurrection emerged in the form of racial reconciliation and integration. As the cast and directing team asked for and regularly experienced Christ's kingly presence among them, as they imagined through their singing and discussions the coming kingdom filled with people, tribes and tongues who have 'every past reconciled'[14] and as they practised being together with all of the positive and negative interactions that were involved, a growing sense of unity emerged.

It is unnecessary to overreach regarding the impacts of such an exercise. What is undeniable, however, is that through God's grace, this church, the collaboration of people who put the musical together and all of the people associated with this project as directors, participants or observers have moved forwards in their journey towards racial reconciliation and integration. Transformation has emerged from genuine relationship, both with God and with each other, and engaging in these relationships has enabled the church to make a small step towards holiness, anticipating in its life and activity just a little more than it has in the past the united and just characteristics of the coming kingdom.

---

14. Consider the lyrics of the final song, for example:
    'Under the mountain, anthem sounding, echoing through our land
    Hate must give way, every tear wiped away, together as one we stand
    No more land be defiled, every past reconciled, together as one we stand ...
    Over borders of culture and colour and land, together in you we stand
    May love reign supreme, as our children dream, together in you we stand
    Arms open wide, an unstoppable tide, together in you we stand'
    Steve Worsley, *The Way of the Raukura: A Parihaka Musical* (Auckland: 2019), 43.

9.3 Future research directions

As this volume has demonstrated, applying the methodology of Third Article Theology to ecclesiology is a rich and fruitful approach – one that rewards careful examination with significant theological and practical insight. The question addressed in this last section, then, is what next steps a research trajectory in this area could profitably take. While there are many possibilities, this discussion is restricted to three significant but diverse examples.

First, there would be value in comprehensively and specifically exploring how through regular ecclesial practices, the Spirit transforms the church through the interrelated mechanisms of presence, practice and imagination. Chapter 5 gave an extensive and detailed examination of the Lord's supper utilizing an eschatological Third Article Ecclesiology approach, and Chapter 6 expanded that with a slightly less extensive discussion of prayer, praise and preaching. While this discussion was sufficient to enable the core features of how our community gatherings and practices lead towards transformation to be understood, there would be significant value in intentionally viewing all the church's activities through the lens of an eschatological Third Article Ecclesiology, working systematically through each to discover and discern ways that the contemporary church can effectively partner with the Spirit's presence in each to effect transformation. This exercise could perhaps be seen as the communal equivalent of the Spiritual disciplines literature, which for all its value faces the valid criticism of being primarily individualistically focused. The complementary (and perhaps even more important) question is how a church's practices and disciplines can contribute to its ongoing communal transformation.

It is worth recognizing just how radically different this understanding of church life as intentionally practising for the kingdom is from the way most think about church these days. Most Western Christians attend church to express their devotion to God. In contrast, an eschatological Third Article Ecclesiology maintains that it is God who 'is the primary . . . agent . . . in the worship encounter'.[15] We receive; he gives. Similarly, most Western Christians believe transformation happens primarily through their daily life and devotions. While not denying God works in all aspects of our lives, this approach maintains, in contrast, that church gatherings are the primary place where the Spirit transforms us. Third Article Theology places the emphasis on the community and its transformation over and above that of the individual. Doing so radically puts our experience in this world into an appropriate perspective. This world is the gymnasium, not the rugby field; it is the rehearsal space, not the concert hall. Just as the Israelites were led through the desert for forty years to prepare them to become true inhabitants of the promised land, so churches are led through this life to prepare us together to become true inhabitants of the coming kingdom. A detailed treatise on how the rhythms of regular church life can transform communities (and the individuals that make

---

15. Smith, *You Are What You Love*, 77.

them up), preparing us to become a people who by their actions genuinely belong in the coming kingdom, would be of immense value.

A second (although much more theoretical) future avenue this research could profitably pursue is to develop an intentionally pneumatological understanding of time. In 1964, the German theologian Heribert Mühlen noted with regret that a book on the Holy Spirit and time had not yet been written.[16] It still has not. There are many reasons for this. One is that the theological understanding of time and space has neither kept pace nor interacted sufficiently with the significantly altered descriptions of time emerging from contemporary physics. Another limiting factor is that the pivotal role of Christ (and particularly Karl Barth's key eschatological insight that the Son became not just flesh but time) in informing a nuanced understanding of not just time and the Spirit but the relation between them has often been neglected. Regarding this last point, the research outlined in Chapter 3, its analysis of the relationship between fallen time, redeemed time and eternity, and its ultimate characterization of time's intrinsically fractal nature, provides a helpful first step in this direction. Utilizing the approach of Third Article Theology, the Spirit could provide an insightful integrating motif enabling a dialogue between the fields of contemporary physics (particularly relativity and quantum theory), eschatology (particularly Spirit eschatology) and Christology (particularly Spirit Christology).

Although investigating the intersection between these fields would require a mammoth research project, the value arising from the initial insights made in Chapter 3 suggests that continuing investigation pushing further in this direction would be of significant value. Such a project would ultimately aim to answer the very fundamental questions of 'What is time?' and 'What is the Spirit's role in time?' by viewing Christology, eschatology and contemporary physics through the lens of the Spirit. Undergirded by a Wolterstorffian, dialogue-based approach, the burgeoning of Third Article Theology provides a unique opportunity for theology and physics to dialogue and interact in a way that has not yet been possible.[17] Doing so could launch a new era of cooperation and mutual enhancement between these traditionally disparate subjects. My (presently untested) hypothesis is that delving deeply into both physics and theology will demonstrate that there are other ways to articulate their interaction than current panentheistic accounts,[18] alternatives which will lead to a much more biblically accurate, systematically rigorous and emotionally gratifying understanding of the relationship between God and creation in general, and eternity and time in particular.

---

16. Mühlen, *Una Mystica Persona*, 279.

17. For a recent overview of the relationship between science and theology viewed through a pneumatological perspective, see Wolfgang Vondey, 'The Spirit and Science', in *T&T Clark Handbook of Pneumatology*, ed. Daniel Castelo and Kenneth M. Loyer (London: T&T Clark, 2020).

18. For example, Ernest L. Simmons, *The Entangled Trinity: Quantum Physics and Theology* (Minneapolis: Fortress Press, 2014).

The final potential future direction this research programme could take is one that has already been alluded to at several points throughout this volume. It is to extend the exploration of Third Article Ecclesiology to missiology. The first steps in this promising research avenue were taken in Chapter 8, but these need to be fleshed out into a monograph-length volume, comparable to this exploration of eschatology. Just as an eschatological vantage point has provided significant insight into the nature and practice of ecclesiology, there is every expectation that a missiological vantage point would have a similarly worthwhile outcome. Moreover, as noted in Section 9.1, the missiological perspective provides the final significant vantage point from which ecclesiology needs to be viewed (following the perspectives of Christology, Trinity and eschatology utilized in this and previous volumes). Consequently, this research avenue would not only describe the unique aspects of ecclesiology when seen from a missiological perspective but also provide the final significant piece of the jigsaw required for constructing an integrated, coherent and complete understanding of a Third Article Ecclesiology. This missiological exploration is the natural next step following on from this research on an eschatological Third Article Ecclesiology.

Each time we say the Lord's prayer, we ask for God's kingdom to come (Mt. 6.10). The significant insight and compelling vision of this volume are that this is not just a prayer for the future but a bold request for the coming kingdom to change our lives at the present moment. For the church is the proleptic anticipation of the coming kingdom. Through enabling Christ's kingly presence, the Spirit draws back to the present church characteristics of the coming kingdom. This enriches, influences and transforms the present church towards its intended *telos*. So, like the apostle John, we will continue to fervently pray that the Lord Jesus Christ will come soon (Rev. 22.20). But as the methodology of Third Article Theology makes so abundantly clear, through the Spirit Christ the king is already among us. So as we wait and pray for that day to come, we shall also pray that Christ's pneumatologically enabled presence will continue to transform our church communities here and now, preparing us to be people who are fit to be true servants and friends of our king.

REFERENCES

Aagaard, Johannes. 'Trends in Missiological Thinking during the Sixties'. *International Review of Mission* 62, no. 245 (1973): 8–25.

Althouse, Peter. 'In Appreciation of Jürgen Moltmann: A Discussion of His Transformational Eschatology'. *Pneuma: The Journal of the Society for Pentecostal Studies* 28, no. 1 (2006): 21–32.

Althouse, Peter. 'Pentecostal Eschatology in Context: The Eschatological Orientation of the Full Gospel'. In *Perspectives in Pentecostal Eschatologies*, edited by Peter Althouse and Robert Waddell, 205–31. Eugene: Pickwick, 2010.

Althouse, Peter. *Spirit of the Last Days: Pentecostal Eschatology in Conversation with Jürgen Moltmann*. London: T&T Clark International, 2003.

Anderson, Willhelm. *Towards a Theology of Mission: A Study of the Encounter between the Missionary Enterprise and the Church and Its Theology*. London: SCM Press, 1955.

Aquinas, Thomas. *Summa Theologica*. Translated by Fathers of the English Dominican Province. London: Burns Oates & Washbourne, 1920.

Arendt, Hannah. *The Human Condition* 2nd edn. Chicago: University of Chicago Press, 1998.

Aring, Paul Gerhard. *Kirche als Ereignis: Ein Beitrag zur Neuorientierung der Missionstheologie*. Neukirchen-Vluyn: Neikirchener Verlag, 1971.

Armstrong, John H. 'Introduction: Do This in Remembrance of Me'. In *Understanding Four Views on the Lord's Supper*, edited by Paul E. Engle, 11–25. Grand Rapids: Zondervan, 2007.

Badcock, Gary D. *The House Where God Lives: Renewing the Doctrine of the Church for Today*. Grand Rapids: Eerdmans, 2009.

Badcock, Gary D. *Light of Truth and Fire of Love: A Theology of the Holy Spirit*. Grand Rapids: Eerdmans, 1997.

Balthasar, Hans Urs von. *The Theology of Karl Barth*. Translated by John Drury. New York: Holt, Rinehart and Winston, 1971.

Barnhill, Gregory M. 'The Paradox of Ecclesiology: A Theological Reading of 1 Corinthians 5'. *Journal of Theological Interpretation* 12, no. 2 (2018): 242–63.

Barr, William R. and Rena M. Yocum. 'Introduction'. In *The Church in the Movement of the Spirit*, edited by William R. Barr and Rena M. Yocum, 1–10. Grand Rapids: Eerdmans, 1994.

Barth, Karl. *The Christian Life: Church Dogmatics IV,4 Lecture Fragments*. Translated by Geoffrey W. Bromiley. London: Eerdmans, 1981.

Barth, Karl. *Church Dogmatics*. Translated by Geoffrey W. Bromiley and Thomas F. Torrance. Peabody: Hendrickson, 2010.

Barth, Karl. 'Die Theologie und die Mission in der Gegenwart'. In *Theologische Fragen und Antworten*, Vol. 3, 100–26. Zollikon-Zürich: Evangelischer Verlag, 1957.

Barth, Karl. *Dogmatics in Outline*. New York: Harper and Row, 1959.

Barth, Karl. *The Epistle to the Romans*. Translated by Edwyn C. Hoskyns. London: Oxford University Press, 1933.

Barth, Karl. *The Resurrection of the Dead*. Translated by Henry James Stenning. London: Hodder & Stoughton, 1933.

Bauer, Walter. *Orthodoxy and Heresy in Earliest Christianity*. Translated by Robert A. Kraft and Gerhard Krodel. Philadelphia: Fortress, 1971.

Bavinck, Herman. *Reformed Dogmatics*, edited by John Bolt, trans. John Vriend. Grand Rapids: Baker, 2008.

Bender, Kimlyn J. *Karl Barth's Christological Ecclesiology*. Aldershot: Ashgate, 2005.

Berkhof, Louis. *Systematic Theology*. Edinburgh: Banner of Truth, 1939.

Blomberg, Craig L. *1 Corinthians*. Grand Rapids: Zondervan Academic, 2009.

Bobrinskoy, Boris. 'Holy Spirit'. In *Dictionary of the Ecumenical Movement*, edited by Nicholas Lossky, José Miguez Bonino, John S. Pobee, Tom F. Stransky, Geoffrey Wainwright, and Pauline Webb, 470–3. Grand Rapids: Eerdmans, 1991.

Bonhoeffer, Dietrich. *Sanctorum Communio*. Translated by Reinhard Krauss. Minneapolis: Fortress Press, 1998.

Bosch, David J. *Transforming Mission: Paradigm Shifts in Theology of Mission*. New York: Orbis Books, 1995.

Brunner, Emil. *The Word and the World*. London: SCM Press, 1931.

Butin, Phil. 'Two Early Reformed Catechisms, the Threefold Office, and the Shape of Karl Barth's Christology'. *Scottish Journal of Theology* 44, no. 2 (1991): 195.

Calvin, John. *Calvin's Commentaries*. Translated by John Pringle. 22 vols. Grand Rapids: Baker Books, 2009.

Calvin, John. *The First Epistle of Paul to the Corinthians*. Translated by John W. Fraser. Edinburgh: Oliver and Boyd, 1960.

Calvin, John. *Institutes of the Christian Religion*. Translated by Henry Beveridge. Peabody: Hendrickson, 2008.

Carr, Frederick David. 'Beginning at the End: The Kingdom of God in 1 Corinthians'. *Catholic Biblical Quarterly* 81, no. 3 (2019): 449–69.

Chester, Tim. *Truth We Can Touch: How Baptism and Communion Shape Our Lives*. Wheaton: Crossway, 2020.

Clark, Jason Swan. 'Just Go to Church'. Paper presented at the Society of Vineyard Scholars Conference. London, 2019.

Coffey, David. 'Spirit Christology and the Trinity'. In *Advents of the Spirit: An Introduction to the Current Study of Pneumatology*, edited by Bradford E. Hinze and D. Lyle Dabney, 315–38. Milwaukee: Marquette University Press, 2005.

Collins, Raymond F. *First Corinthians*. Collegeville: The Liturgical Press, 1999.

Conzelman, Hans. *1 Corinthians: A Commentary on the First Epistle to the Corinthians*. Translated by James W. Leitch. Philadelphia: Fortress, 1976.

Cousar, Charles B. 'The Theological Task of 1 Corinthians'. In *Pauline Theology Volume II: 1 & 2 Corinthians*, edited by David M. Hay, 90–102. Minneapolis: Fortress Press, 1993.

Dabney, D. Lyle. 'Starting with the Spirit: Why the Last Should Now be First'. In *Starting with the Spirit*, edited by Stephen Pickard and Gordon Preece, 3–27. Hindmarsh: Australian Theological Forum, 2001.

Dadosky, John. 'Ecclesia de Trinitate: Ecclesial Foundations from Above'. *New Blackfriars* 94, no. 1049 (2013): 64–78.

de Lubac, Henri. *The Splendour of the Church*. Translated by Michael Mason. London: Sheed and Ward, 1956.

Del Colle, Ralph. *Christ and the Spirit: Spirit Christology in Trinitarian Perspective* Oxford: Oxford University Press, 1993.

Del Colle, Ralph. 'Spirit Christology: Dogmatic Issues'. In *A Man of the Church: Honoring the Theology, Life, and Witness of Ralph Del Colle*, edited by Michel René Barnes, 3–19. Eugene: Pickwick Publications, 2013.

Dempster, Murray W. 'Eschatology, Spirit Baptism, and Inclusiveness: An Exploration into the Hallmarks of a Pentecostal Social Ethic'. In *Perspectives in Pentecostal Eschatologies*, edited by Peter Althouse and Robert Waddell, 155–88. Eugene: Pickwick, 2010.

Dorrien, Gary J. 'Suffering Divine Things (Review)'. *Pro Ecclesia* 11, no. 1 (2002): 103–5.

Eugenio, Dick O. *Communion with the Triune God: The Trinitarian Soteriology of T. F. Torrance*. Eugene: Wipf & Stock Publishers, 2014.

Eusebius. *The Church History: A New Translation and Commentary*. Translated by Paul L. Maier. Grand Rapids: Kregel Publications, 1999.

Falconer, Kenneth J. *Fractals: A Very Short Introduction*. Oxford: Oxford University Press, 2013.

Farrow, Douglas. 'Karl Barth on the Ascension: An Appreciation and Critique'. *International Journal of Systematic Theology* 2, no. 3 (2000): 127–50.

Faupel, D. William. *The Everlasting Gospel: The Significance of Eschatology in the Development of Pentecostal Thought*. Sheffield: Sheffield Academic Press, 1996.

Fee, Gordon D. *The First Epistle to the Corinthians*. Edited by Ned B. Stonehouse, F. F. Bruce, and Gordon D. Fee, The New International Commentary on the New Testament. Grand Rapids: Eerdmans, 1987.

Fee, Gordon D. 'Toward a Theology of 1 Corinthians'. In *Pauline Theology Volume II: 1 & 2 Corinthians*, edited by David M. Hay, 37–58. Minneapolis: Fortress Press, 1993.

Flett, John. *The Witness of God: The Trinity, Missio Dei, Karl Barth and the Nature of Christian Community*. Grand Rapids: Eerdmans, 2010.

Foster, Richard. 'Foreword'. In *The Spirit of the Disciplines*, ix–x. London: Hodder and Stoughton, 1988.

Franklin, Patrick S. 'The God Who Sends Is the God Who Loves: Mission as Participating in the Ecstatic Love of the Triune God'. *Didaskalia* 28 (2017): 75–95.

Frost, Michael and Alan Hirsch. *The Shaping of Things to Come: Innovation and Mission for the 21st-Century Church*. Peabody: Hendrickson, 2003.

Furnish, Victor Paul. 'Theology in 1 Corinthians'. In *Pauline Theology Volume II: 1 & 2 Corinthians*, edited by David M. Hay, 59–89. Minneapolis: Fortress Press, 1993.

Furnish, Victor Paul. *The Theology of the First Letter to the Corinthians*. Cambridge: Cambridge University Press, 1999.

Ganss, George E., William B. Palardy, and S. A. R. P. Chrysologus. *Selected Sermons*. Vol. 2. Washington, DC: Catholic University of America Press, 2004.

George, Timothy. *Faithful Witness: The Life and Mission of William Carey*. Birmingham: New Hope, 1991.

Goheen, Michael W. '"As the Father Has Sent Me, I am Sending You": Lesslie Newbigin's Missionary Ecclesiology'. *International Review of Mission* 91, no. 362 (2002): 354–69.

Gorman, Michael J. *Cruciformity: Paul's Narrative Spirituality of the Cross*. Grand Rapids: Eerdmans, 2001.

Graham, Lon. 'A Showdown or a Put Down? Rethinking an Incident from Early Baptist Mission History'. *Journal of European Baptist Studies* 18, no. 2 (2018): 7–18.

Green, Garrett. 'Imagining the Future'. In *The Future as God's Gift: Explorations in Christian Eschatology*, edited by David Fergusson and Marcel Sarot, 73–88. Edinburgh: T&T Clark, 2000.

Greggs, Tom. *Dogmatic Ecclesiology: The Priestly Catholicity of the Church*. Grand Rapids: BakerAcademic, 2019.
Grenz, Stanley J. *Theology for the Community of God*. Grand Rapids: Eerdmans, 1994.
Guder, Darrell L. *Be My Witnesses*. Grand Rapids: Eerdmans, 1985.
Guder, Darrell L. *The Continuing Conversion of the Church*. Grand Rapids: Eerdmans, 2000.
Gunton, Colin. 'Baptism: Baptism and the Christian Community'. In *Father, Son and Holy Spirit: Toward a Trinitarian Theology*, 201-15. London: T&T Clark, 2003.
Gunton, Colin. *Being and Becoming: The Doctrine of God in Charles Hartshorne and Karl Barth*. 2nd ed. London: SCM Press, 2001.
Gunton, Colin. *The Christian Faith: An Introduction to Christian Doctrine*. Oxford: Blackwell, 2002.
Gunton, Colin. 'The Church and the Lord's Supper: "Until He Comes." Towards an Eschatology of Church Membership'. In *Father, Son and Holy Spirit: Toward a Trinitarian Theology*, 216-34. London: T&T Clark, 2003.
Gunton, Colin. 'The Church on Earth: The Roots of Community'. In *On Being the Church*, edited by Colin Gunton and Daniel Hardy, 48-80. Edinburgh: T&T Clark, 1989.
Gunton, Colin. 'Salvation'. In *The Cambridge Companion to Karl Barth*, edited by John Webster, 143-58. Cambridge: Cambridge University Press, 2000.
Guyette, Fred. 'Jesus as Prophet, Priest, and King: John Wesley and the Renewal of an Ancient Tradition'. *Wesleyan Theological Journal* 40, no. 2 (2005): 88-101.
Habets, Myk. *The Anointed Son: A Trinitarian Spirit Christology*. Eugene: Pickwick Publications, 2010.
Habets, Myk. '*Filioque? Nein*: A Proposal for Coherent Coinherence'. In *Trinitarian Theology after Barth*, edited by Myk Habets and Phillip Tolliday, 161-202. Eugene: Pickwick Publications, 2011.
Habets, Myk. 'Prolegomenon: On Starting with the Spirit'. In *Third Article Theology: A Pneumatological Dogmatics*, edited by Myk Habets, 1-19. Minneapolis: Fortress Press, 2016.
Habets, Myk, ed. *Third Article Theology: A Pneumatological Dogmatics*. Minneapolis: Fortress Press, 2016.
Haight, Roger. 'The Case for Spirit Christology'. *Theological Studies* 53 (1992): 257-87.
Hart, Trevor. 'Calvin and Barth on the Lord's Supper'. In *Calvin, Barth, and Reformed Theology*, edited by Neil B. MacDonald and Carl Trueman, 29-54. Milton Keynes: Paternoster Theological Monographs, 2008.
Hartenstein, Karl. *Die Mission als theologisches Problem: Bieträge zum grandsätzlichen Verstandnis der Mission*. Berlin: Furche Verlag, 1932.
Hauerwas, Stanley. *The Peaceable Kingdom*. Notre Dame: SCM Press, 1983.
Haughey, John. 'Church and Kingdom: Ecclesiology in the Light of Eschatology'. *Theological Studies* 29, no. 1 (1968): 72-86.
Hays, Richard B. *First Corinthians*. Louisville: John Knox Press, 1989.
Hays, Richard B. 'Reading the Bible with Eyes of Faith: The Practice of Theological Exegesis'. *Journal of Theological Interpretation* 1, no. 1 (2007): 5-21.
Hays, Richard B. 'Spirit, Church, Resurrection: The Third Article of the Creed as Hermeneutical Lens for Reading Romans'. *Journal of Theological Interpretation* 5, no. 1 (2011): 35-48.
Healy, Nicholas M. 'Karl Barth's Ecclesiology Reconsidered'. *Scottish Journal of Theology* 57, no. 3 (2004): 287-99.

Healy, Nicholas M. 'The Logic of Karl Barth's Ecclesiology: Analysis, Assessment and Proposed Modifications'. *Modern Theology* 10, no. 3 (1994): 253–70.
Healy, Nicholas M. 'Practices and the New Ecclesiology: Misplaced Concreteness?' *International Journal of Systematic Theology* 5, no. 3 (2003): 287–308.
Helmich, Bo. *Karl Barth and the Beauty of God*. Duke University, 2017.
Heppe, Heinrich. *Reformed Dogmatics*. Translated by G. T. Thomson. London: George Allen & Unwin, 1950.
Hirsch, Alan. *The Forgotten Ways*. Grand Rapids: Brazos Press, 2006.
Hitchcock, Nathan. *Karl Barth and the Resurrection of the Flesh*. Eugene: Pickwick, 2013.
Holwerda, David E. 'Suffering Witnesses – To What End?: A Sermon on Revelation 11:1-14'. *Calvin Theological Journal* 41, no. 1 (2006): 127–32.
Hunsinger, George. *How to Read Karl Barth: The Shape of His Theology*. New York/Oxford: Oxford University Press, 1991.
Hunsinger, George. 'The Mediator of Communion: Karl Barth's Doctrine of the Holy Spirit'. In *Disruptive Grace: Studies in the Theology of Karl Barth*, 148–85. Grand Rapids: Eerdmans, 2000.
Hunsinger, George. '*Mysterium Trinitatis*: Karl Barth's Conception of Eternity'. In *Disruptive Grace: Studies in the Theology of Karl Barth*, 186–209. Grand Rapids: Eerdmans, 2000.
Hütter, Reinhard. 'The Church: The Knowledge of the Triune God: Practices, Doctrine, Theology'. In *Knowing the Triune God: The Work of the Spirit in the Practices of the Church*, edited by James J. Buckley and David S. Yeago, 23–47. Grand Rapids: William B. Eerdmans, 2001.
Hütter, Reinhard. 'The Church as Public: Dogma, Practice, and the Holy Spirit'. *Pro Ecclesia* 3 (1994): 334–61.
Hütter, Reinhard. 'Karl Barth's "Dialectical Catholicity": Sic et Non'. *Modern Theology* 16, no. 2 (2000): 137–57.
Hütter, Reinhard. *Suffering Divine Things: Theology as Church Practice*. Translated by Doug Scott. Grand Rapids: Eerdmans, 2000.
Johnson, Luke Timothy. 'The Body in Question: The Social Complexities of Resurrection in 1 Corinthians'. In *Contested Issues in Christian Origins and the New Testament: Collected Essays*, edited by M. M. Mitchell and D. P. Moessner, 295–315. Leiden: Brill, 2013.
Johnson, Luke Timothy. *Contested Issues in Christian Origins and the New Testament: Collected Essays*. Leiden: Brill, 2013
Johnson, Luke Timothy. 'Life-Giving Spirit: The Ontological Implications of Resurrection in 1 Corinthians'. In *Contested Issues in Christian Origins and the New Testament: Collected Essays*, edited by M. M. Mitchell and D. P. Moessner, 277–93. Leiden: Brill, 2013.
Jones, Paul H. *Christ's Eucharistic Presence: A History of the Doctrine*. New York: Peter Lang, 1994.
Kärkkäinen, Veli-Matti. *Toward a Pneumatological Theology: Pentecostal and Ecumenical Perspectives on Ecclesiology, Soteriology, and Theology of Mission*. Lanham: University Press of America, 2002.
Kim, Kirsteen. 'Foreword'. In *Third Article Theology: A Pneumatological Dynamics*, edited by Myk Habets, xiii–xiv. Minneapolis: Fortress Press, 2016.
Kruger, C. Baxter. 'Participation in the Self-Knowledge of God: The Nature and Means of Our Knowledge of God in the Theology of T. F. Torrance'. PhD Thesis, University of Aberdeen, 1989.

Kuyper, Abraham. *Our Worship*. Translated by Harry Boonstra, Henry Baron, Gerrit Sheeres, and Leonard Sweetman. Grand Rapids: William B. Eerdmans, 2009.

Land, Steven J. *Pentecostal Spirituality: A Passion for the Kingdom*. London: Sheffield Academic Press, 2001.

Langdon, Adrian. *God the Eternal Contemporary: Trinity, Eternity and Time in Karl Barth*. Eugene: Wipf & Stock, 2012.

Leithart, Peter J. 'The Way Things Really Ought to Be: Eucharist, Eschatology, and Culture'. *The Westminster Theological Journal* 59, no. 2 (1997): 159–76.

Lemmer, Hermanus Richard. 'Pneumatology and Eschatology in Ephesians: The Role of the Eschatological Spirit in the Church'. PhD diss., University of South Africa, 1988.

Lewis, Clive Staples. *Mere Christianity*. London: HarperCollins, 2002.

Lewis, Clive Staples. *The Screwtape Letters: Letters from a Senior to a Junior Devil*. London: HarperCollins, 2002.

Liston, Gregory J. *The Anointed Church: Toward a Third Article Ecclesiology*. Minneapolis: Fortress, 2015.

Liston, Gregory J. 'A "Chalcedonian" Spirit Christology'. *Irish Theological Quarterly* 81, no. 1 (2016): 74–93.

Liston, Gregory J. 'Towards a Pneumato-Ecclesiology: Exploring the Pneumatological Union between Christ and the Church'. *Colloquium* 44, no. 1 (2012): 31–58.

Liston, Gregory J. 'Where the Love of Christ Is Found: Toward a Third Article Ecclesiology'. In *Third Article Theology: A Pneumatological Dogmatics*, edited by Myk Habets, 321–46. Minneapolis: Fortress Press, 2016.

Luther, Martin. 'On the Councils and the Church'. In *Luther's Works (Volume 41)*, edited by Eric W. Gritsch, 3–178. Philadelphia: Fortress, 1966.

Macchia, Frank D. *Baptized in the Spirit*. Grand Rapids: Zondervan, 2006.

Macchia, Frank D. *Jesus the Spirit Baptizer: Christology in Light of Pentecost*. Grand Rapids: Eerdmans, 2018.

Macchia, Frank D. *Justified in the Spirit: Creation, Redemption, and the Triune God*. Grand Rapids: Eerdmans, 2010.

Macchia, Frank D. *The Spirit-Baptized Church: A Dogmatic Inquiry*. London: T&T Clark, 2020.

MacDougall, Scott. *More Than Communion: Imagining an Eschatological Ecclesiology*. London: T&T Clark, 2015.

Maclean, Stanley S. *Resurrection, Apocalypse, and the Kingdom of Christ: The Eschatology of Thomas F. Torrance*. Eugene: Pickwick Publications, 2012.

Macy, Gary. *The Banquet's Wisdom: A Short History of the Theologies of the Lord's Supper*. New York: Paulist, 1992.

Mangina, Joseph L. 'Bearing the Marks of Jesus: The Church in the Economy of Salvation in Barth and Hauerwas'. *Scottish Journal of Theology* 52 (1999): 269–305.

Marshall, I. Howard. *Last Supper and Lord's Supper*. Vancouver: Regent College Publishing, 1980.

Martyn, J. Louis. 'Epistemology at the Turn of the Ages: 2 Corinthians 5:16'. In *Christian History and Interpretation: Studies Presented to John Knox*, edited by William Reuben Farmer, Charles Francis Digby Moule, and Richard R. Niebuhr, 269–87. Cambridge: Cambridge University Press, 1967.

Mawson, Michael. 'The Spirit and the Community: Pneumatology and Ecclesiology in Jenson, Hütter and Bonhoeffer'. *International Journal of Systematic Theology* 15, no. 4 (2013): 453–68.

McClendon, James William. *Systematic Theology: Doctrine*. Nashville: Abingdon Press, 1994.

McCormack, Bruce L. 'Witness to the Word: A Barthian Engagement with Reinhard Hütter's Ontology of the Church'. *Zeitschrift für Dialektische Theologie*. Supplement Series 5 (2011): 59–77.
McDonnell, Killian. 'A Response to D. Lyle Dabney'. In *Advents of the Spirit: An Introduction to the Current Study of Pneumatology*, edited by Bradford E. Hinze and D. Lyle Dabney, 262–4. Milwaukee: Marquette University Press, 2005.
McFarland, Ian A. 'The Body of Christ: Rethinking a Classic Ecclesiological Model'. *International Journal of Systematic Theology* 7, no. 3 (2005): 225–45.
McKim, Donald K. *Introducing the Reformed Faith*. Louisville: Westminster John Knox, 2001.
McKnight, Scott. *Kingdom Conspiracy: Returning to the Radical Mission of the Local Church*. Grand Rapids: Baker Publishing Group, 2014.
McQueen, Larry R. *Towards a Pentecostal Eschatology: Discerning the Way Forward*. Dorset: Deo Publishing, 2012.
Meyers, Jeffrey J. 'Concerning Wine and Beer'. *Rite Reasons* 48–9 (1997): n.p.
Migliore, Daniel L. *Faith Seeking Understanding: An Introduction to Christian Theology*. 2nd edn. Grand Rapids: Eerdmans, 2004.
Mitchell, Margaret Mary. *Paul and the Rhetoric of Reconciliation*. Tubingen: Mohr and Louisville, 1992.
Mitchell, Margaret Mary. *Paul and the Rhetoric of Reconciliation: An Exegetical Investigation of the Language and Composition of 1 Corinthians*. Louisville: Westminster/John Knox Press, 1993
Molnar, Paul D. 'The Eucharist and the Mind of Christ: Some Trinitarian Implications of T. F. Torrance's Sacramental Theology'. In *Trinitarian Soundings in Systematic Theology*, edited by Paul L. Metzger. 175–88. London: T&T Clark, 2005.
Moltmann, Jürgen. *The Church in the Power of the Spirit: A Contribution to Messianic Ecclesiology*. New York: Harper and Row, 1977.
Moore, Russell D., Ira John Hesselink, David P. Scaer, and Thomas A. Baima. *Understanding Four Views on the Lord's Supper*. Grand Rapids: Zondervan, 2007.
Mühlen, Heribert. *Una Mystica Persona. Die Kirche als das Mysterium der heilsgeschichtlichen Identität des Heiligen Geistes in Christus und den Christen: Eine Person in vielen Personen*. 2nd edn. Paderborn: Ferdinand Schöningh, 1967.
Neuhaus, Richard John. 'Wolfhart Pannenberg: Profile of a Theologian'. In *Theology and the Kingdom of God*, edited by Richard John Neuhaus, 9–50. Philadelphia: Westminster, 1969.
Newbigin, Lesslie. *One Body, One Gospel, One World: The Christian Mission Today*. London: Wm. Carling & Co., 1958.
Newbigin, Lesslie. *The Reunion of the Church: A Defence of the South India Scheme*. London: SCM Press, 1960.
Otto, Randall E. 'Baptism and the Munus Triplex'. *Evangelical Quarterly* 76, no. 3 (2004): 217–25.
Pelikan, Jaroslov and Valerie Hotchkiss, eds. *Creeds and Confessions of Faith in the Christian Tradition: Early, Eastern and Medieval*. New Haven: Yale University Press, 2003.
Persaud, Winston D. 'The Theology of the Cross as Christian Witness: A Theological Essay'. *Currents in Theology and Mission* 41, no. 1 (2014): 11–16.
Peterson, Cheryl M. 'Who Is the Church?' *Dialog* 51, no. 1 (2012): 24–30.
Peterson, Cheryl M. *Who Is the Church? An Ecclesiology for the Twenty-First Century*. Minneapolis: Fortress, 2013.
Peterson, Eugene. *Practise Resurrection*. London: Hodder & Stoughton, 2010.

Pinnock, Clark H. *Flame of Love: A Theology of the Holy Spirit*. Downers Grove: IVP Academic, 1996.
Pugh, Ben. *SCM Studyguide to Theology in the Contemporary World*. London: SCM Press, 2017.
Purves, Andrew. 'The Advent of Ministry: Torrance on Eschatology, the Church, and Ministry'. In *Evangelical Calvinism: Volume 2*, edited by Myk Habets and Bobby Grow, 95–127. Eugene: Pickwick, 2017.
Rae, Murray. 'Suffering Divine Things (Review)'. *Modern Theology* 17, no. 3 (2001): 397–9.
Riddell, Mike. *Godzone: A Guide to the Travels of the Soul*. London: SPCK, 2011.
Robinette, Brian D. *Grammars of Resurrection: A Christian Theology of Presence and Absence*. New York: Herder & Herder, 2009.
Rosato, Philip J. 'The Mission of the Spirit within and beyond the Church'. *Ecumenical Review* 41, no. 3 (1989): 388–97.
Rosato, Philip J. 'Spirit Christology: Ambiguity and Promise'. *Theological Studies* 38 (1977): 423–9.
Sánchez M., Leopoldo A. *Receiver, Bearer and Giver of God's Spirit*. Eugene: Pickwick, 2015.
Sánchez M., Leopoldo A. 'Sculpting Christ in Us: Public Faces of the Spirit in God's World'. In *Third Article Theology: A Pneumatological Dogmatics*, edited by Myk Habets, 297–320. Minneapolis: Fortress Press, 2016.
Sánchez M., Leopoldo A. *Sculptor Spirit: Models of Sanctification from Spirit Christology*. Downers Grove: IVP Academic, 2019.
Sánchez M., Leopoldo A. *T&T Clark Introduction to Spirit Christology*. London: T&T Clark, 2021.
Sherman, Robert. *King, Priest, and Prophet*. New York: T&T Clark, 2004.
Simmons, Ernest L. *The Entangled Trinity: Quantum Physics and Theology*. Minneapolis: Fortress Press, 2014.
Smith, James K. A. *Desiring the Kingdom: Worship, Worldview, and Cultural Formation*. Grand Rapids: Baker Academic, 2009.
Smith, James K. A. *You Are What You Love: The Spiritual Power of Habit*. Grand Rapids: Brazos, 2016.
Snyder, Howard A. *The Radical Wesley: The Patterns and Practices of a Movement Maker*. Franklin: Seedbed, 1996.
Starling, David Ian. '"Nothing Beyond What Is Written"?: I Corinthians and the Hermeneutics of Early Christian Theologia'. *Journal of Theological Interpretation* 8, no. 1 (2014): 45–62.
Steinkerchner O. P., Scott. 'Time in Heaven: From Glory to Glory'. *New Blackfriars* 100, no. 1087 (2019): 264–83.
Stroup, George W. 'The Relevance of the Munus Triplex for Reformed Theology and Ministry'. *Austin Seminary Bulletin (Faculty ed.)* 98, no. 9 (1983): 22–32.
Studebaker, Steven M. *From Pentecost to the Triune God: A Pentecostal Trinitarian Theology*. Grand Rapids: Eerdmans, 2012.
Studebaker, Steven M. 'The Pathos of Theology as a Pneumatological Derivative or a Poiemata of the Spirit?: A Review Essay of Reinhard Hütter's Pneumatological and Ecclesiological Vision of Theology'. *Pneuma* 32, no. 2 (2010): 269–82.
Tanner, Kathryn. *Christ the Key*. Cambridge: Cambridge University Press, 2010.
Taylor, Charles. *Modern Social Imaginaries*. Durham: Duke University Press, 2004.
Thiselton, Anthony C. *The First Epistle to the Corinthians, The New International Greek Testament Commentary*. Grand Rapids: Eerdmans, 2000.

Thompson, Matthew K. *Kingdom Come: Revisioning Pentecostal Ecclesiology*. Dorset: Deo Publishing, 2010.
Torrance, James B. *Worship, Community and the Triune God of Grace*. Downers Grove: IVP Academic, 1996.
Torrance, Thomas F. 'Atonement and the Oneness of the Church'. *Scottish Journal of Theology* 7, no. 3 (1954): 245–69.
Torrance, Thomas F. *Atonement: The Person and Work of Christ*. Downers Grove: InterVarsity Press, 2009.
Torrance, Thomas F. *Conflict and Agreement in the Church, Vol II: The Ministry and the Sacraments of the Gospel*. Eugene: Wipf & Stock, 1996.
Torrance, Thomas F. 'Eschatology and the Eucharist'. In *Intercommunion*, edited by Donald M. Baillie and John Marsh, 303–50. London: SCM, 1952.
Torrance, Thomas F. *Incarnation: The Person and Life of Christ*. Downers Grove: InterVarsity Press, 2008.
Torrance, Thomas F. *Karl Barth. Biblical and Evangelical Theologian*. Edinburgh: T&T Clark, 1990.
Torrance, Thomas F. *The Mediation of Christ*. 2nd edn. Edinburgh: T&T Clark, 1992.
Torrance, Thomas F. *Reality and Evangelical Theology*. Philadelphia: The Westminster Press, 1982.
Torrance, Thomas F. *Royal Priesthood*. Edinburgh: Oliver and Boyd, 1955.
Torrance, Thomas F. *Scottish Theology from John Knox to John McLeod Campbell*. Edinburgh: T&T Clark, 1996.
Torrance, Thomas F. 'The Modern Eschatological Debate'. *Evangelical Quarterly* 25 (1953): 45–54, 94–106, 67–78, 224–32.
Torrance, Thomas F. *Royal Priesthood: A Theology of Ordained Ministry*. Edinburgh: T&T Clark, 1993.
Torrance, Thomas F., ed. *The School of Faith: The Catechisms of the Reformed Church*. London: James Clarke and Co., 1959.
Torrance, Thomas F. *Space, Time and Resurrection*. Edinburgh: T&T Clark, 1976.
van der Kooi, Cornelis. *This Incredibly Benevolent Force: The Holy Spirit in Reformed Theology and Spirituality*. Grand Rapids: Eerdmans, 2018.
Volf, Miroslav. *After Our Likeness: The Church as the Image of the Trinity*. Grand Rapids: Eerdmans, 1998.
Volf, Miroslav and Maurice Lee. 'The Spirit and the Church'. In *Advents of the Spirit: An Introduction to the Current Study of Pneumatology*, edited by Bradford E. Hinze and D. Lyle Dabney, 382–409. Milwaukee: Marquette University Press, 2005.
Vondey, Wolfgang. *Heribert Mühlen: His Theology and Praxis*. Dallas: University Press of America, 2004.
Vondey, Wolfgang. 'The Holy Spirit and Time in Contemporary Catholic and Protestant Theology'. *Scottish Journal of Theology* 58, no. 4 (2005): 393–409.
Vondey, Wolfgang. 'The Spirit and Science'. In *T&T Clark Handbook of Pneumatology*, edited by Daniel Castelo and Kenneth M. Loyer, 111–20. London: T&T Clark, 2020.
Wainwright, Geoffrey. *Eucharist and Eschatology*. London: Epworth Press, 1971.
Weinandy, Thomas. *The Father's Spirit of Sonship: Reconceiving the Trinity*. Edinburgh: T&T Clark, 1995.
Welker, Michael. *God the Revealed: Christology*. Translated by Douglas W. Stott. Grand Rapids: Eerdmans, 2013.
Wilkerson, David. *The Cross and the Switchblade*. New York: Jove Books, 1977.

Wolterstorff, Nicholas. *Reason within the Bounds of Religion*. Grand Rapids: Eerdmans, 1976.

Wolterstorff, Nicholas. 'The Reformed Liturgy'. In *Major Themes in the Reformed Tradition*, edited by Donald K. McKim, 273–304. Grand Rapids: Eerdmans, 1992.

Wood, Susan K. 'Liturgy: Participatory Knowledge of God in the Liturgy'. In *Knowing the Triune God: The Work of the Spirit in the Practices of the Church*, edited by James J. Buckley and David S. Yeago, 95–118. Grand Rapids: William B. Eerdmans, 2001.

Worsley, Steve. *The Way of the Raukura: A Parihaka Musical*. Auckland: Unpublished, 2019.

Wright, Christopher J. H. *The Mission of God: Unlocking the Bible's Grand Narrative*. Downers Grove: IVP Academic, 2006.

Yong, Amos. *Beyond the Impasse: Toward a Pneumatological Theology of Religions*. Grand Rapids: Baker, 2003.

Yong, Amos. *In the Days of Caesar: Pentecostalism and Political Theology*. Grand Rapids: Eerdmans, 2010.

Yong, Amos. *Mission after Pentecost: The Witness of the Spirit from Genesis to Revelation*. Grand Rapids: BakerAcademic, 2019.

Yong, Amos. *Renewing Christian Theology: Systematics for a Global Christianity*. Waco: Baylor University Press, 2014.

Yong, Amos. 'Introduction: Pentecostalism and a Theology of the Third Article'. In *Toward a Pneumatological Theology: Pentecostal and Ecumenical Perspectives on Ecclesiology, Soteriology, and Theology of Mission*, edited by Amos Yong, xiii–xx. Lanham: University Press of America, 2002.

Zizioulas, John. 'Die pneumatologische Diemension der Kirche'. *IKZ Communio* 2 (1973): 133–47.

AUTHOR INDEX

Aagaard, Johannes 162, 187
Althouse, Peter 45, 50, 54, 187, 189
Anderson, Willhelm 162, 187
Arendt, Hannah 40, 187
Aring, Paul Gerhard 158, 163, 187
Armstrong, John H. 85, 187

Badcock, Gary 5, 9, 51–2, 187
Baillie, Donald M. 27, 195
Baima, Thomas A. 193
Balthasar, Hans Urs von 34, 45, 56, 187
Barnes, Michel René 5, 189
Barnhill, Gregory M. 131, 146–7, 187
Baron, Henry 192
Barr, William R. 163, 187
Barth, Karl (Barthian) 9, 12, 19–22, 25–39, 41–2, 45, 47–9, 56, 59, 64–71, 76–80, 95, 98–104, 107–12, 114, 116, 118–22, 124, 127, 132–3, 162, 185, 187–92, 195
Bauer, Walter 130, 188
Bavinck, Herman 94, 188
Bender, Kimlyn 31, 33–4, 66, 79, 102, 107, 110, 120, 188
Berkhof, Louis 44, 61, 188
Beveridge, Henry 94, 188
Blomberg, Craig L. 81–2, 188
Bobrinskoy, Boris 3, 164, 188
Bolt, John 94, 188
Bonhoeffer, Dietrich 37, 53, 188, 192
Boonstra, Harry 125, 192
Bosch, David J. 158, 162–3, 188
Bromiley, Geoffrey W. 27, 100, 187
Brunner, Emil 158, 188
Buckley, James J. 37, 113, 191, 196
Butin, Phil 64–5, 67, 188

Calvin, John (Calvinism) 46, 60–1, 65, 93–4, 103, 122, 133, 139, 157, 168–9, 188, 190–1, 194
Carey, William 158, 189
Carr, Frederick David 145, 188

Castelo, Daniel 185, 195
Chester, Timothy 94, 188
Chrysologus, Peter 60, 189
Clark, Jason Swar 161, 188
Coffey, David 4, 12, 188
Collins, Raymond F. 151, 188
Conzelman, Hans 130–2, 188
Cousar, Charles B. 137, 139, 144, 147, 188

Dabney, Lyle 2–4, 163, 188, 193, 195
Dadosky, John 150, 188
de Lubac, Henri 160, 188
Del Colle, Ralph 4–5, 188–9
Dempster, Murray W. 50, 189
Dorrien, Gary J. 40–1, 189

Engle, Paul E. 85, 187
Eugenio, Dick O. 70, 189
Eusebius 60, 189

Falconer, Kenneth J. 55, 189
Farmer, William Reuben 140, 192
Farrow, Douglas 68, 189
Faupel, D. 49, 189
Fee, Gordon D. 85, 131–2, 134–6, 139, 141–2, 145, 150, 153, 189
Fergusson, David 16, 189
Fitch, David 161
Flett, John 162, 189
Foster, Richard 86, 99, 189
Franklin, Patrick 161, 164, 189
Fraser, John W. 139, 188
Frost, Michael 160–1, 189
Furnish, Victor Paul 131, 136, 138, 140, 152–3, 189

Ganss, George E. 60, 189
George, Timothy 158, 189
Goheen, Michael 159, 189
Gorman, Michael 54, 56, 141, 189
Green, Garrett 16, 189
Greggs, Tom 176, 190

Grenz, Stanley J.   171, 190
Gritsch, Eric W.   108, 192
Grow, Bobby   46, 194
Guder, Darrell L.   158, 161, 190
Gunton, Colin   11, 13, 33, 46, 66, 78, 190
Guyette, Fred   60, 190

Habets, Myk   2–6, 12, 15, 43–4, 46, 86, 169, 190–2, 194
Haight, Roger   44, 190
Hardy, Daniel   13, 190
Harrisville, R. A.   133
Hart, Trevor   103, 190
Hartenstein, Karl   162, 190
Hauerwas, Stanley   36, 171, 190, 192
Haughey, John   25–6, 190
Hays, Richard   129–30, 152, 190
Healy, Nicholas M.   32, 41–2, 45, 190
Hegel, G. W. F.   37
Helmich, Bo   100, 103, 191
Heppe, Heinrich   61, 191
Hesselink, Ira John   193
Hinze, Bradford E.   4, 163, 188, 193, 195
Hirsch, Alan   160–1, 189, 191
Hitchcock, Nathan   65, 67, 191
Holwerda, David E.   168, 191
Hoskyns, Edwyn C.   95, 187
Hotchkiss, Valerie   20, 26, 46, 193
Hunsinger, George   9, 28–30, 32, 66, 101, 191
Hütter, Reinhard   19–22, 25, 28, 32, 36–42, 45, 48, 53, 71, 77, 79–80, 88, 98–9, 101–5, 107–14, 116, 118–22, 124, 191–4

Johnson, Luke Timothy   131–5, 146–9, 191
Jones, Paul H.   84, 191
Justin Martyr   60

Kärkkäinen, Veli-Matti   6, 9, 54, 163, 191
Kraft, Robert A.   130, 188
Krauss, Reinhard   53, 188
Krodel, Gerhard   130, 188
Kruger, C. Baxter   70, 191
Kuyper, Abraham   125, 192

Land, Steven J.   49, 53, 192
Langdon, Adrian   29–32, 34–5, 45, 65, 68, 192
Leitch, James W.   130, 188
Leithart, Peter J.   84–6, 93, 97, 192
Lemmer, Hermanus Richard   35, 192
Lewis, Clive S.   86–7, 92, 123–4, 192
Liston, Gregory J.   2–6, 8, 12–13, 17, 32, 37, 42, 44, 46, 51–3, 87, 91, 98, 115, 163, 165, 167–9, 173–4, 192
Lossky, Nicholas   3, 188
Luther, Martin   39, 108, 110–14, 117–21, 133, 192

Macchia, Frank D.   4, 6, 46, 49–50, 192
MacDonald, Neil B.   103, 190
MacDougall, Scott   15–16, 82, 84, 99, 192
Maclean, Stanley S.   28, 32, 35–6, 45–6, 192
Macy, Gary   84, 192
Maier, Paul L.   60, 189
Mangina, Joseph L.   36, 192
Marsh, John   27, 195
Marshall, I. Howard   82, 192
Martyn, J. Louis   140, 192
Mason, Michael   160, 188
Mawson, Michael   37, 41, 45, 56, 101, 114, 192
McClendon, James William   158, 192
McCormack, Bruce L.   37–8, 42, 45, 193
McDonnell, Killian   3–4, 193
McFarland, Ian A.   51, 101, 193
McKim, Donald K.   62, 118, 193, 196
McKnight, Scott   25, 193
McQueen, Larry   49, 193
Metzger, Paul L.   69, 193
Meyers, Jeffrey J.   93, 193
Migliore, Daniel L.   62, 193
Mitchell, Margaret Mary   132, 152, 191, 193
Moessner, D. P.   191
Molnar, Paul D.   69, 193
Moltmann, Jürgen   37, 45, 54, 71, 79–80, 133, 187, 193
Moore, Russell D.   84, 91, 193
Moule, C. F. D.   192
Moxnes, H.   133
Mühlen, Heribert   164, 185, 193, 195

Neuhaus, Richard John 83, 193
Newbigin, Lesslie 159, 161, 170, 189, 193
Newton, Isaac 6
Niebuhr, Richard R. 192
Nietzsche, Friedrich 95
Nissiotis, Nikos 38

Otto, Randall E. 62, 193

Palardy, William B. 60, 189
Pannenberg, Wolfhart 37, 71, 79, 83, 193
Pelikan, Jaroslav 20, 26, 46, 193
Persaud, Winston D. 168, 193
Peterson, Cheryl M. 5, 163, 166, 175, 193
Peterson, Eugene 167, 193
Pickard, Stephen 2, 188
Pinnock, Clark H. 4–5, 194
Polanyi, Michael 113
Preece, Gordon 2, 188
Pugh, Ben 3, 194
Purves, Andrew 46, 194

Rae, Murray 40, 194
Riddell, Mike 179, 194
Robinette, Brian D. 15–18, 194
Rosato, Philip 44, 74, 152, 160, 194
Ryland, John Collett 157–8

Sánchez, Leopoldo A. 4, 46, 86, 194
Sarot, Marcel 16, 189
Scaer, David P. 193
Sheeres, Gerrit 192
Sherman, Robert 62, 194
Simmons, Ernest L. 185, 194
Smith, James K. A. 83, 117, 184, 194
Snyder, Howard A. 123, 194
Starling, David Ian 130, 194
Steinkerchner, Scott 64, 194
Stenning, H. J. 133, 188
Stonehouse, Ned B. 83, 189
Stott, Douglas W. 62, 195
Stransky, Tom F. 188
Stroup, George W. 60, 194
Studebaker, Steven M. 38, 48–50, 194
Sweetman, Leonard 191

Tanner, Kathryn 13, 194
Taylor, Charles 82, 194
Thiselton, Anthony C. 132–3, 139, 194
Thomas Aquinas 60, 187
Thompson, Matthew K. 48, 55, 195
Thomson, G. T. 51, 191
Tolliday, Phillip 12, 190
Torrance, James B 7, 160, 194
Torrance, Thomas F. 20–1, 26–8, 30, 32–3, 35–6, 45–9, 54, 59–61, 63–4, 67–71, 76, 79–80, 88, 93, 103–4, 122, 127, 166–7, 187, 189, 191–5
Trueman, Carl 103, 190

van der Kooi, Cornelis 62, 71–2, 89, 195
Volf, Miroslav 13, 41, 163, 195
Vondey, Wolfgang 35, 46, 164, 185, 195
Vriend, John 94, 188

Waddell, Robert 50, 187, 189
Wainwright, Geoffrey 84, 188, 195
Webb, Pauline 188
Webster, John 33, 190
Weinandy, Thomas 12, 28, 169, 195
Welker, Michael 62, 195
Wesley, John (Wesleyan) 60, 123, 190, 194
Whitefield, George 123
Wilkerson, David 123, 195
Wolterstorff, Nicholas (Wolterstorffian) 2, 6–8, 21–2, 118, 122, 124–5, 129, 157, 164–5, 172, 174, 185, 196
Wood, Susan K. 113, 196
Worsley, Steve 183, 196
Wright, Christopher J. H. 158, 196

Yeago, David S. 37, 113, 191, 196
Yocum, Rena M. 163, 187
Yong, Amos 5, 43–4, 47, 163, 196

Zizioulas, John 37–9, 41, 45, 71, 79, 99, 196
Zwingli, Ulrich (Zwinglian) 100, 103

SUBJECT INDEX

absence (of Christ or Spirit)   15, 31, 66, 100, 112
abundant life   72–3, 92–3, 98, 143
Adam   133–4
affections   38, 83
analogy, analogous   7, 9, 11–13, 16–17, 19, 26–7, 30–1, 34, 40, 45–7, 50–1, 53, 57, 63, 88, 101, 117, 128, 134, 167, 175
anhypostasis, anhypostatic   87–8, 91, 98, 102, 104, 117, 128
anointed, anointing   46, 61–2, 122, 178–9
anthropology   5, 15, 43, 164
anticipate, anticipation   1, 7, 15, 22–3, 26, 30, 35, 39, 64, 72, 75, 77–9, 81–5, 88–92, 95–6, 99–100, 105, 110, 121, 125–6, 129, 143, 145, 150, 153–4, 166, 170, 173, 177, 183, 186
apostle, apostolicity   2, 16, 143–5, 147, 153–4, 174–6, 186
ascended, ascension   17, 31, 63, 67–8, 70, 77
asymmetry, asymmetrical   10, 30, 51, 66, 69, 75, 101, 167–8, 175
atonement, atoning   54, 61–2, 67–8, 138, 167

balance, balanced   9–11, 20, 28, 36, 98, 104, 115, 172
baptism, baptized   6, 9, 11, 27, 39, 49–50, 62, 69, 80, 94, 100, 103, 108–9, 152, 175
Barth, Karl (Barthian)   9, 12, 19–22, 25–39, 41–2, 45, 47–9, 56, 59, 64–71, 76–80, 95, 98–104, 107–12, 114, 116, 118–22, 124, 127, 132–3, 162, 185
beer   93, 193
bios (life)   72, 92
blessing   68, 70, 153

body, bodies   17–18, 27, 90, 92, 133–5, 146–8, 150, 159
breath, breathe, breathing   1, 12, 127, 131, 157, 164, 169–70, 172
bride, bridegroom   1, 7, 11, 82, 89, 120

call, called, calling   33, 78, 80, 100, 109, 118–19, 125, 131, 139–40, 160–1, 167
Calvin, John (Calvinism)   46, 60–1, 65, 93–4, 103, 122, 133, 139, 157, 168–9
catechesis, catechism   60–1, 64–5, 67, 93, 120
catholic, catholicize   9, 14, 25, 32, 35, 37–8, 46, 60, 108, 112, 121–2, 145, 160, 174, 176
celebrate, celebration   81–2, 84, 86–7, 89–97, 99, 102–3, 121, 178
Chalcedon, Chalcedonian   5, 9, 20, 26–8, 30, 32, 42, 44, 46–7, 63, 66, 102, 104, 115, 121, 128, 175, 181
Christlike, Christotelic   10, 51–2, 55, 109, 126, 142
Christology
   Logos Christology   5, 20, 44–5, 57, 126
   Spirit Christology   4–6, 10–12, 17, 19, 21, 32, 42–6, 50–1, 57, 86, 126, 185
commune, communal   51, 53–5, 57, 76–7, 82–5, 88, 92, 94, 96, 111, 144–7, 149, 152, 184
communion
   among believers   81, 104
   between God/Christ and church/humanity   10, 51, 68–9, 81, 84, 85, 87, 116, 127, 180
   Eucharist   80, 83, 86–7, 93–4, 97, 100, 103–4, 180
   within Godhead   7, 29, 40, 122, 160, 166, 168
conform, conformity   5, 10, 17–18, 51–2, 54–7, 78, 126

consecrate, consecration 53, 122, 147
correspondence, corresponding 9, 11, 27–8, 34–5, 45, 75, 108, 116, 122, 163, 172, 181
corrupt, corruptible 73, 113, 121, 133
covenant, covenantal 30, 112
created 3, 29, 82, 92, 95, 99, 177
creator, creation 16–17, 27–8, 30, 32, 37–9, 47, 49, 60, 68, 70, 72–4, 82–5, 88, 94, 171–2, 185
creature, creatureliness 17, 30, 34, 37, 51, 85, 88, 123
Creed 2, 7, 20, 22, 26, 39, 46, 129
crucified, crucifixion 22, 63, 66, 136–8, 140–1, 145, 154
cruciform, cruciformity 10, 21, 44, 52, 54–7, 83, 96, 126, 135, 140–1, 179

dialectic 32, 108
dialogical 2, 6–7, 23, 157, 163–5
discern, discerning 4, 49, 54, 60, 109, 124, 138, 147, 167, 184
disciple, discipleship 13, 90, 117, 140, 168, 175
discipline, disciplines 85–6, 157, 178, 181, 184
discontinuity, discontinuous 1–2, 4, 17–19, 21, 25–6, 28, 32, 37, 42, 46, 51–2, 88, 91, 93, 95, 100, 104–5, 125, 143, 167–8, 178
division, divisive 30, 75, 90–1, 97, 109, 119, 152, 171, 176
docetic, docetism 5, 9, 11, 85, 110, 114, 128, 181
dogma 37–8, 108, 120

ebionism 9, 11, 42, 128, 181
ecumenical, ecumenism 3, 6, 44, 60, 74, 109
elements 84, 91, 97
embody, embodied 14, 18, 34, 40, 56, 83, 102, 108, 141, 161, 169
encourage, encouragement 75, 109, 144, 176
endure, endurance 73, 109, 137, 144, 149
enhypostasis, enhypostatic 39–41, 45, 87–8, 91, 98, 101–2, 104, 117, 128
epistemology, epistemological 3, 8, 137–8, 140, 142, 152, 161, 172

eschatology
    Logos eschatology 45–50, 56, 126
    Spirit eschatology 6, 19, 21–2, 43, 45–50, 53, 56–7, 126, 185
ethnic, ethnically 96, 152, 177–8
Eucharist, eucharistic 21–2, 27–8, 41, 69, 77, 79–105, 107, 109–11, 117, 122, 125, 127, 148, 150–1, 175–6
Eutychianism 11, 32, 85, 102, 104, 110, 114, 128, 181
evangelism, evangelization 108–9, 158
evil, evildoer 1, 4, 72–3, 143, 149

faith, faithful 13, 16, 20, 26, 34, 46, 56, 60–2, 78, 80, 91, 93, 100, 113, 117, 123, 130, 147, 158, 175
feast, feasting 83, 89–94, 97
fellowship 9, 14, 80–2, 85, 89–90, 108–9, 112, 148, 153, 175, 177
filial 13, 55, 59, 70, 76, 81, 95
filioque 12, 190
flesh 27, 47, 65, 67, 80, 87, 92, 118, 133, 185
foreign, foreigners 75, 82, 95
foreshadow, foretaste 73, 82–3, 95, 97–8, 102, 104, 124, 136–7, 139, 149, 153
forgiveness 68, 109
fractal 55–7, 96, 117, 126, 128, 181, 185
free, freedom 41, 73–4, 88, 96, 146–8, 171–2, 177, 180
fruit, fruitful 3, 45, 116, 153, 184
fulfil, fulfilment 30, 37, 39, 52, 56, 73, 99, 159, 161, 171
functional, functionality 84, 152, 161

gather, gathering 14, 31, 53, 65, 68, 90, 94, 96, 119–20, 127, 150, 160, 170, 172, 175, 178, 180–1, 184
gift, giver 16, 46, 83, 93, 101, 103, 114, 122, 133, 136, 140, 150–4, 171, 179–81
glory, glorified 27, 47, 52, 54–5, 59, 64–5, 73, 76, 122, 133, 148, 159
glossolalia 55, 131, 139, 154
gospel 22, 37–8, 49–50, 56, 103–4, 108–10, 118–25, 127, 130, 135–6, 145, 159, 161, 164, 170
grace 7, 26, 29, 61, 69, 80, 100–1, 111, 122, 160, 166, 182–3
grammar, grammatical 2, 15–18

Subject Index

grows, grown, growing 1, 40, 42, 51–2, 73–5, 98, 102, 117, 120, 123–4, 133, 142–3, 145, 147, 153, 169, 176, 179–80, 183
guide, guidance 38–9, 44, 52–4, 115, 117, 150, 167, 172
guilty 87, 110

heal, healing 30–1, 71–2, 74, 91, 171
hear, heard, hearers 68, 118–19, 121, 149
hearts, heartbeat 74, 85, 88, 96–7, 104, 116–18, 180
heaven, heavenly 16, 31, 49, 61–5, 67, 69, 82, 96, 116, 133–4, 137
hermeneutics, hermeneutical 129–30
hide, hidden, hiddenness 72, 91, 137, 140, 153
history, historic 4, 10–11, 16–18, 21, 31, 52, 56, 60, 77–8, 81, 109, 123, 130–1, 175, 181
holiness 22, 27, 47, 72, 94–6, 98, 115, 117–18, 128, 136, 143, 152, 154, 174, 176, 182–3
honour, honouring 5, 90, 97, 142, 144
hope, hoping 17, 35–6, 55–6, 79–80, 83, 86, 99, 123, 135–6, 139, 179
humanity 73–4, 141, 171
    interaction between God and 30–1, 34, 35, 51, 55, 59, 61, 64–5, 67–70, 78, 81, 103, 124, 137
    of Christ 5, 12, 17–18, 21, 27, 30, 33, 49, 64, 67–71, 125
    of church 9, 10, 12, 73
hungry 96–7, 143, 151
hypostasis, hypostatic 12–13, 27, 29–30, 39, 46–7, 53, 63, 99, 125, 169

illuminate, illumination 7–11, 22, 66, 90, 122, 131–2, 137, 154, 166–7, 170, 174–5
image, imagery 2–3, 13, 16, 21, 52, 54–7, 86, 89–90, 96, 120, 143, 167
imaginary 82–3, 127, 138, 140–1
imagine, imagination 15–16, 21–2, 80, 82–5, 88–90, 92–3, 95–101, 104–5, 107, 110, 114–16, 118, 121, 123–5, 127–8, 130, 135–7, 139, 141–2, 144–6, 149, 151, 154, 175, 179–84

imbalance 21, 28, 32, 36, 104
immanence, immanent 12–14, 29, 91
incarnate, incarnation 10, 14, 17, 26–7, 33, 44, 46–7, 51, 53, 57, 63, 66–70, 80, 125, 157, 160, 167, 169
individualism, individualistic 40, 84, 90, 94, 135, 145, 147, 152, 161, 184
indwell, indwelling 9–10, 17, 40, 47, 87, 91, 116, 159
inscape 167–8
inspired, inspiring 10, 66, 84, 89, 104, 111–12, 121–2, 171, 181–2
intercede, intercession 64, 68–70, 111

journey, journeying 51–2, 98, 151
joy, joyful 55, 73, 90, 92–4, 96, 98, 143
judge, judgement 32, 63, 65, 73–4, 83, 87, 90, 97, 142–4, 149, 151, 179–80
justice 34, 71, 73–5, 80, 89, 96–8, 110, 116, 124, 127, 143, 151, 171, 180
justification 3, 13, 34, 37, 46, 56, 133, 163

king, kingship 1, 21, 23, 49, 55, 59, 62, 64–5, 67, 70–2, 74–6, 79, 81, 85, 88–9, 95–6, 125–7, 129, 143, 173, 176, 178, 180, 182–3, 186

lamb 72, 81–2, 89, 95–6, 102
liberty, liberate 61, 73–4, 147, 171
liturgy, liturgical 3, 113, 118, 121–2, 124, 151, 164, 188

loaf 90, 92, 151
logos 5, 9, 20, 40, 44–50, 53, 56–7, 87, 126
longing 26, 74, 83, 88, 96, 99, 101–2, 104, 116, 118, 127, 139, 180–1
love, loving 12, 73–4, 89, 117, 153, 161, 164, 171

manifest, manifestation 35, 39, 55, 59, 76, 97, 99
marks (of the church) 18, 36, 39, 124, 128, 140, 174
marriage 94, 149
mature, maturity, maturation 46, 51, 93, 135, 139, 142, 144–5, 153–4
mediator, mediation 9–10, 14, 29–33, 51, 66, 68–70, 88, 99–101, 103, 127, 145, 180

metaphor, metaphorical   51, 93, 124, 143, 147
method, methodology   1–5, 13, 15, 19, 21, 42–4, 50, 59, 75, 86, 184, 186
miracle, miraculous   33, 83, 179, 181
missio Dei   158, 162–3, 165
missiology, missiological   8, 23, 157, 159–68, 170–5, 186
missional   10, 99, 157–66, 168, 170
missions, missionary   109, 158–64, 168, 170
multicultural   177, 182
munus triplex   21, 36, 59–65, 67–71, 73, 75, 193–4
mystery, mystical   13–15, 39, 91, 100, 169

narrative, story   10, 18, 54–5, 96, 117, 128, 158, 161, 183
Nestorianism   11, 103–4, 110, 128, 181
noetic, noetically   18, 26, 32, 34–5, 49, 64, 66–7, 76, 79, 88, 93, 97, 100, 125–6, 179

obey, obedience   44, 52, 54, 57, 69, 109, 115, 117, 123–4, 126, 142, 144–5, 149–50, 167–8, 172
offices (of Christ)   21, 59, 61–2, 64–5, 67, 70, 75–6, 85, 109, 126–7
oneness   11, 54, 167, 174
ontic, ontically   18, 26, 32, 34–5, 49, 64, 70, 76, 79, 88, 125–6, 179
ontology, ontological   9–10, 13, 17–18, 38, 48, 59, 69–71, 81, 84–5, 87, 97, 133–6, 138, 140, 142, 147–9, 159
oppress, oppressor   54, 73–4, 95, 171

participation
  in Christ's offices   21, 59–60, 67–9, 76, 99, 122, 127, 133, 162, 169
  in Christ's time   48, 52, 64, 72, 126–7
  in church practices/Spirit's transformation   39, 77, 81–4, 87, 91, 98, 103, 114
  in the coming Kingdom   39–40, 81, 96
  of church in Christ/Trinity   7, 11, 13, 30, 32–3, 37, 49, 54–5, 62, 64, 66, 70, 81, 83, 92, 95, 115–18, 122, 124, 140, 150, 160, 168, 170, 174, 176
pathos, pathic, pathically   38–40, 99, 101, 113–14, 121

pattern, patterns   9, 30, 55–6, 66, 69, 72, 74, 83, 123, 125–6, 140, 169
Paul, Pauline   16–18, 22, 35, 54, 56, 60, 69, 73, 84–5, 90, 95–7, 112, 125, 130–55, 173, 176–7
peace, peaceable   93, 97, 168, 171
Pentecost   4, 48, 50, 55, 123, 163
Pentecostal, Pentecostalism   5–6, 44–5, 47–50, 53–4, 56
perfect, perfection   11, 27, 36, 47–8, 61, 74, 78, 127
perichoresis   12, 29
person, personed, personal   12–14, 28, 38, 55, 66–7, 77, 86, 91, 144, 164, 174
physical, physicality   17, 55, 72, 92–3, 97, 101, 148, 167
poiesis   38–40, 98
power, powerful   17, 31, 33, 35, 54, 61, 72–4, 88, 91, 95, 102, 117, 122, 134, 136, 138–40, 142, 144–5, 148–9, 159, 182
practices (of the church)   1, 21–2, 25, 37–42, 45, 48, 53, 56, 77, 80, 85–9, 91, 98–9, 101–5, 107–13, 118–20, 123–5, 127–8, 130–1, 145, 152, 175, 178, 181, 184
practise, practising   55, 89, 91, 96, 101, 109, 116, 118, 124, 128, 131, 181, 184
praise   22, 96, 103–19, 122, 125, 127, 135, 180, 184
pray, prayer   22, 86, 94, 108–19, 122, 125, 127, 169, 178, 182, 184, 186
preach, preacher   16, 68, 108, 118–23, 135, 137, 184
presence
  of Christ in the church through the Spirit   1, 20–3, 38, 49, 59, 63, 66, 73–5, 78, 80, 82–91, 105, 110, 112, 125–9, 137, 141–9, 151, 154, 167, 172–3, 175–6, 178, 180–6
  of Christ in the practices of the Church (e.g. Eucharist)   31, 96–103, 114–18, 120–5
  of the Spirit in the church   9–10, 39–40, 51–3, 73, 168
  of the kingdom   20, 35, 76
priest, priesthood   14, 21, 26, 46, 49, 55, 59–62, 64–5, 67–71, 74–6, 81, 85, 95, 114, 127 160, 176, 180

proclaim, proclamation   22, 34, 37, 39, 66, 68, 72–3, 97–8, 102–3, 108–10, 118–25, 127
progress, progression   34, 41, 43, 92, 166, 178–9
proleptic, proleptically   1, 7, 15, 22–3, 39, 59, 77, 79, 81, 91, 105, 125–6, 129, 166, 170, 173, 177, 186
prophet, prophecy   21, 49, 55, 59–71, 74–6, 79, 81, 85, 95, 100, 107–9, 127, 151, 176, 180
purpose, purposeless   17, 19, 27, 47, 99, 110–11, 115, 120, 122, 173
purvey, purveyor (church as)   74–6, 172

race, racial   78, 96–7, 149, 173, 176–81, 183
redeemed, redemptive   3, 17, 27, 33–4, 47–50, 59, 62–3, 77, 99, 125–6, 179, 185
reformed, Reformation   14, 59–62, 64–5, 67, 75–6, 84, 94, 103, 118, 122, 124
reign, reigning   62, 67, 71–5, 78, 85, 89, 115, 127, 145, 171, 183
renew, renewal   9, 44, 60, 69, 72, 82, 88, 104, 118, 137, 144, 162, 171
restore, restoration   30, 70, 90
resurrect, resurrection, risen   15–19, 22, 27–8, 31–3, 36, 42, 45–50, 52, 55–6, 63, 65–8, 70, 72–3, 77–9, 81, 83, 95–6, 117, 125–9, 131–7, 139–41, 145–6, 148–51, 154, 167, 175, 179–80, 183
reveal, revealing   8–9, 21, 28, 31, 50, 57, 59, 61–6, 72, 76, 81, 91, 96, 131, 137, 140, 150, 152, 167–8, 171–2, 195
revelation   1, 13, 15–16, 32–3, 59, 63, 65–7, 70, 72, 76, 89, 92, 95, 100, 163, 168, 175
richer, richness   54, 75–6, 161
righteousness   72–3, 85, 171, 180
royal   26, 46, 69, 74–6

sacrament, sacramental   3, 9, 11, 14–15, 27, 31, 41, 55, 66, 69, 80, 88, 94, 97, 99–100, 102–4, 122, 164, 174–5
sacrifice, sacrificial   54, 61–2, 65, 68, 73, 167

salvation, salvific, save   30–3, 36, 38–9, 46, 49, 55, 59, 63–4, 66–7, 76, 78, 93, 99–100, 135–6, 140, 149, 170
sanctify, sanctification   38–9, 69, 86, 108, 112–13, 116, 118
Scripture, Scriptural   5, 7–8, 15–17, 22, 26, 35, 43, 71, 118, 121–2, 129–30, 175
send, sending   31, 159, 161, 164
sequel (church as)   10, 51, 167
simultaneous, simultaneity   2, 12, 29–30, 39, 55, 77–8, 83, 87, 89, 95–7, 116, 127, 130, 134, 160, 164
sin, sinfulness   19, 27, 34, 41–2, 47, 51–3, 56, 70, 73, 79, 88, 102, 104, 114–15, 121, 124, 135, 138, 148
sociological, sociopolitical   14, 40, 42, 54
sons, sonship   11–13, 28, 87, 169, 174, 195
soteriology, soteriological   6, 13, 15, 32, 40, 43–4, 62, 70, 101, 138, 161, 164
spirate, spiration   12, 39
status   70, 99, 140, 144–5, 147
submit, submission   52, 96
subordinated   9, 32
suffer, suffering   38–41, 44–5, 52, 54–5, 57, 59, 67, 70, 72, 76, 88, 92, 96, 99, 101, 108–9, 113, 120, 126, 142, 144–5, 149–50, 167–8, 171–2, 183
supper   33, 39, 80–2, 84–6, 89–94, 96–7, 99–100, 102–3, 108, 184

teleological   25, 27–8, 32–7, 39, 42, 47–8, 54–5, 57, 77–9, 98–100, 105, 107, 112, 115, 120, 126, 178
telos, telic   1, 18, 23, 26, 35, 38, 40, 44, 49, 51, 54, 64, 67, 75–6, 79, 89, 101, 110, 125–6, 143, 150, 173, 179, 186
temple   90, 144, 148
temporal   26–30, 34, 42, 45, 47, 63, 80–1
thankfulness, thanksgiving   86, 93, 100, 109, 111–12, 137
timebound   19, 60, 62, 64–5, 67, 70, 77, 79, 125, 178
tradition   15, 18, 20, 26, 41, 46, 59–60, 65, 76, 118, 130

tribe, tribal   96, 177, 181–3
Trinity, trinitarian, triune   2, 4–5, 7–9, 11–15, 23, 28–31, 33, 37–40, 43, 48–50, 69–70, 78, 91, 113, 115–16, 122, 157, 160–6, 168–70, 172–5, 182, 185–6
truth   3, 5, 17–18, 35, 40, 61, 65–6, 71–6, 80–1, 84, 86, 89, 93–6, 98, 104, 110, 116, 119, 121, 123, 127, 136, 140, 143, 167, 171–2

unite, uniting   1, 10–11, 17, 21, 27, 46, 51–3, 57, 69, 74, 77–8, 81–2, 87, 89, 92, 96–7, 140, 142, 148, 153, 171, 175, 179, 181, 183
unity   1, 29–30, 66, 69, 73–4, 80, 85, 89–91, 94, 97–8, 102, 124, 130, 133, 137, 142–3, 145, 151, 154, 171–2, 175, 179–81, 183

vicarious (humanity of Christ)   49, 59, 62, 64, 67–71

weak, weakness   33, 46, 91, 123, 133–4, 137, 140, 143, 182
wedding   81–2, 85, 89, 92, 94, 96, 102
Wesley, John (Wesleyan)   60, 123, 190, 194
wine   86, 92–5
wise, wisdom   5, 72, 84, 95, 137–40, 142, 144–5
witness   5, 16–18, 31, 38, 42, 45, 64, 66, 68, 76, 100–1, 103–4, 108–12, 114, 116, 119–20, 122, 124, 127, 157–8, 161–4, 167–8, 175–6, 180
Wolterstorff, Nicholas, (Wolterstorffian)   2, 6–8, 21–2, 118, 122, 124–5, 129, 157, 164–5, 172, 174, 185
worship, worshipful   7, 18, 22, 53, 80, 82–3, 98, 103, 114–17, 122, 125, 150, 152, 159–60, 166, 169, 175, 177–8, 184

zoë (life)   72, 92, 116
Zwingli, Ulrich (Zwinglian)   100, 103

www.ingramcontent.com/pod-product-compliance
Lightning Source LLC
Chambersburg PA
CBHW062228300426
44115CB00012BA/2263